THE
BECKHAMS

Ger
Luv
Auntie
Caroline
x

THE
BECKHAMS

ANDREW MORTON

MICHAEL O'MARA BOOKS LIMITED

First published, under the title *Posh & Becks*,
in Great Britain in 2000 by
Michael O'Mara Books Limited
9 Lion Yard, Tremadoc Road
London SW4 7NQ

Michael O'Mara Books Limited paperback edition first published,
as *Posh & Becks*, in 2001. Updated paperback edition published in
2003. This revised, retitled and updated edition published in 2007.

A CIP catalogue record for this book is available
from the British Library

ISBN 978-1-84317-277-2

1 3 5 7 9 10 8 6 4 2

Photograph Acknowledgements

www.expresspictures.com 1 (*both*), 2 (*both*); East News/Rex Features
3 (*inset*); © Spice Girls/RetnaUK/Retna Ltd, USA 3 (*main image*);
EMPICS Entertainment/PA Photos 4; Richard Young/Rex Features
5 (*above*), 11 (*below*); Tim Rooke/Rex Features 5 (*below*), 16;
Retna/Soulla Petrou 6 (*above left*); Terry Williams/Rex Features
6 (*below right*); www.mirrorpix.com 7, 10 (*both*); Steve Wood/Rex
Features 8 (*above*); Dave Gaskill/ *The Sun* 8 (*below*); David Jones/
PA Archive/PA Photos 9; Anthony Upton/Rex Features 11 (*above*);
Bongarts/Getty Images 12 (*above*); Getty Images 12 (*below*),
15 (*above*); AFP/Getty Images 13, 14 (*both*), 15 (*below*).

Designed and typeset by Martin Bristow

Printed and bound in Great Britain
by Cox & Wyman, Reading, Berks

Contents

The celebrity is a person who is known
for his well-knownness.

DANIEL BOORSTIN,
The Image (1962)

One

Dream Team

It is possibly the greatest sporting show on earth, watched by an estimated one billion people from 232 countries. As a spectacle the Super Bowl is an unrivalled money-making machine, featuring advertisements lasting for just thirty seconds that cost up to £1.3 million. Yet in spite of the hype and hard sell, the Super Bowl still exudes the feeling of a gigantic family day out, where catchy beer commercials and the chessboard intricacies of gridiron coexist.

For the watching audience, the event has the routine and familiarity of an old friend come to visit. The commentators are as venerable as the entertainment; comforting, unsurprising and reliable. Everyone knows what to expect – apart from the score. So the watching millions could be excused for being somewhat perplexed when a good-looking, blond, English soccer player joined the likes of the rapper LL Cool J, TV homemaker Martha Stewart and former attorney general Janet Reno at a celebrity party hosted by NFL wide receiver Chad Johnson for a commercial during the 2007 Super Bowl.

As England soccer captain and one of the most talented players of his generation, David Beckham was known to the watching American audience, but not well known. As football in the USA remains the preserve of youngsters, women and the growing Hispanic community, his fleeting appearance in the commercial was one way of introducing him to America's sporting family, which he was soon set to join.

Like a favoured if wilful son leaving the family home, his decision in January 2007 to quit Spanish club Real Madrid and finish his football career playing for the Los Angeles Galaxy in California was greeted with the collective disbelief and breast beating. Even the British Prime Minister Tony Blair was moved to comment on his career move, praising the soccer superstar for his outstanding contribution to sport. 'In a world where celebrity comes too easily, David deserves fame,' said Blair. 'The phenomenal interest in his move to the US is a reflection not just of his talent, but his understanding of the importance of sport as an industry.'

It showed how far the gas fitter's son from the impoverished East End of London had come. That the great and good were ruminating about his career was an acknowledgement that the one-time Manchester United star, whose ability to make a ball swerve and dip inspired the title of the hit movie *Bend it Like Beckham*, is one of a rare breed. Like Michael Jordan, Tiger Woods and Muhammad Ali, he is a man whose personality transcends his sport. Idolized by many in Britain, Europe and the Far East, it is expected that the Beckham Effect will help transform America's Major League Soccer, bringing awareness, enthusiasm and acceptance.

However David Beckham is not a solo performer. His life changed the moment he first spotted Victoria Adams dancing in a pop video with her all-girl group, the Spice Girls. A generation of wannabes adopted their slogan of 'Girl Power', tapping into the exuberance and cheekiness of the five-strong combo where Victoria played the role of aloof, pouty Posh Spice to perfection. When they first met, she was enjoying worldwide acclaim, and rubbing shoulders with the likes of South African President Nelson Mandela and Prince Charles. Wealthy, too, Posh Spice had helped the band to an amazing eight number-one hits and record sales of more than 55 million worldwide.

On their own, David and Victoria would have enjoyed their brief time in the spotlight: she in a successful all-girl group, him as a sumptuous soccer player and handsome poster boy. Together they have become a unique double act: Posh and Becks, universally admired and criticized, but never ignored. Like any other commercial concern, fame is a business and the Beckhams, particularly Victoria, are skilful entrepreneurs. As celebrity watcher Sharon Crum argues, 'It's actually very easy to build celebrity, but talent is not enough. You have to create a team, like Team Madonna.'

Since their marriage in July 1999, Team Beckham's every move has been slavishly chronicled by an eager media, with the couple transforming modern celebrity into pseudo-religious status. They have become ersatz royalty and an international marketing combo: brand Beckham. Such is their fame that when two professional Posh and Becks lookalikes went shopping in a Tokyo department store in 2003, their presence provoked near riots.

David and Victoria's wedding, held in a castle in Ireland complete with his-and-hers thrones, a coat of arms and fluttering initialled pennants, sealed the couple's coronation as royalty for the common man. Souvenir mugs, tea towels and plates were produced to commemorate the occasion – just like a royal wedding – while their first home in the Hertfordshire countryside, north-east of London, is known universally as Beckingham Palace. When their first son Brooklyn was born, the event was choreographed like a royal birth; the delighted father talking to waiting reporters, the daily bulletins about the health of mother and baby son, and the departure home in a convoy of blacked-out limousines and official police outriders. Again, when Victoria succumbed to viral meningitis in August 2000, official announcements about her recovering health led the TV news. Perhaps more importantly, when David broke a bone in his left foot shortly before the 2002 World Cup, Prime Minister Tony Blair earnestly told fellow politicians that the health of the injured England captain was the most important matter facing the nation at the time. Clergy led prayers and newspapers printed an exact facsimile of his foot so that well-wishers could lay their hands on the image and transfer healing energy.

Such is the Beckham appeal and ubiquity that historians, who like to define a period with the name of the reigning monarch, talk about calling the beginning of the third millennium the 'new Victorian era'. 'We may even begin to gauge our times by David Beckham's haircuts or sendings off,' claims Professor Ellis Cashmore, a lecturer at the University of Staffordshire, who uses Beckham to illustrate the influence of sport on modern culture and society. 'Nobody embodies the spirit of the times as well as David Beckham.'

In an age where participation in organized religion has declined and belief in the afterlife diminished, celebrity – the one chance we have of immortality – has become the new nirvana. As the American novelist Norman Mailer once noted, celebrities, be they from Britain or Hollywood, are the new gods. In Hollywood, where star-spotting is a business complete with maps and bus tours, the Beckhams will fit in perfectly. For the House of Beckham already has many devotees. Not only are they celebrated in waxworks in Madame Tussauds in London, but a twelve-inch high statue of David has been placed at the foot of the main Buddha image in Bangkok's Pariwas Temple. 'Football has become a religion and has millions of followers,' explained the temple's senior monk, Chan Theerapunyo.

On their amazing journey, David and Victoria Beckham have become all things to all men; role models for family life, gay icons, sex symbols, fashion leaders, and the king and queen of conspicuous consumption. David, for example, thought nothing of spending £40,000 on a romantic weekend in Paris to celebrate Victoria's thirty-third birthday in April 2007. Even though he has lived in Madrid for the last three years, David Beckham is seen as a stylist supreme. The man who has famously worn everything from a sarong to a white suit is a regular on the annual lists of the world's most stylish men. 'Still the biggest influence on Britain's High Street,' says Dylan Jones, the editor of style magazine *GQ*.

Victoria has skilfully reinvented herself, transforming her image from opinionated pop tart to svelte fashionista, the creative force behind her own label that includes jeans, sunglasses and handbags. Aware that as a mother of three in her thirties she is not going to remain on the front pages for ever, she has embarked on a new career path as a fashion stylist, working with her new A-list friends such as Hollywood actresses Katie Holmes and Jennifer Lopez. As commentator Ashley Rossiter notes, 'Victoria has gone from pop star to successful musician, to mother to married woman. She never loses her edge. She's made herself a fashion icon and is the current darling of the fashion designers.'

However, their status comes at a price. As icons and style arbiters they have been mocked and caricatured, copied and adored, simultaneously appearing on the 'Most Annoying' as well as 'Best Dressed' lists. As the novelist David Lodge has observed, 'Being a celebrity changes your relationship with the world. From being a private person you become also a public property, the object of envy as well as admiration, fair game for criticism, interrogation, ridicule and spite.'

Even though Victoria became used to facing an audience of screaming fans and David the taunts and jeers of opposing soccer supporters, at times the almost visceral reaction to their real-life soap opera was still surprising. A video of David sleeping, shot by the artist Sam Taylor-Wood, was so well-received that it inspired comparisons with work by the seventeenth-century religious painter Caravaggio when it went on display at London's National Portrait Gallery. During a book signing in a London

14

department store in 2006, Victoria was touched and taken aback by the fact that numerous fans – mainly women – burst into tears in her presence.

Sadly, this worship is not always so benign. As numerous stars have discovered, celebrity attracts the loners, the weirdos, the faceless; unknown individuals who want to hurt them and destroy their lives. Over the years the Beckhams have faced apparent kidnap attempts and death threats that have made them suspicious of everyone. Crass, thoughtless behaviour becomes the norm. Even the former Spice Girl was taken aback when one of the detectives investigating a spate of death threats against herself and her family asked the singer for advice on how his guitar-playing son could break into the music business. At the time she was naturally more worried about being the victim of a mad stalker.

Accompanied by bodyguards and surrounded by high-tech security, the Beckhams have spent a small fortune ensuring safety for themselves and their three boys. Over time they have learned to trust no one, not only for safety's sake, but because they know that an offhand comment is likely to end up as front-page news. They feel they can only confide in each other or their immediate family. Experience has taught them that everyone, from beauticians and hairdressers to bodyguards and nannies, is vulnerable to the chequebook wielded by tabloid newspapers. Even David's father Ted surprised his famous son when he failed to mention that he was producing an affectionate tribute book about his boy.

The couple's decision to actively court publicity inevitably means that every aspect of their private life, even their trash, is pored over. But the

Beckhams did have a choice. A couple who could have followed a similar celebrity trajectory, chart-topping pop singer Louise Nurding, voted Sexiest Woman of the Decade by *FHM* magazine, and her husband, former England player Jamie Redknapp, deliberately decided to distinguish between their public and private life. As Louise has said, 'It's hard enough being married and making it work, so we just don't need the added pressure of every move we make being written about. I didn't marry him for a photo opportunity. I married him because I wanted to spend my life with him.'

The daily spotlight on the Beckhams is unremitting. It is not just the daily soap opera of their lives that is chronicled by magazines and tabloid newspapers either, because every day they exit their front door they are followed by a phalanx of paparazzi. When Mel C, who grew used to publicity when she was with the Spice Girls, joined Victoria for a day out in Madrid even she was shocked by the media scrum. 'It's like people living in your head,' she noted perceptively.

While the couple have invited media intrusion into their lives, at times they find the attentions of the paparazzi too much, and have been known to become verbally and physically aggressive towards some irritating photographers. Victoria's body tightens and fists clench in tense anticipation, while David has had several physical altercations. On one occasion the police were called following a rowdy incident at a motorway service station.

David has freely admitted that he has a little black book containing the names of those upon whom he will one day take his revenge. As psychologist

Dr Glenn Wilson observes, 'They haven't grown into fame gracefully and have discovered that it is a two-edged sword. They have fed the media intrusion while never really getting used to the idea that they are substitute royalty.' In fairness, though, David is increasingly philosophical about his fame and the intrusion that comes as part of the territory. 'I would like to have a more normal life, but I don't think that's going to happen,' he says. 'I just wanted to be a footballer and the fame came with it. I'm not complaining, because I enjoy a lot of it.' Certainly, when he joins the LA Galaxy in July 2007, he will have to keep smiling whatever tricks are played by the paparazzi. He knows that he is going to be on show 24/7, not just as a celebrity, but also as an ambassador for the sport.

These sporadically sour media encounters do not gel easily with their presenting image as down-home folk who happen to be international superstars. They portray themselves as a couple deeply and playfully in love. David is a devoted father who enjoys spending time having soccer kickabouts with his boys, while Victoria is the acme of normality, citing 'toast' as her favourite food and loving nothing more than spending the day in comfy clothes, and watching reality TV with her husband in the evening.

While she went blonde in 2007 to give her that 'sun-kissed LA skater girl' look for when she moves to California, and has been photographed dining at the fashionable Ivy restaurant in Beverly Hills with her friend Katie Holmes, Victoria predicts that life in Hollywood will not be all partying and high jinks.

'Am I going to start going to nightclubs with Britney Spears every night? Possibly not,' she says.

Indeed she gives the impression of being rather starstruck herself after her encounters with A-listers such as Penelope Cruz, Demi Moore and Tom Hanks at the parties she attended in between house-hunting.

What intrigues the media – and the public – is the sense that not far beneath the surface image of domestic bliss and marital harmony lie demons of doubt, insecurity and unhappiness, especially with Victoria. People find her fascinating not because she is talented, but because she is tormented; revealed in stories about her self-inflicted dietary regimes, her obsession with publicity, her shockingly skinny figure and seemingly surgically enhanced cup size.

Bullied at school and with few childhood friends, Victoria has spent a lifetime wanting the world to look at her. She has succeeded by virtue of relentless ambition, shrewd choices and a healthy dollop of luck. 'I'm the girl next door who got lucky,' she says, a statement that is self-deprecating, honest and yet contains the seeds of her insecurity. Her identity as an individual seems to be defined by her celebrity, her life measured out in newspaper and magazine column inches. Those who have been around her note that her mood is largely defined by the way the public perceives her, via the distorting prism of the press. Every day she flicks through the tabloids in search of any photographs or references to herself, her husband or her boys. There is always one subject of overwhelming interest: Victoria Caroline Beckham.

Her dreams of celebrity hide deeper yearnings. As consultant psychiatrist Dr Paul Flowers observes, 'There is a sense that she is powerfully propelled and has a relentless desire to be loved and cared for.

In her mind, carrying this tremendous sense of neediness and unfulfilment, she thought that fame was accompanied by satisfaction and contentment. This is precisely not what it brings.' It remains to be seen how Victoria, who has found validation in her new career as a fashion stylist, copes in the land of the eternal dream and cruel illusion.

LA is a place where size zero is the norm, and thus is somewhere Victoria should feel at home, as a vegetarian who has been known to survive the flight from London to LA on a cup of ginger tea and a handful of raw vegetables. Her wraith-like physique has prompted several TV documentaries to examine size zero women in an effort to understand Victoria's troubled psyche. Journalist Kate Spicer, who endured the brutal dietary regime necessary to reach this shape, came to the following conclusion: 'I feel a peculiar sense of power and control, an air of aloof removal from other women. The pursuit of thinness is a way of losing yourself in one problem and ignoring all the other issues in your life.'

It hardly helps her equanimity that her husband is beautiful – and lusted after by both men and women. So while she complains publicly that she has 'no bum at all' and that she looks really 'awful naked' because of the loose skin on her stomach, David was happy to pose pouting and half-naked for a fashion exhibition held at London's National Portrait Gallery in early 2007. At one point he even asked celebrity photographer Steven Klein if he should wear black nail varnish. Klein, who has worked with the likes of actor Brad Pitt, acknowledged David's positive attitude to his looks: 'Like Brad, he's completely at ease with his masculinity, his femininity, his sexuality. With being looked at. Men work on their bodies. They want to be looked at.'

David enjoys being a gay icon as much as he is happy to be voted the world's sexiest dad by lingerie chain Victoria's Secret. He presents a blank canvas on which others can paint their fantasies; a star cast in the old-fashioned mould: silent, stylish and talented. As Professor Ellis Cashmore argues, 'He doesn't do or say anything to undermine people's notions of him. He is a kind of an everyman. There is something there for everyone.'

He seems relaxed with his own stardom, a sublimely skilful football player who has largely accepted the fame that came with his talent. Matter-of-fact and self-effacing with a strong streak of exhibitionism, with David what you see is not necessarily what you get. 'Nobody knows me apart from the people I want in my life,' he says. While Victoria acknowledges that he is more talented, better looking and more stylish than her, it seems that his calm appearance is something of an illusion as well. During a television interview he admitted that he suffers from Obsessive-Compulsive Disorder to the point where he feels compelled to throw out drink cans in the fridge if there is an uneven number. The condition causes panic attacks, and symptoms include shortness of breath, sweating, nausea and an overall feeling of dread.

Perhaps his condition, which can be treated by hypnosis or drugs, explains why he badly wants a fourth child, preferably a girl, to even things up at home. Certainly this domestic ambition has helped calm gossip about the couple's eight-year marriage, which has been dogged by rumours of his alleged infidelities, especially during his time in Madrid when he was linked to a series of single women, notably his Spanish interpreter Rebecca Loos.

The couple stay together not only because of their complex emotional dynamic, but because they are a brand, a unique combination that has companies such as Motorola, Gillette, adidas and others beating a lucrative path to their door. It has helped propel David into the ranks of the highest-earning sportsmen in the world, as the soccer star is currently estimated to be worth £125 million by the *Sunday Times* Rich List, though his deal with LA Galaxy may well double that in five years.

It is no coincidence that this ground-breaking deal was brokered by his agent Simon Fuller, whose background is in entertainment – he is the brains behind TV phenomenon *American Idol* – and not sport. He recognized, even before David and Victoria themselves, that as a couple they were about much more than sport and music; rather they were about lifestyle as entertainment. As Andy Milligan, media consultant and author of *Brand It Like Beckham*, observes, 'The move to the US is the missing piece in the global brand jigsaw. Hollywood is the lifestyle and entertainment capital of the world, and David and Victoria are very much a lifestyle brand.'

Indeed it is a move that has ensured that the Beckhams are probably the most famous British export since The Beatles. It has been an incredible journey for two young people who believed in the power of their childhood dreams and were determined to make them come true.

Two

Dreams of Wealth and Fame

She was a young girl dreaming of fame and footlights, but in her wildest imaginings Victoria Caroline Adams could not have anticipated the extent to which her childhood fantasies would be realized, or where teenage ambition, dedication and hard work would take her.

'I always dreamed of being rich and famous,' Victoria has said. Certainly a love of music and dancing is in her blood. Her father Anthony Adams, a working-class North Londoner, enjoyed a short-lived career as a pop singer in the sixties with a band called The Sonics. The band covered Beatles' songs and had a stab at writing their own, but when their manager died The Sonics split up.

For Tony Adams fame was to be elusive, but not so fortune. When not performing with the band he worked as a sales representative from his home in Edmonton, North London, and with the help of his wife Jackie he began to build up a lucrative business.

Jacqueline Doreen Cannon was working as an insurance clerk when she and Tony first met, although she had also trained as a hairdresser. She, too, lived in North London, in a modest terraced house in West Green near to White Hart Lane, the Tottenham Hotspur football ground. The couple married in the local parish church in West Green on 25 July 1970, a month after Ted Heath became Prime Minister following a surprise victory for the Conservatives in the General Election.

Four years afterwards, Victoria Caroline Adams was born on 17 April 1974 followed by a sister, Louise, in 1977 and a brother, Christian, in 1979.

In the 1980s Tony and Jackie started up Glade-realm, an electrical wholesale business, selling goods locally and exporting them to the Middle East. Tony devoted long hours to the business, which paid off handsomely – the family soon moving to the Old School House, a large, wood-beamed house in Goff's Oak, a leafy commuter village just north of the M25 in Hertfordshire. Although it is less than twenty miles from London, Goff's Oak is a rural area with unspoilt woods, commons and secluded lanes – in many respects a world away from the surroundings in which Tony and Jackie grew up. The family was also able to enjoy foreign holidays to such places as Spain and the Canary Islands.

While Victoria was disappointed whenever her father was late home, according to her mother she has inherited his ambition and work ethic – as well as his love of performing. As soon as she could walk Tony would dance with her around the living room, and it wasn't long before the little girl was dancing and singing her way through the house. Her favourite record as a child was Stevie Wonder's 'Sir Duke', which Tony sentimentally requested DJ Ed Stewart to play on the radio as Victoria and David drove to the airport on the way to their wedding.

At the local junior school in Goff's Oak, Victoria showed early promise as a stage performer, on one occasion taking the lead role in a performance of *The Pied Piper*. Former teacher Sue Bailey recalls, 'Victoria was always such a pleasant child, very pretty, not at all loud or pushy. She worked hard and came from a lovely family. She was always in school productions, very keen on drama.'

When she was eight she persuaded her parents to enrol her at the Jason Theatre School for after-school classes. School principal Joy Spriggs recalls the fact that Victoria stood out from her fellow pupils, winning numerous dance medals. 'The very first time I saw Victoria dance I knew she was special,' she once said. 'Victoria ate, slept and drank dancing.' On one occasion Victoria, dressed in yellow top hat and tails, tap-danced to 'If My Friends Could See Me Now', the song that Shirley MacLaine made famous in the hit musical *Sweet Charity*.

Victoria would show off her routines to her class-mates and badgered teachers so that she could always be the star of any school show. The smell of greasepaint and the thrill of performing on stage were a constant delight to her. She would watch such musicals as the 1978 film *Grease* starring John Travolta and Olivia Newton-John over and over, learning the words to the songs and playing out the roles. She also loved the early 1980s band The Kids From Fame, spawned from the television series of the same name, which followed the lives of talented young people from the New York High School of Performing Arts.

One of her sister Louise's childhood memories is of her and Victoria dancing to the song 'Making Your Mind Up' by the 1981 Eurovision Song Contest winners Bucks Fizz. At the end of their Eurovision routine, the two boys famously tore off the girls' long skirts to reveal shorter ones underneath, and Jackie Adams made her daughters similar skirts so that they could mimic the routine. However, Victoria's passion for song and dance did not entirely impress her sister. 'She used to get all the fancy outfits and I'd get all the boring ones or have to be the man. I wasn't happy about that,' reflects Louise.

Louise was not the only one to be a touch envious. While Victoria had been a happy pupil at junior school, her teenage school years at local state school St Mary's in Cheshunt were marred by bullying. Although as a younger child Victoria had met with praise for her theatrical efforts, her ambitions now provoked teasing and ridicule.

As far as her fellow pupils were concerned she was a show-off. The fact that she worked hard and preferred to go to after-school dance classes rather than hanging out with the in-crowd led to her being dubbed 'Goody Two Shoes'. More seriously, she began to be threatened and abused, and often ended up in the school loos crying her eyes out and counting the minutes before she could go home. She suffered sleepless nights and used to plead with her teachers to escort her to the school gates at home time. 'Victoria had a bad time at senior school,' says Louise. 'People didn't like her because she didn't go out every night and hang around street corners. Instead she used to go to a lot of singing and dancing lessons.' Victoria herself admits, 'I always used to cry when holidays ended. I hated school and never wanted to go back.'

At an age when fitting in with rather than standing out from the crowd is important, neither did it help Victoria that her parents' lifestyle was showily opulent. Aside from having the largest house in Goff's Oak, and the only one with a swimming pool, Tony Adams also drove a gold Rolls-Royce. Although Goff's Oak and Cheshunt could be described as generally affluent areas, such displays of wealth did not go down well at the Cheshunt comprehensive. Victoria would plead with her father to take her there in his delivery van instead, but she had already been marked out as different and for having airs above her station – ironically, the same things that would lead Spice Girls manager Simon Fuller to christen her Posh Spice, the name that would gain her the fame and fortune she craved.

It was, without doubt, the unhappiest period of Victoria's life – a time of intense loneliness that stripped the extroverted youngster of her confidence and left a deeply troubled teenager in its place. A later boyfriend, Stuart Bilton, recalls that Victoria was, 'a quiet person, not majorly outgoing', and says that 'she made enemies at school because her dad was rich.'

Tony and Jackie were very protective parents, but this may have exacerbated Victoria's problems. As Louise has said, 'When we were younger we weren't allowed to go out on our bikes. We weren't allowed to play on the street with the other kids. We could do anything we wanted, as long as we didn't leave the house or the garden.' Cut off from other children in the neighbourhood, the siblings had become each other's best friends, although not without the inevitable bickering and rivalry that such close proximity effects. The Adams were, essentially, interdependent – a close-knit family with few friends in the outside world. At home Victoria was loved and safe, but as she was discovering, the outside world was a tougher place and one for which she was not prepared.

Much later, when she was away from home at theatre school or on tour with the Spice Girls, she would suffer from intense bouts of homesickness, crying and calling her mother from all parts of the globe. 'I miss seeing the windows all steamy when my mum has burnt the dinner and there's a chair wedging the door open so that the fire alarm doesn't go off,' she said. For Victoria, home represented her deep yearning for security and safety. In the years when most young people crave independence, Victoria repeatedly longed for or flew back to the family nest. Indeed, after Victoria and David bought their own properties, the couple, along with baby Brooklyn, still spent a good deal of their time at the Old School House – the only place where Victoria felt truly comfortable.

However, it must be said that Victoria's brother and sister went through school with few problems. It cannot have helped Victoria's self-esteem to see how popular Louise was with her fellow classmates, and that, while she was reduced to moping about the house, Louise had a healthy social life. So could much of the blame for her unhappiness lie with

Victoria herself? Certainly it is easy to see how her self-absorption and obsession with her looks would have come across, even by teenage standards, as mere vanity.

Though she was attractive, Victoria had become very insecure about and concerned by her looks. She would spend whole weekends in her bedroom experimenting with make-up, and used to get up for school two hours early so that she could achieve a look she felt brave enough to face the world with. She would also get her mother to write notes to excuse her from physical education because she didn't want to mess up her carefully styled hair.

Matters were made worse by the fact that Victoria was plagued by teenage acne – an embarrassing problem for any teenager, but devastating to a girl planning a career in which looks and image are important. Victoria was, of course, teased about her skin, too. She recalls four girls known as 'the Mafia' who made her life hell, calling her 'Acne Face' or 'Sticky Vicky Victoria'. Neither did it help that Jackie had enrolled all three children with a modelling agency, and while Louise was chosen for numerous TV and magazine jobs, Victoria was overlooked. 'I used to work more than her [Victoria], but then I got bored of going to castings,' recalls Louise.

In spite of her troubles, deep down Victoria was still determined that one day she was going to be somebody, and although her self-confidence was severely dented, her fierce ambition remained unquenched. At sixteen, as soon as she could, she left St Mary's with few qualifications, but with her heart set on going to stage school. She knew it was not going to be easy, but she was delighted when she gained a place at the Laine Arts Theatre School in Epsom, Surrey. It meant living away from the comfort and consolation of home in rented accommodation, but it was a new chance for Victoria.

It was around this time that she fell headlong in love with Mark Wood, a security consultant who lived near her parents. In her unhappy schooldays Victoria appears to have had little to do with the opposite sex, aside from the occasional crush on such teen idols as Matt Goss from the British band Bros. Thus, believing herself to have met the love of her life, she agreed to get engaged before she left for the theatre school, even though she was only seventeen. In the event it was a short-lived infatuation that ended acrimoniously, Mark complaining afterwards that Victoria 'only loved herself'.

Putting bullies and broken hearts behind her, Victoria embarked on her theatre course with enthusiasm. Unfortunately, while she was hard-working and keen, the theatrical promise she had shown as a child failed to shine through at Laine Arts, and as a consequence Victoria was not picked for auditions. Nor did many of her teachers have much faith in her abilities, frequently telling her that she did not have that special something to make it in the world of entertainment. One of her teachers recalls, 'Victoria was a very nice girl. She never gave us any problem. She worked very hard' – hardly glowing praise for an aspiring star.

Even though being a starring success meant the world to Victoria, strangely she was not discouraged by such comments, and seemed to be acquiring a thicker skin. Toughing it out was something Victoria had learned she must do. In spite of the less than encouraging reports she received at Laine Arts, she persevered and graduated, aged nineteen, only to join the ranks of a huge community of performing hopefuls, turning up for auditions to find herself a new face amongst a thousand others. However, there was to be no starving in any garret for this struggling artist. Although she was forced to sign on the dole, she had the security that her parents were behind her chosen career and, perhaps more importantly, that they were also willing to help her financially. They were in no hurry for her to fly the family nest and were also happy to indulge their daughter's preference for designer clothes and accessories.

Victoria had her first real break when she answered an advert she had seen in the showbiz magazine *The Stage*. Smart, keen and pretty, she turned out to be just the girl a band called Persuasion was looking for. The other members overlooked the fact that she had no real singing experience and for the next few months she toured the country with the group.

Her love life was also looking up – thanks to her sister, who introduced Victoria to her boyfriend's best friend Stuart Bilton, a local boy who worked as a florist and part-time model. Once again Victoria jumped in feet first and, according to Stuart, 'drove him mad to go out'. A determined Victoria got her man, however, and they were together for three years. While they went out frequently, Stuart remembers that what she enjoyed best was relaxing at home, watching sentimental movies on television.

Although Victoria enjoyed her time with Persuasion, it was not turning out to be the career she had dreamed of. Unbeknown to the other band members she returned to scouring *The Stage* for more attractive propositions. At an audition in the winter of 1994 for a part in the movie *Tank Girl*, she shared a bag of popcorn in the foyer of the Trocadero cinema in London's West End with another wannabe, ginger-haired Geri Halliwell.

The result was another rejection, another blow to the ego – and another week waiting for the arrival of *The Stage* to see if opportunity would finally knock on their doors. A few weeks later, each noticed independently an ad in *The Stage* for an all-girl band. Those who were 'streetwise, ambitious, determined and outgoing' were asked to apply. Victoria needed no second invitation. She and 400 other hopefuls were each permitted a 30-second audition, her song and dance routine seeing her through to the short-list. The girls were selected by the father-and-son team Chris and Bob Herbert, who, backed by financier Chic Murphy, had the idea of creating an all-girl group to match the success of boy bands such as Take That, East 17 and New Kids on the Block. It was a purely commercial pop exercise, dreamed up by enterprising businessmen. Girl Power was the last thing on their minds.

After a second audition in April 1994, Victoria, Geri, Mel Brown, Melanie Chisholm and student Michelle Stephenson were chosen for the group. They had to give up all other work, holidays, and other auditions to concentrate on turning themselves into a group, provisionally called Touch. For a time they shared rooms at a bed and breakfast in Surrey. Victoria, who arrived with two huge suitcases filled with clothes, roomed with Geri. Glamorous it was not. The girls, now on the dole, rehearsed in

Trinity Studios in Woking, Surrey, a rundown dance hall run by a music charity.

Their first musical efforts were as woeful as the surroundings. Pianist Ian Lee recals: 'They sounded absolutely awful. Geri had problems singing in tune and none of them could move together. After a few days you could see something gelling, but it was not an overnight miracle.' In fact it took two years of hard work before they became 'an overnight success'. 'They worked like slaves to get things right,' he said. While it helped that Victoria, Mel C and Mel B had dance training, the girls were regularly working from early morning until late into the evening, endlessly practising their routines and their singing. Occasionally they would put on an impromptu show for visiting council dignitaries. 'They loved the opportunity to show off,' Lee remarked. 'They were a laugh and we all got on really well.'

The girls later moved to a three-bedroomed semi-detached house in Maidenhead, Berkshire, with Victoria now sharing with Michelle who was never as committed as the others. She eventually left to be replaced by blonde Emma Bunton, then just eighteen. As the youngest in the group, she was, like her new room-mate, often homesick; Victoria ferried her regularly to her mother's home in North London. 'I like going out with Victoria because she goes to posh places,' said Emma. 'When you catch her on a funny day, you won't stop laughing. She's got a really dry sense of humour.'

She needed it. Communal life in the house in Maidenhead was something of a shock after leafy Goff's Oak; the morning rush for the bathroom, the washing-up rota and of course the queue to use the house phone. Mealtimes were as haphazard as their different, rather faddy diets. Geri, who has admitted suffering from the eating disorder anorexia nervosa, had ongoing problems, while the other girls had their own quirks. Mel C loved mashed potatoes and tomato ketchup, Emma dieted on baby food, while Victoria existed on a diet of cheese and crackers with the occasional bagel with honey. Only Mel B made herself proper meals.

Of course there were rows and personality clashes, but when the girls looked back on those days they remembered only the good times. As Victoria has said: 'We know each other so well, and we've all seen each other happy, sad, crying, what-ever, that we're totally comfortable with each other.' While the girls got on well, Victoria's personality got rather submerged in the group dynamics. Victoria was a little intimidated by the experience of Geri, the oldest girl in the group, and Mel B's raucous, argumentative nature, and she was creatively over-shadowed by Mel Chisholm who was acknowledged as the best singer in the band. Certainly Geri and Melanie Brown were the accepted leaders of the group, fighting like cat and dog over everything from choreography to singing style. 'Geri would stand there with her arms by her sides and her fists clenched as Mel would have a go at her for singing out of tune,' recalls Ian Lee. 'Mel Chisholm would always act the peacemaker and the other girls would just watch in stunned silence.'

Victoria had other talents, as Geri revealed in her autobiography: 'I had a wild imagination and chaotic creativity, but I didn't have the skills or training to channel them properly. Mel C had a great voice, but was camera-shy and introverted; she hated even talking on the telephone. Mel B had amazing energy, but was a loose cannon who never quite knew what she was aiming at or why it was important to her. Victoria perhaps wasn't the most creative, but she had something far more valuable and important to the group – a sensible and normal outlook on life. She could keep our feet on the ground when our ambitions outstripped our abilities.'

It was Victoria who paid closest attention to the contracts that their musical mentors asked them to sign in February 1995, when they considered their act was good enough to launch on to an unsuspecting world. After consulting with her businessman father, Victoria convinced the others that the percentage their then managers wanted to take was too high. One evening, while the girls were sitting chatting in their house in Maidenhead, Victoria put forward the suggestion that they should leave Bob and Chris. It was an idea seized on by the others, particularly Geri. The girls were no longer raw recruits, but a well-trained, professional outfit who knew they had something special to offer. They were well rehearsed, their strengths were amplified, and their weaknesses downplayed. In short they had what it takes. As Ian Lee remarked: 'You could see they were going to make it.'

It was not going to be easy. After a major bust-up with the Herberts in April 1995, the girls were left homeless, hawking their talents around Tin Pan Alley. They travelled to Sheffield to team up with songwriter Eliot Kennedy, who had penned hits for Take That, while in London two other songwriters, Matt Rowe and Richard Stannard, helped them write the song that was to make their name, 'Wannabe'.

They realized that they needed a manager who was as ambitious as they were. They found him in the shape of Simon Fuller, who already had Annie Lennox and disco diva Cathy Dennis on his books. At their first meeting the girls, then still on the dole, talked about their hopes and dreams. They wanted movies, merchandising, TV specials, the lot. 'We want to be as famous as Persil Automatic,' quipped Victoria. For his part, Fuller told the girls that they would make it big, with or without him, but if they followed his guidance he would take them in the direction they wanted to go.

They took him at his word and agreed to allow him to act for them. First Fuller had to sort out the mess the girls had left behind, settling their contractual dispute with the Herberts and then setting about finding a record deal for the band. While some have seen this story as a triumph of artist over management, others, more cynically and perhaps realistically, describe the changeover as treating the girls rather like professional footballers, selling them from one management to another for a sum neither side would disclose.

No matter, over the next few months and years, Victoria quietly learned at the feet of the master, her business brain soaking up the way their new smooth-talking Svengali operated. She realized almost instinctively that success in showbiz was not just about talent but, more importantly, hard work, enterprise and control. The control of image mattered most; planning, placement, public relations and promotion were all vital ingredients.

Understandably she lost her famous self-control when the girls celebrated signing their first recording contract with Virgin Records in July 1995. At a champagne reception on the rooftop of Virgin headquarters, they signed a rumoured £2 million deal. On the way home Victoria, high on drink and the exhilaration of the day, threw her knickers out of the taxi. That same effervescent spirit – and acute sense of publicity – was on show a few months later when the girls performed 'Wannabe' around the bronze statue of Red Rum at Kempton racecourse, much to the annoyance of race officials. It was their ebullient high spirits and comradeship, later defined as Girl Power, that impressed those who were working with them on their first single and album. Producer Matt Rowe recalls, 'Everything was there, right from the beginning, the attitude, the philosophy, the Girl Power thing. They had all the ideas for the songs, and we'd sort of piece them together like a jigsaw puzzle.'

The puzzle started fitting together in early 1996, when a video of their first single was shown on cable TV and proved such a success that it was repeated seventy times in a week. After the video came the release of the single in Japan to test the commercial waters. The bean-counters need not have worried; 'Wannabe' sold more than any of The Beatles' records. In July 1996, 'Wannabe' was released in Britain. Two weeks later, it went to number one where it remained for nearly two months, selling 1.25 million copies in Britain alone. It was eventually knocked from the top spot by teen idol Peter Andre, Victoria's mother's favourite singer. During the endless rounds of interviews and TV appearances, the girls hardly had time to consider how they had come so far so fast. 'When I was little I always thought: "I want to be famous,"' said a rather perplexed Victoria at the time. 'But you could never dream of what's happened to us. It's a bit out of the ordinary.'

Indeed their boundless energy and joie de vivre seemed to capture a national mood. The girls were loud, proud and sometimes lewd, and didn't seem to be afraid of anybody. As Mel B noted, 'The whole concept of Girl Power is about being aware of yourself, of not taking any crap from anyone and getting what you want. Not in a horrible way, but in a nice way.' Politicians and prelates all used lines from the song's lyrics to make a point, whether it were about the economy or the health of the nation. Behind the aggressive can-do, sexually charged energy and attitude radiated by the group, were five down-to-earth suburban girls who loved their mothers and believed in traditional values: marital fidelity, the superiority of friendship with other girls to transitory male boyfriends and individual endeavour. When they proclaimed former Prime Minister Margaret Thatcher the original Spice Girl, they were speaking more accurately than they knew. 'They obviously have very clear political views,' said Conservative Central Office. 'They are a go-ahead group and we are a go-ahead party.'

In many respects, of all the Spice Girls Victoria Beckham represented the creed of Girl Power. She was an archetypal suburban girl from the Home Counties; politically conservative, culturally disinterested and focused, almost obsessively, on home and family values. At the same time, while she was always dismissed as the least talented Spice Girl, in the longer run she proved herself to be more disciplined, more cunning, more astute and ultimately more successful than the others. In a group defined by ambition itself, she has showed herself to be the most relentlessly ambitious.

After the success of 'Wannabe', the Spice Girls soon proved that they were not simply one-hit wonders. The hits simply came rolling out. In October 1996 their follow-up single 'Say You'll Be There' took the charts by storm, while their much-anticipated album trounced all competition in the Christmas charts. As Mel B remarked at the time: 'It's all happening so fast. One day we were no one, the next we were beating George Michael to number one.' They were dubbed 'Oasis in a Wonderbra' by *Smash Hits* magazine.

The pace was astonishing. Just five months after the world had first heard of them, they followed in the footsteps of royalty and Hollywood celebrity to switch on the Christmas lights in London's Oxford Street.

There was no let-up. Even though they had taken Britain by storm, they still had to conquer America. With three number ones under their collective belt, the Spice Girls arrived in New York in January 1997 ready to do battle. The relentless schedule was beginning to tell. Victoria went down with flu, but struggled through a host of personal appearances, interviews and photo shoots. Their hard work paid off; they stormed to the top slot in the all-important Billboard charts in February. Before they could draw breath they returned to Britain to perform the opening set for the Brit Awards at London's Earls Court. The year before they had come as nobodies, now they were feted as pop royalty, nominated in five different categories. 'Things just seem to get better and better,' observed Victoria at the time.

Their performance was a triumph, Geri's micro Union Jack dress stealing the show, especially when she revealed rather more of herself than was intended in front of an estimated 30 million TV audience. 'Everyone's seen them before so I don't give a damn,' she said later.

Still there was no let-up. In March 1997 they sent themselves up for charity, their video of the hit single 'Who Do You Think You Are?' being mimicked by celebrity lookalikes, including the portly comedienne Dawn French who played Victoria. When she was trying to get into character, Dawn asked the famously po-faced Spice Girl why she never smiled. 'Because I get dimples,' came the reply. 'They make me look thirteen.'

That same month Victoria emphatically broke her golden rule when she was introduced to a dashing young England soccer star who would change her life for ever.

Three

A Star is Born

While Victoria Adams was making a splash on the front pages, a shy young man with a winning grin was making headlines on the back pages. Manchester United star David Beckham was being hailed as the new George Best, a devastating combination of sex appeal and football talent.

David had a rather more humble upbringing than Victoria. His parents were also from a working-class background – his father, David Edward Alan Beckham, known as Ted, was the son of a gas fitter from the East End, while his mother, Sandra Georgina West, was a hairdresser. Ted was a fitter's mate when he met Sandra. As Victoria's father had dreamed of playing in a successful band, Ted, a lifelong Manchester United fan, had dreams of playing football professionally. He had trials for two amateur clubs as a teenager, but never made the grade.

No doubt when Ted asked Sandra's father Joseph West, a printer from Islington, North London, and an ardent Tottenham Hotspur supporter, for her hand in marriage, there was much joshing about team allegiances. Ted and Sandra exchanged vows in front of close family and friends at the St John the Baptist church in Hoxton, East London, in September 1969, before going on a short honeymoon on the south coast of England. The couple lived in a terraced house in Leytonstone, East London, Ted following in his father's footsteps to become a fully qualified gas fitter. Three years after they married, their first child Lynne was born. Then, on 2 May 1975, David Robert Joseph Beckham came kicking and screaming into the world. By the time his younger sister Joanne was born in the early 1980s, David's talent for kicking a ball around was already shining through, and he joined his father at weekends to watch the Sunday League side that Ted organized.

The family later moved to Chingford in Essex where David attended Chase Lane Junior School and later the local comprehensive, Chingford High. It was fortunate for David that his father recognized his son's talent at an early age. In fact there is the sense that David was the vessel for Ted's thwarted football ambitions. He was keen to share his great passion for the game with his young son, spending hours practising with him, teaching him the fundamentals of touch and control, while indulgently allowing him to stay up way past his bedtime to perfect his dead-ball kicks and corners.

It was an early indication of David's meticulous dedication to his chosen profession – he was often the last to leave training during his Manchester United career – as well as of his perfectionist character. Away from the field, the unassuming youngster exhibited similar qualities of control and self-discipline; keeping his room immaculate, folding his dirty washing or carefully tracing cartoon characters from comic books.

It was obvious from an early age that this open-faced, shy young man was destined for more than Sunday football on the Hackney Marshes. Tongue-tied off the pitch, his right foot did the talking for him and by the age of eight he was the star player for Ridgeway Rovers in the Enfield District League, scoring 101 goals in three seasons.

He was part of a group of eager youngsters, which included Matthew Barham, Danny Fielder, Ritchie Sutton and Alan Crafer, who have remained friends long after many of them have hung up their boots. 'They were all soccer crazy seven-year-olds,' recalls team manager Stuart Underwood. 'They were very close-knit.'

At Chingford High his friends nicknamed him the 'Little Devil', after Manchester United's club nickname, Red Devils, and while he was unlikely to make the grade academically, his skills on the football field were outstanding. He was also a promising athlete – winner of the local 1,500 metre race four years running. His sports teacher at school, John Bullock, recalls, 'he was always focused on football. He had blond fluffy hair, his shirt would be hanging out, his tie half undone and he almost always had a football under his arm.'

David had his first taste of international success when he was just eleven, when his team played in a competition in Holland in 1986. While the rest of the boys were overawed and excited by their foreign adventure, David, according to his childhood friends, seemed to take it in his stride. The right-winger won the game, whipping in the winning goal from one of his trademark crosses. It was an early indication not just of his raw talent but also of his temperament, that combination of belief in his own ability, inner calm and technical focus that is common to all top athletes.

David achieved his first breakthrough on the path to stardom courtesy of television. In 1986 he spotted an item on the British children's TV programme *Blue Peter* about Bobby Charlton's Soccer Skills Tournament and badgered his mother to let him enter. It was thanks to his grandfather Joseph West, who gave him the £125 fee, that the eager eleven-year-old was able to take part in the nationwide competition to uncover England's future football talent.

While he amassed the tournament's highest points total ever, easily winning the event that was completed at Old Trafford, the Essex schoolboy also had his first taste of the jeers that he would have to endure throughout his professional career. United were playing Spurs later that day and a number of fans had already taken their seats in the stadium, so when it was announced that the boy from Chingford supported the home team, he was booed off the pitch by supporters of the London club. It may have been harmless fun, but it was an early brush with the dark emotions and tribal allegiances of the game this fresh-faced youngster was soon to dominate.

At the time the Spurs fans would have had every right to be perplexed by his preferred choice of clubs. In November 1986 Manchester United was well and truly in the doldrums. The club was second from bottom of the First Division after fifteen matches – a dreadful run of form that resulted in the departure of the flamboyant manager Ron Atkinson and his replacement by the dour but successful Scotsman, Alex Ferguson.

By contrast Spurs, David's local club and his grandfather's team, had twice won the FA Cup during the 1980s as well as collecting European silverware in the shape of the UEFA Cup in 1984. More than that, the cup-winning side contained an array of creative talent, most notably England star Glenn Hoddle, one of David's childhood heroes. In addition, they were just a bus ride away from home. But seductive, slinky and accessible as Spurs seemed, another club had stolen his heart.

Of course his father's fanaticism for the Reds played its part in the courtship – every year David was given a replica United kit for Christmas – but he was independently wooed when he saw the likes of Bryan Robson, Gordon Strachan and Norman Whiteside play for United against Spurs at White Hart Lane. As he recalled in his club biography: 'All I ever wanted to do was play football for Manchester United . . . There was never another team for me.'

As his schoolmates gradually drifted away, more interested in chasing girls than footballs, David's loyalties to the game remained constant. Former teammate Ritchie Sutton, now a computer operator, recalls, 'When we were fifteen we started going down the pub. David didn't come because he wanted to go to the park and play football.' Nor did he want to go to discos or parties with the other lads. As David himself says, 'I gave up a lot when I was younger. It wasn't easy but I knew what I wanted to do. United was the dream.'

It was not long before talent scout Malcolm Fidgeon came knocking at the family home in Chingford. He remembers that 'He [David] was very frail and tiny, but he could do things the other boys couldn't and I thought he wouldn't disgrace himself if he was given the opportunity of a United trial.'

There were also other suitors vying for David's hand. It was rumoured that West Ham and Arsenal were interested, and he had a trial for Spurs, although the club's then manager Terry Venables' courtship of the youngster was lukewarm. As far as David was concerned there was no choice in the matter – he was joining the Reds, signing schoolboy terms on his fourteenth birthday. During the school holidays he regularly travelled to Manchester for trials or simply to hang around the training grounds, soaking up the atmosphere. 'I was in love with the place,' he said. When he was sixteen it was no surprise that David chose to sign for Manchester United as an apprentice, swapping his part-time job collecting glasses from punters at Walthamstow Greyhound Track in East London to a far more prosperous career away from family and friends. Even though he moved into accommodation in Manchester, he and his parents remained just as close, Ted and Sandra clocking up thousands of motorway miles to support their son and his dream – a footballing prodigy straight out of the pages of a schoolboy comic book.

As a new recruit he was in awe of his manager, star-struck by the senior players he now rubbed shoulders with, and utterly thrilled at the chance to play soccer full time. Photos of him from that time reveal a wide-eyed innocent with a shy, cheeky smile, a teenager with an engaging enthusiasm for his chosen career.

While his father was thrilled that his son had chosen Manchester United, as important to Ted and Sandra Beckham was the charming but firm figure of manager Alex Ferguson. While Ferguson's belief in and promotion of his youth teams was to be central to the club's success, it was his genuine interest in and concern for his young charges that was reassuring to their parents. 'It was good to know that he was in safe hands,' recalls Sandra. 'The support we've got from Alex and the club has been fantastic.' Little things about the manager – like his ability to remember names and dates, and the fact that he took the trouble to turn up when David was given a cake by United staff to celebrate not only his fourteenth birthday but signing for the club – made a lasting impression on Ted and Sandra.

Together with Alex Ferguson they were the triumvirate who carefully guided David's life and budding career. David has often admitted, 'Everything I have done in football, I owe to my Mum and Dad.' However, he has also acknowledged his debt to his United manager. Throughout his illustrious career, Ferguson has set great store by his club's youth policy, nurturing and husbanding his young talent as carefully as a grower of rare orchids.

Born in Glasgow during the war years, Alex Ferguson's self-control, discipline and will to win have made him the outstanding football manager of his era. He is a man who values hard work, loyalty and commitment. For Ferguson soccer comes first, middle and last. He has no time for distractions, particularly drinking and partying, and woe betide the player who stretches his patience or resists his strict regime. As numerous idols of the terraces have found to their cost, it is a quick route to the transfer market.

The shrewd Scotsman has seen too many promising careers cut short by burnout, booze and injuries. As with his contemporaries, Ryan Giggs, Gary Neville and Paul Scholes, David was rested, substituted and kept away from the media glare until Ferguson felt he was ready. It is a policy that paid rich dividends.

At times, though, his concern for his young charges was reminiscent of an old-style schoolmaster, a stern disciplinarian who brooked no opposition or breaking of the strict club rules. It was not unusual for him, for example, to ring the landlady to ensure her football charges were tucked up in bed before 10 o'clock on the eve of a match. Stories of him throwing soft drinks at recalcitrant players are, by his own admission, only a slight exaggeration. Yet Beckham has acknowledged, 'There's not one player at United who doesn't have some kind of fear of the gaffer, but it's not dread of him, more a respect for what he stands for. And what he's done for us all.' As gifted as he was, David, like most of the team, had suffered the 'hairdryer treatment', enduring a close-range verbal blast from the manager. In many respects, though, as a mild and well-behaved squad member, David was the model young professional.

While his former school reports had regularly criticized his homework, or lack of it, at Old Trafford he willingly put in endless hours of training after the normal day was over, practising free kicks, corners and dead-ball situations. Indeed, in his autobiography, tellingly entitled *Managing My Life*, Ferguson singled out Beckham for his diligence: 'David Beckham is Britain's finest striker of a football not because of God-given talent, but because he practises with a relentless application that the vast majority of less gifted players wouldn't contemplate.'

There were other qualities that marked him out: hard work, courage and a touch of arrogance, which are often the hallmarks of a successful athlete. England World Cup winner Nobby Stiles was in charge of the United youth team during this period and recalls how, as team captain, Beckham was not afraid of his responsibilities. On one occasion, despite having missed a penalty in open play during an important semi-final game in the Milk Cup Youth Tournament, he was the first to volunteer when it came to a penalty shoot-out. 'He was determined to stand up and be counted and he has continued to show that great character,' Stiles recalled. 'He has taken a tremendous amount of stick over the last few years, but the great thing about David is that he doesn't let it get to him.'

Away from the ground he was equally dedicated. Rather than nights on the town, he regularly stayed in at his lodgings, reserving his energy for the next day on the pitch. He was happy to relax watching the TV, reading books by writers such as Stephen King, or listening to his preferred rap music. When he did go out it was with his fellow apprentices in the youth squad, notably Gary and Phil Neville, Ryan Giggs, Ben Thornley and Dave Gardner. Even in this ambitious and highly talented group of friends, David stood out as being, at times, rather prissily conscientious. After a night out at the cinema rounded off with a pizza, David was ribbed by his friends when he ordered milk rather than beer. Worried that he was too scrawny for the big time, he thought this would build up his body.

In a profession where discipline and team spirit are paramount, Ferguson took a dim view of individualism, and as a result the normal teenage opportunities to rebel or to stand out from the crowd were strictly limited. However, there had to be some outlets for the youngsters to show off their success and the fruits of hard labour. In David's case he developed a passion for fast cars, which he personalized, and also a taste for playing the dandy in designer clothes.

As well as devoting much time to his image and appearance, David also started to put more effort into his social life. Whereas, when he was younger, he had had no time for the opposite sex, he now started to date girls whom he met through the Manchester United circle. He briefly dated blonde air stewardess Lisa Rys-Halska, and his short romance with Julie Killelea, a part-time model and daughter of wealthy United supporter Robert Killelea, was talked of in the press as a 'real love match'.

David had other relationships, but his girlfriends complained of a lack of commitment, receiving the impression that he would rather be making passes on the soccer pitch than in the bedroom. Model Leoni Marzell dated him on and off for a year, but admitted that he only came alive when talking about football to her father at their home in Waltham Abbey. When he made a date with former Miss UK Anna Bartley, after meeting her at a Manchester United supporters' club function, his social skills left her distinctly underwhelmed. 'He took me to a restaurant but said almost nothing,' the former psychology student was reported as saying. 'He wasn't great at conversation.' Others were more charitable. 'He was the perfect gentleman,' remembers Belinda Gibson, the sister of former Tottenham and Manchester United player Terry Gibson, who dated him for two months.

In spite of the easy access to friends and family of other players, and to the beautiful and glamorous hangers-on who adorned the Manchester United circle, David had yet to meet the woman for him, but while his love life might not have been running smoothly, his career was in top gear. By 1996 he had already won the League Championship and FA Cup titles with his club and had been picked to play for England by his childhood hero, then team coach, Glenn Hoddle. He was so thrilled to be elevated to such illustrious company that the young man even took along his autograph book to collect signatures. And it was while he was with the England team that the missing piece in an otherwise seemingly perfect young life fell within his grasp.

He was relaxing in a hotel in Tblisi, Georgia, in November 1996 with his room-mate and best friend Gary Neville when he noticed a video of the Spice Girls' second number-one hit, 'Say You'll Be There', playing on the TV. He recalls, 'I pointed at the screen and told Gary, "That's the girl for me and I am going to get her." It was her eyes, her face. She's my idea of perfection. I was sure just from seeing her on that video that she was the one I wanted, and I knew that if she wanted me we would be together forever.'

In fact the pop video, complete with fast cars, laser guns and special effects, portrayed Victoria as a screen dominatrix, dressed from head to foot in a black PVC cat suit, sporting a dark wig. She was only glimpsed in very short bursts as she played the part of fantasy screen babe, Midnight Miss Suki.

While David fell for the challenge of the dominant, unattainable woman, when Victoria was making the film, romance was the last thing on her mind. She was forced to perch on the back of a car in the searing 112°F heat of the Mojave Desert for an hour while the director got the shot he wanted.

Coincidentally, a few days after he returned from the match that England won, Victoria appeared in *The Sun* newspaper wearing a Manchester United strip, which she had donned to please her manager Simon Fuller who was a keen United fan. As it happened, around the same time Victoria's romance with Stuart Bilton was fizzling out. Her whirlwind lifestyle, mixing with such luminaries as Prince Charles and former South African President Nelson Mandela, was not something that Stuart felt he could relate to. She was away touring for months at a time and inevitably their relationship foundered.

Victoria, too, remembers that she was attracted to David some time before the couple met in person, having favoured his photograph over those of other footballers in a soccer magazine interview she was shown. 'I fancied David long before I met him,' she recalls. 'I had no idea who he was, but I just

51

remember thinking he was gorgeous. He just seemed ideal – sensitive, sexy, good-looking, funny, confident but not arrogant – all the qualities I look for in a man.'

Interestingly David Beckham may not have been the only one she had eyes for. Apparently, when the Spice Girls were just struggling wannabes, she idolized his teammate Ryan Giggs.

While Stuart Bilton was recovering in hospital following a serious skiing accident during a holiday with Victoria's father and other friends, Victoria found herself with an opportunity to get a closer look at the sexy footballer whose looks had caught her eye. She went to watch David play at Chelsea – with tickets supplied by her manager – and after the game went to the players' lounge. The couple waved to one another across the crowded room, but both were too shy to make closer contact.

It was an intensely frustrating moment for David. 'It was the moment I'd waited for and I blew it,' he said. Fortunately for him, Victoria's appetite was whetted. The relationship with Stuart was over and when, on 15 March 1997, Simon Fuller again tried to play Cupid, giving her and fellow Spice Girl Melanie Chisholm tickets to see David in action against Sheffield Wednesday, she jumped at the chance. Victoria may have set her sights on the midfielder, but according to one source she forgot to take her glasses along to the match and had no idea which of the men in action was David. This time, though, she was not going to let her quarry escape, and she walked purposefully over to him in the players' bar to compliment him on his game. 'We really did get on from that first moment,' she recalled. 'I could see he was shy which I thought, for someone so well known, was really attractive.'

David duly asked her if she wanted to go out for dinner, and while she declined his invitation, she did give him her phone number and left him to mull over a suitably direct Spice Girls-style message.

'If you don't ring me,' she said, 'I'm going to kick you in the bollocks the next time I see you.'

Wisely, he gave her a call.

Four

Diary of a Long-Distance Lover

It was a long-distance romance that they conducted by mainly by mobile telephone, and which was punctuated by occasional meetings when their diaries allowed, which was not too often. As with his previous girlfriends, David was a rather bashful suitor. It wasn't until the fourth date that he and Victoria even shared a kiss. But their courtship, which began in March 1997, was off to a sure if slow start. It didn't help that Victoria, along with the rest of the Spice Girls, was based mainly in Ireland to avoid paying tax on her earnings. So David chartered private planes to see her in concert or drove hundreds of miles for brief romantic liaisons.

It mattered little. Both were utterly love-struck. Whenever they could be together the couple were soon inseparable, preferring to stay at home and cuddle on the sofa, watching television and eating takeaway curry than be out having nights on the town. When, more often than not, they were forced to be apart, Victoria would go to bed wearing one of David's football shirts.

Inevitably they spent hours on the telephone, discussing the minutiae of their lives. If, for example, David was in a restaurant he would ring up Victoria, wherever she was in the world, to talk about what he should have for a starter. Then he would call again to debate the main course. Even though she trusted her lover implicitly, there were the inevitable doubts and worries. Indeed Victoria has admitted that she phoned David late at night to check that he was home safely. Left unsaid was her fear that he could be with another woman. 'Are they going out? What are they doing? . . . it's always in the back of your mind when you're so far away,' she confessed.

David's United colleagues were quick to see the changes in him, and the United number seven found himself being teased mercilessly by his teammates for the amount of time he spent chatting on the phone. Ryan Giggs especially liked to ring up David's mobile phone pretending to be Victoria and cooing 'I love you' before bursting into laughter. Meanwhile Gary Neville observed, 'He was coming to training every day and he was like a little schoolboy.'

While the United players teased him, Alex Ferguson took a stronger stance – not impressed to find that if his formerly model player was not on the telephone to his new love, he was chartering planes to see her in Ireland during her time as a tax exile. David also flew to Barcelona to watch a Spice Girls concert and appeared backstage at another show at Wembley Arena. In Spring 1997, when the team was on the coach to play in a vital European Cup semi-final against Borussia Dortmund in Germany, the gaffer brusquely told his star player – who was the 1997 PFA Young Player of the Year – to curb his endless mindless chatter on his mobile phone and concentrate on the match. It was an early sign of things to come.

First the couple tried to keep the romance a secret from the world, but soon grinned at the eager press cameramen, who had not been slow to wake up to the fact that the combination of a world-class footballer and a world-famous pop star was a media gift from heaven. The paparazzi were on their tail – snapping away at Victoria leaving David's house or during the couple's romantic weekend away in St Tropez. 'We seemed to have every photographer in the world following us, which was really difficult,' said Victoria. Then, when she was photographed coming out of a bridal shop in June 1997, it sparked premature speculation that the couple were about to announce their engagement.

Yet their love for each other deepened and proved more than capable of withstanding the problems of distance, career commitments, and the considerable distractions of a romance being played out in the public eye. In the early months of their relationship, the couple's overriding concern was for each other. It was noted that they acted like teenagers who were head over heels in love for the first time. There was almost a childlike innocence about their relationship. They shared a bond that deepened with every passing day.

In spite of the distance and difficulties, they realized that their lives had much in common. Significantly they shared and understood the pleasures and pressures of being at the height of a career they loved, but they also both came from close-knit and loving families whose values were important to them. Neither had looked for or had the chance to explore a wild adolescence, and both were highly dedicated perfectionists who were prepared to do whatever it took to get to where they wanted to be.

What they wanted from each other was trust and understanding, but also the reassurance of mutual admiration. In a sense they were each other's trophies – both slightly disbelieving that they had won each other, but immensely pleased and flattered to have done so. It is a common phenomenon in the world of celebrity. As psychologist Dr Glenn Wilson has explained, while David and Victoria are deeply in love, their status gives them the opportunity for mutual worship, transferring their fantasies on to one another. They not only bolster each other's egos, but in mirroring each other they fulfil their narcissistic tendencies.

Victoria has admitted that much of her initial attraction to David was because she saw in him someone like her – well known and well off. They also started to exchange expensive presents and began their ongoing preference for his-and-hers items. They were spotted wearing matching designer Rolex watches, and while Victoria claims it was just a laugh that they sometimes dressed identically, it was also a public statement that they belonged together, as well as being guaranteed to generate publicity.

'Everyone used to ask if my initial attraction to David was the fact that he was famous. I always said it wasn't, but actually that was a lie. If someone is really talented, as a footballer or an artist or an academic, the point isn't that they are famous, but they are talented and dedicated. The fact that we are in the same position makes us equal and it is quite ironic the way our careers run parallel. When we first met I was on my first album and he was playing in his first proper first-team season . . . We are equally famous and attract equal attention.'

Equally famous, but there were crucial differences. To David playing football for Manchester United and England was the horizon of his ambitions. As far as he was concerned, celebrity took second place. In his eyes, fame was just a by-product of being a successful professional footballer. By contrast, Victoria's supreme ambition, the goal she had had since childhood, was to be famous and admired. For her, celebrity is an achievement in itself, her work with the Spice Girls a vehicle to allow her to fulfil her dream. Similarly, while it can be said that both of them have been lucky, and that both owe their success to the careful nurturing of others – in David's case Alex Ferguson and the Manchester United machine, in Victoria's Simon Fuller – success was more gradual for David. His talent has been unquestioned since he was a small boy, and increasingly recognized and praised as he matured into an undoubtedly first-class player. In contrast Victoria's success was achieved quickly, and in spite of rather than because of any real talent she could demonstrate.

As one commentator noted: 'Home Counties children David Beckham and Victoria Adams could easily have met in a West End nightclub, fallen in love, married and lived happily ever after like thousands of other anonymous couples. Two things prevented it – his prodigious football talent and her good fortune in being plucked from obscurity for the Spice Girls. Beckham, as arguably the most talented English footballer of his era, would no doubt be famous whoever his wife was.'

Whatever the debates about her talent, Victoria was working at such a pace that it was remarkable she even found time to make a phone call – let alone fall in love. During 1997, the girls no longer had a life; they had a schedule that was brutal and unrelenting, a 'sleep-deprived tunnel of non-stop work' which, according to Spice Girls biographer David Sinclair, would 'have broken many sane people'. While Victoria and the other girls were multi-millionaires with all the trappings of super-stardom – chauffeurs, secretaries, private jets, personal stylists, publicists and accountants – they were shackled day and night to a money-making treadmill. In the background, orchestrating the lucrative operation, was the canny figure of Simon Fuller.

In the spring of 1997, the Spice Girls appeared in New York before embarking on a punishing three-week tour of the Far East, which included visits to Taiwan, South Korea and Bali. In May they barely had time to celebrate being given the Ivor Novello award for the International Hit of the Year and Best-Selling Single, both for 'Wannabe', when they began work on making an album and film – *Spiceworld: The Movie.* Billed as a madcap comedy, the movie took a light-hearted look at their lifestyle: the press conferences, rehearsals and concerts. They spent an exhausting six weeks spent filming, working from six in the morning until late at night in various locations in London. Big name stars such as Richard E. Grant, Lenny Henry and Elton John joined in the fun.

In September the busy bandwagon kept on rolling when the girls could be found rehearsing hard for their first live concert in Istanbul, Turkey. Simon Fuller controlled their every movement with a rod of iron. When Geri pleaded for a week off, he refused, and if any of the girls were in danger of being led astray he would move in to break up the party. They were beginning to feel that they were in a prison. Little wonder, then, that Geri nicknamed their rehearsal venue, a mansion outside Cannes in southern France, 'Spice Kampf'.

The harsh truth was that far from living the philosophy of Girl Power, the Spice Girls were effectively disempowered. They were living a lie and had been from the beginning. When the Spice Girls were launched, the idea was propagated that the all-girl group had done everything themselves. The legend was soon born that the can-do, can-have girls danced into the offices of Virgin's managing director, Ashley Newton, and spiced up his life. They performed a song-and-dance routine and he was immediately struck by their star appeal. He himself said of the day that the girls gatecrashed their way into his life: 'When we saw them singing in our office we realized they weren't some pieced-together vision by some male Svengali. They have their own agenda.'

It was a refrain picked up by the girls themselves. 'We've had so many people say they managed us,' argued Melanie Brown. 'But we've all been in the music industry for years and we've done it ourselves. We do everything ourselves; we're completely into Girl Power and there's nothing us lot can't handle.'

In truth, as music critic Chris Blackhurst noted, they were 'an ersatz ensemble put together with the overriding purpose of making money for them and their backers. Behind those pouting poses, cheeky grins and Girl Power salutes, there is a programme of cynical media manipulation and calculating exploitation.'

They were a band created by businessmen for the purpose of making money, not promoting sexual equality or liberation. They had become the most marketable and marketed band in history. Their fans were able to buy an enormous array of merchandise, from Spice dolls, cameras, watches, lights and books, to videos and clothing. Then there were lucrative deals with, among others, Walkers Crisps, Polaroid, Cadbury's, Benetton, and Pepsi Cola. They were paid £500,000 to launch Channel 5; and a personal appearance by the girls would cost upwards of £50,000. They weren't so much a pop group – after all they hadn't even done a live concert until Istanbul – more a recording and marketing phenomenon. Commentator Martin Samuel noted, 'Far from espousing Girl Power, what they appear to demand of their fans is meek consumerism.'

Businessman Michael Sparkes confessed that he had put the group together like any other piece of merchandise, admitting, 'I suppose you could say that they are all my own work. I made their sound, their management company made their image.' Similar sentiments are shared by pianist Ian Lee. 'I couldn't believe it when all these stories came out about how the girls did everything themselves,' said Lee. 'They are a put-together band.'

A male writer composing a feature on the Spice phenomenon dreamed up even their nicknames – Posh, Sporty, Ginger, Baby and Scary. Their first Svengali is more measured in his appraisal. 'It's true that I put the band together,' says Chris Herbert, 'but the girls always had their own energy and input. The way I describe it is that I put the ingredients together and the girls added the Spice.'

Everyone, from songwriters to publicists to the girls themselves, propagated the myth. For those at the centre, the Spice Girls themselves, it was hard to cope with the gulf between the image and the reality. During those days they used words like 'guilt' and 'feeling naughty' if they gave in to their true needs and desires. Melanie Chisholm took refuge in the gym, while Victoria Adams engaged in long phone calls to her family and her boyfriend David. 'Sometimes it is difficult when you are in America and all you want is a cuddle,' she said. On tour she became very homesick, crying every day because she wanted to return to her family.

Home represented security, stability and a chance to be herself. For even her name, Posh Spice, was not really her character. While she liked designer clothes, she was a girl from the suburbs whose parents had earned their money by hard work and resilience. As Mel C said, 'She's not posh. She might wear posh clothes, but she's as common as the rest of us.'

While they had money, acclaim and fame, and meetings with the great and the good from the world of politics, show business, arts and entertainment, they knew in their hearts that it had been achieved as much by the image-makers and their manager as by their own endeavours. Like virtually every pop group before them, they wanted to be able to express themselves in their own way, not only artistically but as individuals. They were tired physically and mentally, as well as increasingly unhappy at the way their lives were simply out of their control. One source close to the group observed that by autumn 1997, the girls were exhausted and near hysteria. They had 'recently seen frightening symbols of their loss of power and control'.

In the beginning, when they were making their way, such a status had been acceptable; now the girls wanted a change of direction. They had enjoyed huge success very quickly, but now felt they needed time to take stock and work out their future aims, rather than simply being a money-making machine. Inevitably their thoughts moved towards a change in management. Matters were coming to a head.

In the autumn of 1997, the leaders of the group, Mel B and Geri Halliwell, discussed the prospect of parting from Simon Fuller. After the rigours of the Far East tour they felt that Victoria would agree. According to some accounts, Geri was allegedly angered by the friendship between their manager and the youngest Spice Girl, Emma Bunton.

Initially the girls, now fractious as well as worn out, discussed the delicate matter of splitting from their manager between themselves. Then they brought in their lawyers. In November 1997, while Fuller was recovering from back surgery in London's Cromwell Hospital, the girls informed him that his services were no longer required. A reported £10 million pay-off sweetened the blow.

Although the band had lost their extensive entourage and the back-up provided by Fuller, they were winning back their lives. It was described in the media as the ultimate act of Girl Power. More accurately, it was the girls' first real enactment of their much-repeated slogan. 'I feel much more in control since we sacked our manager,' said Victoria. 'We're much happier doing it the way we're doing it now. Now we make our own decisions because that's the way we've always wanted it.' Similar sentiments were expressed by the other girls. Mel C revealed that they had wanted to leave Simon Fuller's control for a long time, but they had all felt too frightened. 'The day we left Simon was such a huge release for me,' she explained. 'Until that day I'd feel guilty if I didn't go to the gym every day, but now if I don't feel like going, I don't go and I don't care.'

It was a time for all of them to readjust, to sit down and think what stardom really meant for them. How could they do what they really, really wanted rather than dance to someone else's tune? In a way it was a story as old as pop itself. The tension between management and artiste, the differences between members of the group as they tried to do their own thing. The girls had been brought together by blind ambition, now they had a chance to see their way more clearly, to explore their innate talent. Ironically Fuller was fired just as the girls were voted best band in the world at the MTV Awards in Holland. They had reached the summit of pop fame thanks to their guide and mentor. Now they wanted to reach for the stars on their own.

First indications were not good. Just a few days after the departure of Fuller, they seemed to suffer a collective fall from their platform boots. They were booed off stage during an awards ceremony in Spain because they asked photographers to leave and refused to perform until they did so. The rumpus had developed because the group was being fiercely protective of its image to prevent anyone making money from selling pictures of them, but the timing was inconvenient to say the least. It is an added irony that at the centre of the row was the issue that had caused the split in the first place – control. Indeed it followed hard on the heels of a similar occurrence in India and another in Stockholm while Fuller was still in charge. At the same time, first reports suggested sales of their second album in Britain and America were disappointing, while *Spiceworld: The Movie* had opened to less than ecstatic reviews. It looked as if public opinion was turning against the most marketed band in pop history. Everyone was waiting for the stars to fall to earth.

But one member of the band was truly in heaven. Shortly after saying goodbye to one important man in her life, her manager, Victoria accepted her boyfriend's proposal of marriage. Certainly speculation in the media was at fever pitch when Posh Spice was photographed in December wearing a £13,000 diamond-studded cross – her Christmas present from David. Victoria laughed off the notion of a Posh wedding. 'I don't see any ring, do you?' she jokingly told reporters.

Behind the scenes, her father Tony Adams was visited by David to ask for his eldest daughter's hand in marriage – the most nerve-racking moment in his life. He need not have worried. David had proved to be a big hit with the Adams family, especially with Jackie, whom he had won over not just because of the self-evident fact that he adored her daughter, but because he was down to earth – happy to offer to wash up after a meal with the family. Having been given permission, David in the true tradition went down on one knee to ask Victoria to be his wife. She did not hesitate in saying yes, but then produced her own ring. 'Don't forget Girl Power – will you marry me?' she reportedly asked.

In January 1998, a mere ten months after their first meeting, the couple announced their engagement, appearing before the media at a photo call somewhat reminiscent of royal occasions. Victoria had flown in from Los Angeles where she had been promoting *Spiceworld: The Movie*, and linked up with David at the elegant Rookery Hall Hotel in Nantwich, Cheshire. The couple actually overslept and there was hardly a moment to prepare themselves for the inevitable photographs – the press conference having been set for 11 a.m. In the event, they were forced to keep everyone waiting.

As they proudly showed off their rings – hers a diamond solitaire costing over £40,000, his a diamond and gold band she had chosen with the help of her parents at a Hollywood jeweller – Victoria told the world's media it was just what she wanted, adding somewhat coyly that it had all been 'a big surprise'. Meanwhile, David told reporters, 'I could not be happier right now. I have my dream woman.'

Two, it seemed, were set to become one.

Five

Queen for a Day

The romance between David Beckham and Posh Spice captured the imagination of the nation. Neither press nor public could get enough of the prince and princess of soccer and pop. When the couple were introduced to HRH the Prince of Wales, a headline in a celebrity magazine shrieked: 'The King and Queen meet Prince Charles.' The irony was not intended.

While the tabloids loved the couple, the fans on the soccer terraces loved to bait the player for his choice of future bride. The routine jeers and taunts he suffered solely as a Manchester United star were nothing compared to what he experienced once he started dating Posh Spice. Chants about her preferred sexual position became commonplace. Sometimes the fans' relentless antagonism had the desired effect and led to him making rash challenges and petulant fouls; other times the abuse simply made him play better. As a result of the hostility, Victoria would often keep away from the stadium. She knew that David was always concerned about her well-being, unable to relax until he knew that she was safely seated. Worried that his agitation could affect his performance, she chose to stay away.

In any case, Victoria had enough to deal with without spending a Saturday afternoon watching a game she didn't really understand while enduring the foul abuse of football supporters. A few weeks after the couple announced their engagement in January 1998, Victoria had to deal with the break-up of her own ersatz family, the Spice Girls.

The first indication that all was not well was when Geri failed to appear with the rest of the Spice Girls on the National Lottery TV show on 28 May 1998. Hiding her anger and sense of rejection, Victoria said diplomatically, 'Geri is feeling poorly at the moment.' In reality, though, Geri was simply disillusioned, exhausted and wanted out. A few days before, on their journey back from a gig in Helsinki, Finland, the girls had all exchanged strong words about the way the band was going. Geri had made no secret of the fact that she had been discussing her future career plans in TV with presenter Chris Evans.

A strong-minded firebrand, Geri had been the de facto manager since the split with Simon Fuller in November 1997. Could the Spice Girls survive as a foursome? The next gig on the Scandinavian leg of the spring tour was in Oslo, Norway, and the four girls decided to soldier on without her, filling in her vocals and dance routines. Victoria's reaction to Geri's departure expressed her feelings of rejection and confusion: 'I really miss Geri a lot. I felt very lonely after she'd gone. I was really upset and gutted. The next minute I wanted to punch her in the head. We'll get through it though.'

The Spice Girl offices in central London contained evidence of the way the girls really, really felt about the friend who had abandoned them. Photographs of all the girls adorned the walls, including a life-size portrait of Geri Halliwell. There was one difference though: her picture was upside down, her legs spread out in a 'V' sign. It was a telling indication of the sense of betrayal and bitterness felt towards her at that time.

While Victoria and the rest of the girls publicly put a brave face on Geri's departure, it could not have happened at a more stressful time. They had a prestigious tour of America scheduled for June, which could truly establish the band as worldwide musical force. Victoria had other worries – David was playing for England in his first ever World Cup tournament that month and was understandably nervous.

Much had been expected of him during the build-up to the tournament, and so there was surprise bordering on astonishment when the England coach Glenn Hoddle dropped him from the team, arguing that he did not feel the national playmaker was 'focused enough' for the opening match against Tunisia. A question of temperament exacerbated by David's celebrity lifestyle had given Hoddle pause for thought. While his club manager Alex Ferguson had been privately worried about David's off-pitch behaviour, the Scotsman took issue with the England manager when Hoddle forced the young player to face a media conference to discuss his decision to leave him out of the team, calling it 'an example of bad human relations'.

In response David answered the hail of public criticism in the most effective way known to him, by proving his brilliance on the pitch. In the second game against Romania, he came on as substitute to replace the injured Paul Ince, and making his presence felt, linked up with striker Alan Shearer to help set up Michael Owen's equalizing goal. Despite his efforts, a late winner from Romania led to a 2–1 defeat for the England team. Against Colombia, however, the result was very different. From a free kick outside the Colombian penalty area, he scored a scintillating goal to give England a 2–0 lead that they clung to until the final whistle.

However, within days his triumph turned to disaster in a match against Argentina, when he became only the second England player to be sent off in a World Cup tournament. During a match in which England had the upper hand, the Argentinian midfield player Diego Simeone scythed Beckham down. As Beckham lay poleaxed, Simeone bent down and gave his hair a tug. The red mist took over, and Beckham flicked him with his foot, a petulant gesture that had Danish referee Kim Milton Nielsen reaching for the red card. When the remaining ten-man English team eventually lost the match on penalties, David Beckham's moment of madness was widely regarded as the main cause of the national side's defeat.

As Alex Ferguson noted, he could not have been more vilified if he had committed murder or high treason. Fans ignored Glenn Hoddle's plea that Beckham should not be made the scapegoat for England's premature exit from the World Cup. An effigy of him was hung and burnt outside a pub, West Ham fans planned a mass showing of red cards to the luckless international at their next game against Manchester United, while the nation's football pundits had a field day analysing his shortcomings. When David returned for training at Old Trafford he needed police protection.

It was an experience seared into his soul, one that he has acknowledged he will never be allowed to forget. He was hounded with a cruel intensity that would have broken lesser men. 'I just hope I handled it with dignity. It's certainly made me mature a lot as a person and a player,' he admitted. He drew much of his strength from Victoria. Indeed the first thing he did after the sending-off, when he was sitting alone in the dressing room, was to phone her. Then he followed the advice of Alex Ferguson who was the first person to call him after the incident. He told him not to worry and go to New York and be with Victoria. 'That gave me a huge lift,' he recalls, 'because I was only twenty-three at the time.'

Once he landed in the Big Apple he knew he would have to go into hiding until the fuss died down. The first indication that it was going to get ugly was when he got into a New York taxi and a paparazzo jumped in the other side. His unplanned diversion to the States did have a happy consequence, though, as it meant that he could spend some important quality time with his fiancé to make arrangements for their much-anticipated wedding.

While David was quietly licking his wounds, his wife-to-be was taking the States by storm. On 15 June the remaining Spice Girls triumphantly launched their American tour in Miami. During the two-hour concert Geri's name was not mentioned once, the quartet covering her vocal spots and dance routines seamlessly. 'Luckily, America went exceptionally well,' said Victoria proudly. 'It could really have been a bad time for us and there were a lot of people trying to be negative. And now I feel a bit sorry for Geri.'

The US tour was very gruelling, with venues in the middle of nowhere and long journeys in between. Victoria found it especially difficult. Halfway through the visit she discovered that she was pregnant, and was unlucky enough to suffer with regular morning sickness. Ironically, the couple had been in the midst of financial discussions regarding exclusive pictures of their wedding when Victoria realized she was expecting her first child. The couple, who negotiated a reported £1 million deal with celebrity magazine *OK!*, were surprised but thrilled by the news. 'It came at a perfect time in our relationship,' recalled Victoria later.

As a true trooper, she accepted that the American roadshow had to go on. During the hectic tour, Victoria could hardly bear the sight of food, let alone eat it. She joked that she would go through a dance routine, some of which were toned down because of her delicate condition, and then rush to the side of the stage to be sick.

Her morning sickness was compounded by her homesickness. The USA was a long way away from the alluring comforts of Goff's Oak. Comparing it with Europe, Victoria commented, 'I preferred the food in Europe, especially since you can usually find a Marks and Spencer there, and it does make a big difference when there's a huge time gap and you want to pick up the phone and ring somebody.' Her loneliness was magnified by the fact that David eventually had to return to Britain while she had to stay on, so the couple had to revert back to keeping in touch via endless phone conversations.

Nor did it help her mood when the press gleefully revealed that David had been secretly dating Page Three girl Emma Ryan while she was on tour. They had had a couple of dates and enjoyed late-night chats on the phone, and he had even got her complimentary tickets for a home game. He had conducted his flirtation – the couple stopped short of an affair – with the connivance of one of his friends, Tim Bower, a fashion store manager.

The tabloid tale of subterfuge, flirtation and romantic chatter brought all her fears and insecurities to the surface, to the extent that she even gave serious thought to calling off the wedding. In public Victoria put a brave face on the newspaper story, joking that she did not regard his silly behaviour as another 'red card' offence. It did, though, give her considerable cause for concern.

Publicly the couple seemed utterly in love with one another – and their unborn child. Once she had come through the difficult early weeks, Victoria seemed to enjoy showing off her growing voluptuousness, while David was a besotted father-to-be. He was seen openly kissing her bump while the couple were on holiday in Marbella, Spain, and expressed his views on his impending fatherhood with an uninhibited joy. 'I can't put into words what I feel for him; it's like a bond that started when he was in Victoria's stomach. It's unbelievable,' he said. There was talk that he had considered spending £100,000 on an ultrasound scanner to watch the baby grow inside Victoria, as well as reports that they had a special twenty-minute home movie made of their unborn child while she was in America.

During her pregnancy she was a perfect example of the new breed of celebrity women like Madonna, Demi Moore and Mel B who were proud to be pregnant. They celebrated their womanhood and unborn child, wearing skimpy outfits that showed off their bulge or, as with actress Demi Moore, appeared naked on the covers of magazines. Their bulges were beautiful, not something to hide away under voluminous outfits.

So Victoria and David happily posed for pictures when she was highly pregnant, while she spoke in no-nonsense, practical tones about how she was going to bring up her child, speaking confidently of not hiring a nanny, of taking the infant into the recording studios in a backpack and bringing him up in a down-to-earth manner: 'Straight in the cot, because you have to draw the line somewhere, although I have heard there are some babies who never sleep . . . aren't there?' She was constantly keen to assert both in words and deeds that she was in control of her pregnancy, in control of her life, indeed in control of her future.

Yet all the money and technology in the world could not ensure that the baby would be born healthy. Like many mothers-to-be, Victoria was convinced there was going to be something wrong with her precious infant. A self-confessed born worrier, she fretted continually in spite of endless reassurance from her mother and David. 'It's something you have very little control over,' she remarked. This contrast between the public way Victoria liked to project herself as an independent young woman in charge of her life and her private thoughts where she was less certain and confident, was made manifest with baby Brooklyn.

The sense of anticipation was almost palpable, the excitement at fever pitch. It may have been a grey, miserable March evening, but those outside the unprepossessing Portland Hospital in central London knew they were part of celebrity history. The private hospital, which had seen the arrival into the world of the Duke and Duchess of York's children, Princesses Beatrice and Eugenie, was the scene for another celebrity occasion. The birth of Brooklyn Joseph Beckham at 7.48 p.m. on 4 March 1999 was greeted with the kind of fanfare normally granted a royal event. This was not just the birth of a child, but the creation of a dynasty: Brooklyn the acknowledged heir apparent. His was by far and away the most famous of the 2,000 births of that day, and that evening it featured prominently on television news bulletins, knocking the bloody war in Kosovo off the front pages of tabloid newspapers. 'That really freaked me out,' observed Victoria. 'Anyone would think I'd given birth to a royal.'

Certainly the choreography bore all the hallmarks of a royal birth. First there came the official bulletin announcing that he was delivered by Caesarean section, weighed in at 7 lb and was six days early. The waiting gaggle of camera crews, photographers, radio and print reporters as well as excited fans outside the hospital were duly informed that the proud father was in attendance and that mother and baby were doing fine. Naturally the footballer was 'over the moon' at his son's birth.

Then there was the arrival of the showbiz aristocracy, bearing gifts for the infant as he lay in his crib. The Spice Girls brought balloons, champagne and flowers, Elton John sent a giant teddy bear as well as a set of silver bowls from Tiffany, while Donatella Versace gave him designer baby outfits. Finally, after five days resting in her private suite, it was expected that, like royal parents, Victoria and David would make a brief appearance so that they could show the baby off to the world. Not this time. The new House of Beckham had different ideas.

Instead the happy trio made their royal getaway in a well-planned, high-speed operation. A limousine with blacked-out windows pulled up at the back entrance to the hospital and seconds later sped off with an escort of police motorcyclists acting as outriders, stopping traffic as the convoy made their way to Victoria's parents' home in Hertfordshire. The elaborate security blanket covering the sleeping infant almost seemed to signify that baby Brooklyn – named after the New York borough where he was conceived – was in some ways even more precious and protected than a royal prince.

As his parents were keen to make clear, his privacy was of paramount importance. They talked warmly about their love for their son, how David was the perfect husband, changing nappies and feeding the youngster, and how Victoria could hardly bear to be away from the infant for a second. The Beckhams were the ideal happy family, doting on each other and their child, self-professed role models for a generation. When the couple went out shopping they were keen to protect him from intrusive photographers, shielding his head with their hands. 'He's the one thing that is totally private to us,' Victoria argued.

Her idealized notion of life with Brooklyn came down to earth with a bump in the months after he was born – much as many had predicted. As mother Louise Young observed, 'We've all given fish-eye looks to first-time pregnant women who sport charming naivety. Have they ever noticed that babies squeak when you put them down? Does she know that as soon as you've dressed babies, they crap? As soon as you've changed them, they're hungry? As soon as you've fed them, they need winding? As soon as you've winded them, they're sick? I predict rude awakenings. Possibly several times a night.'

Sleepless nights and constant worrying was indeed the reality for Victoria who, like millions of mothers before her, discovered the difference between great expectations and the mundane reality. Not that Brooklyn was the easiest of babies in the early months. In May 1999, when he was just two months old, Victoria held his hand and cuddled him as he was given a general anaesthetic before a hernia operation. The couple have admitted it was the most upsetting thing they had ever endured, naturally concerned about their son during his hour-long operation at the Portland Hospital. Besides his hernia, from which Brooklyn effected a full recovery, he has since suffered from all the usual childhood ailments, and he is particularly prone to ear infections, which is not surprising given his jet-set lifestyle. More worrying for his parents was his apparent inability to hold down his food when he was younger, a condition that famously caused him to be sick over his father's suit on his wedding day.

Victoria has confessed that she is a 'paranoid' mother, always worrying about Brooklyn's health. In the early months she would often go into his bedroom in the night and put a mirror next to his mouth to check that he was still breathing. When the singer, who helped launch a national meningitis campaign, heard that her sister's daughter Liberty was running a high fever, a symptom associated with the killer illness, she may well have suspected the worst. Fortunately, the youngster only had a minor ailment and quickly recovered.

Not only was she learning how to bring up baby, she was also making sure that her big day was going to conform to her childhood dreams. However, marrying her Prince Charming called for patience, determination and an ever open chequebook. It took fourteen months, hundreds of phone calls, letters, visits and meetings to plan the event. Victoria and her mother masterminded the celebrity wedding of the year with a little help from a small army of assistants, organized by Peregrine Armstrong-Jones, the brother of Princess Margaret's former husband, Lord Snowdon. If the birth of Brooklyn marked the beginning of the Beckham dynasty, then the wedding represented the couple's coronation.

The event, which took place on 4 July 1999, exactly four months after Brooklyn's birth, seemed to capture the spirit of Posh and Becks as individuals, a couple and a culture; a curious combination of childlike narcissism, conspicuous consumption and Disneyesque innocence. Billed as the wedding of the year, the sense of illusion and self-delusion was encapsulated in the fact that the couple, who publicly professed such intense love for each other, turned what is traditionally seen as a spiritual union into a photographic shoot. The abiding and certainly symbolic image of the wedding is of a weary David and Victoria huddled over a light box in the early hours of the morning, choosing photographs for the special issue of *OK!* magazine, when they should have been enjoying their first night together as a married couple. As profile writer Stuart Jeffries astutely observed, 'When *OK!* magazine devoted two issues to her wedding, it became disturbingly apparent how far she [Victoria] was prepared to go to bask in the public eye.'

It was a far cry from the romantic illusion of marriage Victoria held in her heart, an ideal expressed in the scrapbook of bridal pictures she had kept from her childhood. Once the couple had decided to marry she apparently took out her scrapbook and went through it, ticking off wedding ideas that she had cherished since she was tiny. 'It will be her childhood dream come true,' a friend was quoted as saying.

The couple decided to theme their wedding on a fairy tale because they believed they had a storybook romance, and, as Victoria admitted, they were just big kids at heart. Indeed David has listed tracing Disney cartoons and colouring them in as one of his hobbies. During their courtship he often faxed his efforts to Victoria, adding a love note to the drawing. 'They have a lot of fun together too – he chases her around the house or they jump like kids on the bed, giggling and being generally soppy. They are very sweet together,' a friend observed.

But these were children who could afford to turn the world into a giant playground. They spent

£500,000 transforming Luttrellstown Castle, an elegant eighteenth-century house outside Dublin, into a royal fairyland that owed more to Walt Disney than House of Windsor. It was themed a la Hollywood on the story of Robin Hood, the outlaw who stole from the rich to give to the poor, the marquee and grounds decorated with greenery, twigs, apples, acres of velvet fabric in burgundy, dark green and cardinal purple as well as 15,000 fairy lights. They chose the theme music from the Disney cartoon *Beauty and the Beast* to make their grand entrance before the assembled throng, and took to the dance floor to the strains of the theme from the animated movie *The Lion King*. The grand finale of the evening was a spectacular four-minute firework display that would not have disgraced the Magic Kingdom itself.

As with every successful Disney production, romantic and real royal history were combined. The genuine eighteenth-century chapel in the castle grounds, which was restored for the wedding, had enchanted Queen Victoria when she saw it during a visit in 1849. 'I do so wish Albert and I had married here,' the Queen admitted, moved by the sense of peace and tranquillity inside the small chapel. More than a century later, Victoria was equally entranced choosing the place, now named Queen Victoria's Folly, as the setting for the crowning event of her life. Royal jeweller Slim Barrett, who had worked with the late Diana, Princess of Wales, lent the bride a £100,000 diamond and gold coronet for her big day, the piece later being auctioned for charity.

These authentic royal connections were elaborated upon in the other arrangements for the day, which were more reminiscent of Hollywood notions of royalty. The 255 guests, including the Spice Girls and Manchester United players, received invitations on parchment embossed with gold leaf and bearing a specially designed coat of arms with a swan, a crown and the words 'Love and Friendship'. When they arrived at the imposing castle, it was indeed like a scene from the Magic Kingdom. A rich purple flag emblazoned with David and Victoria's crest and their initials fluttered in the breeze, and a trumpet fanfare was played from the battlements while six-foot-long silk 'flames' shot from the castle turrets. Once safely inside the thick stone walls, the favoured few were given the imperial purple-carpet treatment.

As they descended the impressive staircase to the banqueting marquee, they were serenaded by liveried attendants in Irish costume. Afterwards they toasted the bride and groom from solid silver goblets, and the newly-weds accepted their plaudits, holding court in his-and-hers red and gold thrones. Before the happy couple cut the tiered cake, which was decorated with nude figures of David, Victoria and Brooklyn, the groom gave an insight into his wife's mindset and the dynamics of the relationship. 'I will always love and look after Victoria and treat her like a princess, because that's how she likes to be treated,' he told the guests.

This was a princess who liked to take command. She omitted the word 'obey' from the marriage vows, while David had meekly obeyed her wishes that he cancel his proposed stag night, and treat the wedding day as if he were in training for a big match.

Just as she gave the impression of controlling their partnership, so Victoria organized a wedding that was very much in their image. She left nothing to chance, calling Peregrine Armstrong-Jones five times a day. 'We knew what we wanted and discussed every detail with Peregrine. I could have left everything to him, but I wanted to be hands on,' she said. The dress, for instance, which was designed by American Vera Wang, took three transatlantic trips to New York for fittings for Victoria before she and her mother were satisfied with the £60,000 gown. 'It is very Scarlett O'Hara,' said Victoria.

On the big day, as David went for a relaxing round of golf, Victoria prowled the castle corridors, taking personal charge of last-minute details. She gave three musicians from the eighteen-piece Starlight orchestra their marching orders because they 'didn't look right'. Like the rest of the band, the trio had been practising for six weeks beforehand. The eleventh-hour decision led to accusations that she was a 'nightmare control freak'.

Ultimately though, beneath the sentiment and saccharine, this was more than a wedding: it was an elaborate money-making scheme, not just for the Beckhams but also for the magazine that had paid a king's ransom for exclusive rights to the event. So all the guests, who were helicoptered in to avoid photographers lurking outside, suffered the indignity of being frisked for cameras before they entered the reception where no photography was permitted.

The proceedings crawled to a virtual standstill because of the demands of the official photographers, while dozens of security men and sniffer dogs patrolled the 560-acre grounds to keep out unwelcome media visitors. 'The main thing was that we wanted everyone to feel really comfortable and enjoy themselves,' said Victoria, without a trace of irony.

Naturally the whole affair attracted a battery of criticism not just because of the vulgar display, the royal pretensions and the conspicuous consumption, but because the couple were cashing in on their romance by selling their wedding day. The fact that this is a regular practice among stars around the world was conveniently forgotten by those selfsame critics. More interestingly, when *she* discussed the couple's £1 million payday, Victoria offered a telling insight into those values she holds dear. 'We wanted everything to be under control and to be safe,' she said in a TV interview. 'The best way to do that was to have control over the pictures, the way they were taken, nobody pushing or shoving.' Those words again, control and safe, are sentiments that seem to dominate her life.

Feisty yet sensitive to the merest hint of criticism, Victoria came out fighting to defend her fairy-tale wedding which was, as far as she was concerned, 'a dream come true'. The money spent and the decisions taken were a reflection of the couple's desires, as well as their sense of humour. 'A lot of stuff is tongue-in-cheek. We don't care what people say as long as we're happy and our families are happy, that's all that matters,' the new celebrity queen protested.

She was not queen for long, though, as despite the couple's pleadings David was ordered back to Old Trafford for pre-season training by his manager Alex Ferguson, forcing them to abandon a ten-day honeymoon in the Indian Ocean. Instead of sunning themselves on a faraway desert island, the newly-weds spent a few days in the south of France at the home of composer Andrew Lloyd Webber before flying home so that David could join his teammates. On his return, however, David found himself reduced to playing in the reserves. While it may have been Ferguson's way of bringing his star player back down to earth after the glamour and glitter of his wedding in Ireland, it did little to improve Victoria's opinion of him – or the world of soccer.

A few weeks later, in August, she could be excused for thinking that her marriage was jinxed. While they were staying in a London hotel, David shame-facedly admitted that he had lost his diamond-encrusted wedding ring after a night of heavy drinking with his friends Ryan Giggs and Dave Gardner. Doubtless Victoria was furious not just because of the loss of such a sentimental possession, but because it seemed a harbinger of misfortune. Fortuitously, though, a hotel cleaner found the valuable piece of jewellery. Once again Lady Luck seemed to be smiling on the glamorous new royals.

Six

Servant
of Two Masters

It was a scene of high drama and keen emotion as
Victoria Beckham, her face streaked with tears,
paced anxiously around the living room of her
parents' house. Her mother Jackie and her father
Tony tried in vain to calm her down as her mood
lurched between frustration, fear and anger. Fans of
the Spice Girls would never have recognized the sobbing, swearing young woman as sultry Posh Spice,
the singer with a trademark scowl and an air of cool
sophistication. In the early hours of Saturday morning, though, Victoria Beckham was simply a terrified
young mother reduced to near hysteria over the
safety of Brooklyn, her baby boy.

She had returned to her parents' mock-Tudor
home in Hertfordshire earlier that evening in
September 1999, after spending a day in the recording studios with the other three members of the
Spice Girls. Their 'Girl Power' slogan was the last
thing on her mind that night, as she felt frightened,

alone and very, very vulnerable. Her world had become a living nightmare from the moment her father had told her about a telephone call from the police. They had received information from several sources that an attempt to kidnap baby Brooklyn and perhaps Victoria herself was going to be made that weekend. It was a threat they were taking very seriously indeed.

At first, as anyone would, Victoria couldn't believe what she was hearing. Certainly she and her husband had received death threats in the past. On one occasion they had been sent bullets on which David's name had been scratched. Such was their concern that for the previous few weeks they had hired a private bodyguard to watch over their six-month-old son. She knew too that extra marked and unmarked police cars had patrolled near her parents' home in Goff's Oak, where she and David had been living on and off since their marriage just a few weeks before.

Somehow though the danger hadn't seemed real. Now here was a policeman telling her about the imminent threat to her son's life. The hysteria surrounding David's sending off in the World Cup paled into significance as, for the first time, she saw the real flipside of celebrity, the dark side of the brightly-lit world she now inhabited. And it was scary. 'It's every parent's worst nightmare, something happening to their child,' she later remarked.

David, who had been with his England teammates at their training camp, had driven home the moment he'd been told of the danger to his son. He was accompanied by Kevin Keegan, England coach at the time, and the team physiotherapist Gary

Lewin. The newly-weds were comforted by Keegan's presence. They both admired his honesty and compassion, believing him to be more tolerant than his predecessor, Glenn Hoddle, as well as being sensitive to the emotional needs of the players who came under his wing. Unusually, Victoria, who has always had little time for the world of football, had nothing but praise for him. 'Kevin Keegan is such a supportive manager,' she said.

The former European Footballer of the Year tried to put the matter into perspective. He told them that during his days with Hamburg he and his family had also received threats, so he understood how upset the Beckhams would be feeling. There were, however, pressing practical matters to be considered. Keegan had already named his team to face Luxembourg in a European Championship qualifying match at Wembley that afternoon. With England's finest player expected to be fit and in the starting eleven, it would create a firestorm of media interest if Beckham deliberately stood down.

Nonetheless, the worried father was adamant that he would not take to the field while his son's life was in danger. He was not prepared to leave either Victoria or Brooklyn until he was certain they were safe. Keegan assured David that the decision to play or not was entirely his own. There were other concerns as well. Later in the day Victoria was due at the private Wellington Hospital in St John's Wood, North London, to undergo cosmetic surgery. It was the only time in her hectic schedule that the operation could be performed and it would be another year before she would again have the chance – and the necessary time to recuperate away from prying eyes. She intended to use the villa of her friend Sir Elton John, in the south of France, which happened to be available.

As heads were scratched and they tried to break the impasse, it was suggested that the whole family should leave Goff's Oak and stay with the England soccer squad at Burnham Beeches, which was under round-the-clock police protection. David agreed to the plan and at three o'clock on Saturday morning he, his coach and the physio left to organize rooms for Victoria, Brooklyn and her parents at the team headquarters. An hour later, a convoy of cars swept down the driveway of the Adams' family home, and made the thirty-five minute journey to the England enclave. When they arrived, David, Victoria and their son were able to snatch a few hours' sleep before the footballer went off to join to his teammates for light training later that morning. While Victoria checked into hospital, Brooklyn remained in safety with Victoria's family.

It was hardly the ideal preparation for a major international match. Nor was their ordeal over. Over the next few months threats and fear of kidnap stalked their daily lives. Gruesome images with sinister messages were regularly sent to them. One particularly sick picture showed defaced newspaper photographs of Victoria and Brooklyn with bullet holes through their heads and blood pouring out. The message was chilling: 'You are going to get what's coming to you.'

Most worrying was the stalker's accurate knowledge of the details of their lives, which added a new side to their fear. Perhaps their every move was being watched. Certainly the police regarded the threats as genuine, putting taps on their phones and carefully monitoring their mail, testing the envelopes and postage stamps for telltale signs of DNA that could identify the anonymous stalker. Victoria's spokesman Alan Edwards confirmed, 'I have received a large number of calls on a regular basis from police to inform me that the gang's plan [to kidnap Brooklyn and Victoria] is still active.'

It was later revealed, according to well-placed sources, why the police were taking the threats so seriously: it seemed that similar threats had been made to Victoria's former colleague, Geri Halliwell, as well as to an unnamed member of the royal family. The unprovoked knife attack on former Beatle George Harrison at his home, and the point-blank shooting of TV presenter Jill Dando earlier that year, were a terrifying reminder to David and Victoria of how real the threats could be. As Victoria often said, 'I don't want to end up like Jill Dando.'

Since their elaborate wedding just two months before when, sitting on the marital throne, they were feted as Britain's new royal couple, Mr and Mrs Beckham's experience had not lived up to the promises in the brochure of celebrity. The normal stresses of being newly married, of staying with Victoria's parents, and of sleepless nights with baby Brooklyn, who was often ill in the early months, were compounded by the added pressures of stardom.

David had barely recovered his equilibrium after the fallout following his World Cup red card – fans still routinely abused him from the terraces – and now he had to contend with serious death threats to his precious wife and child. Aged only twenty-four, it was almost too much to bear. He worried about them dreadfully: 'I'm thinking all the time about my little boy and Victoria. All the time, every minute.' Concerns not just about their general well-being, but now also their safety forced the young man into an ever tighter group of family and trusted confidantes. The strain told in his body language; the watchful eyes, a constant wariness in his gait in readiness for paparazzi ambushes, and a face contorted with anger often replaced the once cheeky grin. On and off the pitch he seemed a changed man. 'Gone is the fun-loving lad of a few years ago,' remarked Alex Ferguson, 'and in his place is a seriously private person, with inner reaches that few can penetrate.'

An already stressful lifestyle was exacerbated by the fact that the newly-wed found that he was now the servant of two masters – his manager and his wife. Ferguson expected him to live and breathe soccer, and live near to the ground in Manchester. His wife needed him by her side when she went to glamorous parties in London, and wanted him to stay with her at her parents' home in Hertfordshire. Even though they had a £300,000 apartment in Alderley Edge in Cheshire, which was only a short drive from his training ground, Victoria preferred life down south. It meant that he was forever commuting 370 miles between Hertfordshire and Manchester, and risking his manager's wrath in the process. He was damned if he did and damned if he didn't. It was a recipe for disaster that was not long arriving.

Only a matter of weeks into the new season, David was handed a record club fine of £50,000 – the equivalent of two weeks' wages – for breaking a club curfew. In September, Victoria and David, wearing a silk headscarf, had made a high-profile arrival at designer Jade Jagger's party in Covent Garden during London Fashion Week. There was just one problem. It was only hours before his team flew to Austria for an important Champions' League game against Sturm Graz and he should have been resting rather than partying. It had proved the last straw for Ferguson, and Beckham was duly penalized for compromising the team at such a crucial time. The punishment symbolized the manager's growing concern about his star player; the fact that he no longer joined his teammates for lunch after training, his celebrity lifestyle and what he considered the malign influence of his wife on his game. 'Everybody knows that I have not always seen eye to eye with Beckham,' said the manager. 'The showbiz element in his life, made inevitable by the pop-star status of his wife, Victoria, has sometimes caused me to worry about a possible threat to his chances of giving maximum expression to his huge talent.'

Yet even though the fine was substantial, the penny did not seem to drop. Just days after he was handed the financial reprimand and, shortly before a crunch match against rivals Chelsea, David left training in Manchester, but instead of heading to his Cheshire home he drove 185 miles down Britain's clogged motorways to join Victoria and Brooklyn in Hertfordshire. He surely realized that by heading south, just prior to another important fixture, he was tempting fate – and another heavy fine – again.

If he had hoped for a relaxing evening with his wife and child when he arrived, he was to be disappointed. Victoria had agreed to join her Spice Girl friend and colleague Emma Bunton, who was launching her television career by hosting the fifth anniversary celebrations of the pop-music channel VH-1. So he was called upon to chauffeur Victoria to the event at the Atlantis Gallery bar in London's East End, risking the attention of the inevitable posse of waiting photographers. He must have known he couldn't afford to be snapped again at such a high-profile bash so soon after his last dressing-down from Ferguson. It was just a question of whiling away a few anonymous hours while Victoria caroused in yet another VIP bar.

One wonders whether he thought all the trouble was worthwhile. Here was one of Britain's most talented football players – whose boots sold at auction at Christie's for £13,800, whose signed shirts could sell for £7,500 apiece and whose fans have been known to rummage through dustbins outside his hairdresser's salon for locks of his golden gelled hair – reduced to skulking around London like a man on the run.

After a couple of hours he returned to the venue, where he was seen but not captured on camera, to pick up Victoria and her party, and drive them home. He would have had little time for rest before the next morning's training session back in Manchester. A snatched night's sleep and a 370-mile round trip was hardly the best training for a professional athlete upon whose slim shoulders rested the hopes and ambitions not only of Manchester United supporters, but also millions of England fans.

Days later, when Manchester played Chelsea at Stamford Bridge on the first Sunday of October 1999, they lost 5–0, their worst result in three years. Beckham was substituted midway through the second half, and his lacklustre performance did not go unnoticed. 'Beckham looked like he was sulking, well and truly cheesed off that football is interfering with his social life,' observed the *Daily Mirror*.

During the 1999 season it was noted too that there was a real streak of petulance about his behaviour on the pitch. During the Sturm Graz game he was lucky not to be sent off. At Anfield he was involved in an ugly stamping incident with Liverpool skipper Jamie Redknapp. There were also allegations that he made obscene gestures to the crowd at Elland Road where Leeds United supporters were baiting him about his wife. In January 2000 he was given a red card for a vicious challenge during the World Club Championships in Brazil. Such was the concern that Graham Bean, the compliance officer for the Football Association, wanted to meet him to discuss his disciplinary record. Serious questions were now being asked about his temperament – although few of his critics had to endure the unseen stresses facing the player.

Furthermore, the famous short fuse on the pitch was becoming more apparent away from the terraces. Often when he was driving he became very aggressive with those he considered to have 'cut him up' on the road. Even autograph hunters were catching the rough edge of his tongue. Normally he was very considerate with fans – 'I don't like bad manners, I never have done, which is why I never refuse autographs,' he has asserted – but persistent autograph hunters known as 'giffers' would get short shrift. On one occasion when a Liverpool youngster asked for his signature, the boy received a torrent of abuse. 'He is so unpleasant and rude that I wouldn't bother asking him again,' said the youngster. 'David and Victoria upset a lot of people with their attitude.'

Photographers who have been snapping him since he arrived as a raw teenage talent became regular targets for abuse. When one cameraman took a picture of the Beckhams leaving the Daisy and Tom children's store in central Manchester, David's reaction was instantly aggressive. He ran across the road and threatened to stab the photographer if he took another picture.

Beckham is certainly not the first celebrity to have clashed with cameramen. It is part of the psychology of stardom. As the comedian Fred Allen observed, a celebrity is 'a person who strives to become well known, then wears dark glasses in order to avoid being recognized'.

There was though a deeper malaise. For all his medals and trophies, and the adulation and acclaim, David Beckham was leading an unsettled life on the road; a long-distance commuter with no fixed abode and a suitcase his constant companion. It was a life that reflected the irreconcilable demands of his wife and his manager. The battle for the heart and mind of David Beckham was more than just a fight between two stubborn, determined and strong-willed individuals: it was a clash of culture and generations.

As far as Ferguson was concerned, in the male-dominated world of professional football, the role of a player's wife was simple: to ensure a well-ordered and preferably quiet home life so that the player put on his finest performance on, rather than off, the pitch. Enter into this equation a multi-millionairess who was both more famous and richer than her player partner; a powerful, ambitious woman used to the trappings of success and the glamorous lifestyle of a pop superstar.

Victoria's complete lack of interest in the sport was summed up by a remark she made after David had scored a sublime goal from a dead-ball kick. She had dutifully watched his performance on television and when he phoned her after the game she congratulated him, but added, 'Your roots really need doing.' On another occasion, in May 2000, after he had scored his fiftieth goal for Manchester United, Victoria genuinely thought it was his fiftieth goal that season. However it was a blunder that only endeared her to him all the more.

On the few occasions during the 1999–2000 season that she watched him play, Victoria made it clear that she regarded her visits to Old Trafford as more of a duty than a pleasure, a necessary function to show loyalty to her husband.

Few could blame her for being reluctant to attend matches in Manchester. The vicious chants sung by the away fans against herself and Brooklyn at the ground, as well as continual death threats sent to her home, made her wary of risking too much public exposure at soccer games. For a long time the shouts of the fans upset Brooklyn and she had to put cotton wool in his ears to protect him. Not that it was much better for her, as the stares of fans as well as the attentions of amateur photographers usually made it an uncomfortable experience.

Safety was always her main concern. On arrival at the ground she was the only footballer's wife whose car was permitted to drive right up to the entrance of the stadium. When she got out of the car, stewards made a cordon so that she and her party only had to walk a few paces before they were safely inside. Once inside she spent little time actually watching a match, preferring to stay in the club crêche with her son. After the match she would wait in the players' lounge for David, rarely speaking to anyone else apart from his mother. With a couple of exceptions, she did virtually nothing to build a rapport with players' partners or United staff. It was apparent even to casual observers that she found the whole experience a trial.

The one occasion she did seem to enjoy was when she watched Brooklyn and his father walk on the pitch when Manchester United were presented with the League Championship trophy on 6 May 2000, following a 3–1 defeat of Tottenham Hotspur at the last home game of the season. David, who organized a special kit for Brooklyn, did a lap of honour with his son, all the while watched by Victoria and their respective parents.

The happy event did little to change her thoughts on the beautiful game, though, especially where her son was concerned: 'I would definitely prefer him to be a golfer. It's a better profession than a footballer.'

Her indifference towards and ignorance of the sport David loved, as well as the geographical distance from his place of work, meant that the orbit of his world had shifted on its axis. 'Football's not the only thing in my life any more,' David himself admitted. 'Things that were important before just don't seem as important now that I have Brooklyn and Victoria.'

The effect of Victoria on a national soccer treasure inevitably sparked hostile debate. There were public accusations that she hated Manchester, she wanted

Right: Displaying precocious talent on the football field, David was a star player for Ridgeway Rovers in the Enfield District League.

Below: A youthful David Beckham makes his ambitions clear . . .

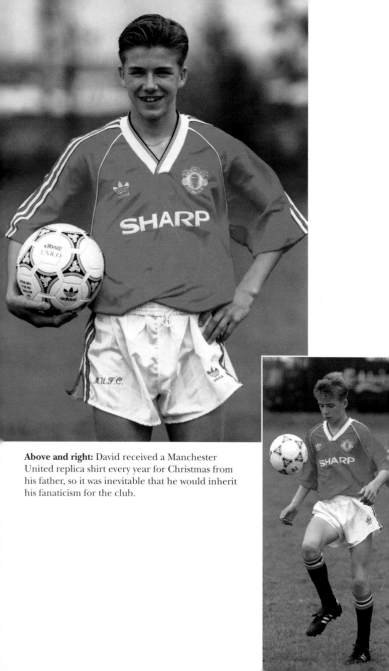

Above and right: David received a Manchester United replica shirt every year for Christmas from his father, so it was inevitable that he would inherit his fanaticism for the club.

Above: At school Victoria was an able student and an aspiring performer.

Right: Setting new trends from an early age, Victoria displays signs of a keen interest in the world of fashion.

Above: The Spice Girls – (clockwise) Victoria, Mel B, Mel C, Emma and Geri – pictured in July 1996, the month in which their first single 'Wannabe' was released – it reached the number one spot within two weeks.

Left: The Spice Girls at Madame Tussauds help raise money for charity on Red Nose Day, 6 February 1997.

Below: The Spice Girls and Prince Charles at a Prince's Trust concert held at Manchester Opera House in May 1997.

Posh and Becks – the early days

Left: Victoria visits David at his Manchester home.

Right: In January 1998 the worlds of music and football were united following the announcement of Victoria and David's engagement, only ten months after they first met. 'I could not be happier right now,' David told the world's media. 'I have my dream woman.'

Below: David and Victoria grow accustomed to hoards of press photographers snapping their every move.

Right: Dressed in matching black leather (which Victoria later described as an embarrassing fashion faux pas), the couple attend the Versace Club in June 1999, a month prior to their much-feted wedding.

Below: The *Sun* newspaper puts a spin on the 'regal' nature of the Beckham's fairy-tale wedding.

David to leave Old Trafford for a London club or one in Europe, and that her relationship with Ferguson was less than cordial. While she made no secret about her lack of interest in football, she publicly denied these stories, branding them 'hurtful and unfair'. 'I know how much it means for David to play for United, so I'd never put him in a position like that,' she said, emphasizing that she was happy living in Manchester. At the time, observers saw her utterances as an attempt to be tactful. As sports journalist Harry Harris commented, 'Behind the scenes Victoria would prefer to live in London. The reality is that she doesn't like Manchester although she has been very diplomatic about it.'

In *Forever Spice*, however, she did refer to earlier tension between David and herself over his desire to play for Manchester United. 'We had a bit of a dispute on the phone because he is re-signing his contract in Manchester. I was a bit hurt because I was hoping deep down he would sign for a London club.' In a later interview, Victoria admitted, 'I'd be lying if I said we're going to be here for ever and ever. Footballers move abroad at some stage in their career so I'm sure we will.'

It seemed that Victoria was constantly thinking of ways to enable David to spend more time in the south with her and her family. The manager ruled out suggestions that Beckham could commute by helicopter as too dangerous, and also rejected a scheme to convert a camper van so that David could sleep while a chauffeur drove him on the motorway. Even though Stansted airport was only half an hour's drive from Goff's Oak, the player did not dare travel south by air, as word would soon have got back to his boss.

The continuing conflict between his professional and personal life was perfectly illustrated at Christmas 1999. The couple argued over her desire to spend the festive season with her family in Hertfordshire, even though he had an important league game at home against Bradford City on Boxing Day. The bickering went on for several days and, as was usually the case, Victoria prevailed. So on Christmas Eve, while Victoria appeared on a TV show, David drove down to Goff's Oak after training. He stayed at the Adams' home on Christmas Day, driving north late in the evening for the match a few hours later.

David was left with the worst of all worlds, shuttling up and down the motorway at all hours of the day and night, snatching a few precious hours with his son and wife before returning to training or a game. It was a lifestyle that would certainly have surprised Ferguson, who was under the mistaken impression that the player was permanently based in his Cheshire apartment.

David himself had denied that he was commuting frequently between London and Manchester: 'If I was travelling up from London at six every morning, I think the strain would start to tell.'

While Victoria was seen as the enemy within, ironically it was Brooklyn Beckham who caused the biggest rift between player and manager. The first occasion was the night of Ferguson's testimonial dinner in Manchester in the autumn of 1999. The Beckhams arrived at 8.55 p.m. for an event due to start at 7 p.m. By the time they were seated by a stony-faced Ned Kelly, the head of Manchester United security, the event was well under way.

Nevertheless, the snub was not deliberate. Brooklyn had not been able to settle down for the night and as the minutes ticked by he grew more and more agitated. As he would not respond to the babysitter's attempts to soothe him, the couple had had to delay their departure until he had quietened down. By the time the domestic crisis had been resolved, the couple were very late for the important event, and destined for critical column inches in next day's papers.

However it was another episode involving David's concern over Brooklyn that led to his most damaging fallout with Ferguson. On the night of Thursday 17 February 2000, Brooklyn, then eleven months old, spent a restless night at Goff's Oak, continually being sick and running a temperature. At dawn the next day it was a very worried and tired David Beckham who left his son behind to drive to Manchester to join his teammates in training for that Sunday's top of the table clash with Leeds United. When he departed Brooklyn was still unwell, and as David headed north he grew increasingly anxious about his son's condition.

After driving on the motorway for an hour or so he had got himself into such a state of worry that he decided to turn back and miss morning training. However, when he contacted the club to inform them of his domestic problem, they had probably assumed that he was at home in Alderley Edge in Cheshire, near to the training ground. As luck would have it, Victoria was later photographed with her sister Louise in London's Knightsbridge on a shopping spree, proving the couple were a considerable distance from their Cheshire home.

While Brooklyn had made a good recovery from his ailments on the Friday, David's relationship with his manager was now on the critical list. When he reported for training on Saturday morning, he faced an angry and very public tongue-lashing from Ferguson, who told him to sort out his priorities because the club came before everything else. Then he unceremoniously kicked him out of the Carrington training ground, shouting: 'Get out of here, get off the pitch and get out now.' He was dropped for the match at Elland Road, fined £50,000, and suffered the ignominy of watching the game, boots in hand, from the sidelines. It was, crowed the *Daily Mail*, a triumph for discipline and integrity over celebrity and distraction.

For David Beckham it was a salutary experience. His parents, who had driven to Leeds to watch the match as they did for all his games, were mortified. Unlike Victoria and her family, they knew the manager, and were only too aware of his strict attitude and his history of ditching players who got too big for their boots. A surprised Ted Beckham first heard about the bust-up in a brief phone call from David, who told him he had been dropped. Seemingly anxious not to make a bad situation any worse when questioned about the circumstances, the player's father said, 'I don't want to upset the apple cart. Whatever has happened is between David and the club.'

David's parents would no doubt have been fearful, probably with good reason, that he was jeopardizing his glittering career at Manchester United. Afterwards, Ferguson believed that his tough approach had brought Victoria and David to their senses, noting, 'The after-effects of the episode were entirely positive. It brought home to David the seriousness of my attitude about how he should prepare for games. Living in the south of England was not fair to me, the club, his teammates or the fans who have supported him so loyally. Nor in football terms was it fair to him.'

In reality, Victoria had already bought a luxury mansion in the Hertfordshire village of Sawbridgeworth, just a few miles from her parents' home, which was quickly nicknamed 'Beckingham Palace'.

It seemed the battle between pop queen and football knight was set to run and run.

Seven

A Bridge Called Brooklyn

In December 1999, when Victoria Beckham arrived for a thirty-seventh birthday lunch at the fashionable Ivy restaurant in central London, hosted by Elton John for his partner David Furnish, she caused a sensation.

She was wearing a figure-hugging, off-the-shoulder, red, leather mini dress, and the change in her figure was unmistakable. On that chilly winter's day when other guests such as Elizabeth Hurley and actress Helena Bonham Carter had wrapped up well, the five-foot-six-inch singer, who weighed barely 90 lb, seemed to want to flaunt her sculptured facial features, jutting collarbone and stick-like legs.

Her breasts though seemed larger and more defined. The girl who used silicone 'falsies' on TV because she was self-conscious about the modest size of her bust, fiercely denied that she had had breast surgery – even though she had checked in for an operation in a private hospital the previous September.

Commentators were unconvinced: 'I'm afraid Mother Nature really doesn't do acorn shoulders and melon breasts on the same torso.'

A few weeks later, in February 2000, Victoria was keen to expose herself again, this time for London Fashion Week where she wore a pair of hot pants and an evening dress slashed to the thigh. While she admitted that she was 'so petrified that she could hardly speak', she went ahead with her catwalk routine. Indeed she was so keen to parade her body that when her friend, designer Maria Grachvogel, was making the outfits she insisted on showing as much flesh as possible. 'We discuss the designs for the clothes she makes for me. She says, "Let's put the split to the knee" and I always say, "No, make it higher – thigh high."'

On the same day that the *Daily Mail* newspaper advised its readers on how to 'lose a stone in a flash', they observed with horror Victoria's new shape. Under the headline 'Skeletal Spice', the paper asked the burning question of the day: 'Should she be a role model for teenage girls prone to anorexia?'

As with her husband and his woes on the soccer field, Victoria Beckham was now a national lightning rod for debate. In a country where an estimated 1.5 million people, overwhelmingly women, suffer from some kind of eating disorder, Posh Spice's problems struck a chord. It seemed that she had joined a long line of other female stars, notably *Friends* favourites Courteney Cox Arquette and Jennifer Aniston, *Ally McBeal*'s Calista Flockhart and actress Elizabeth Hurley, whose lives under the spotlight had impelled them to become, according to one critic, 'like some dreadful mockery of famine victims'. It was all so ironic. For this was the same girl who when asked what she meant by Girl Power had replied, 'We're saying you don't have to be skinny and six foot tall and have no spots and be beautiful, 'cos we're not like that. We're normal shaped girls.'

Understandably Victoria was hurt by the furore about her body shape, not just for herself but for her mother. 'I could have a nervous breakdown,' she said. 'This is also saying that my mum hasn't brought me up right. It's saying that I've got a problem and no one has recognized it and no one is offering me any help. My mum is really upset about this.'

She argued that her own mother had lost 40 lb after giving birth to her brother Christian, that her husband David was perfectly happy with her new shape, that she ate healthily and that bringing up baby Brooklyn was such hard work that she was always on the go. 'It's irresponsible to say I'm anorexic. After a baby you are dashing about all day. I never sit down,' she revealed, adding that she had a responsibility as a role model to young fans who could get the wrong idea. 'I'm not anorexic, I'm not bulimic and I'm not a skeleton. I'm seven and a half stone, very fit and I feel great,' she retorted.

Her mother Jackie also waded in, phoning an afternoon TV show to assure viewers that her daughter was perfectly healthy. 'Victoria is working very hard and she's looking after a baby,' she argued, omitting to mention that with her daughter's busy schedule it was often her small army of surrogate parents who helped with Brooklyn.

Once again, in the life of Victoria Beckham there was a difference between what she stated defiantly in public and what went on when the microphones were switched off and the notepads put away. She subsequently admitted that she was so worried that she went to see a family doctor to discuss her condition. He told her that she was 14–21 lb underweight for her height and frame. 'It did worry me. I did go to the doctor's because I started to get paranoid,' she confessed to TV talkshow host Michael Parkinson. Far from her family being untroubled by her figure, there were reports of rows between her and David over her eating habits, while her mother was said to have urged her to have a full check-up.

By any standards the previous year had been a traumatic period in her life. A new husband, a new baby, a new home, a new Spice Girls album and tour, and a life under constant public scrutiny; it would have taxed any woman. Victoria was no exception and years later she admitted what the world could see – that she was suffering from an eating disorder.

Certainly she had the mindset of other skinny celebrities, with a strict diet equating to a misguided control over her life and hence her fame. As commentator Shane Watson argued, 'Vulnerable squashy bodies belong to vulnerable weak people. An obsessive attitude to physical perfection is now the mark of the seriously ambitious.'

At first glance her daily eating regime was a dietician's dream. She eschewed fatty foods and was careful about what she ate and drank. A typical day's menu was fat-free Sugar Puffs in the morning, fat-free chicken tikka and plain salad for lunch, or fat-free tuna, prawns or swordfish and plain steamed vegetables in the evening. She never ate chocolate or other sweets, preferring instead to binge on fat-free crisps, munching through five bags in a day. It was, however, a more varied diet than during the height of her Spice Girls fame, when she lived off raw and boiled vegetables.

At some point during the 1990s she was diagnosed with polycystic ovaries, a condition that can, ironically, cause excess weight and body hair as well as facial acne, from which Victoria suffered. She was advised to stick to a low-fat, low-sugar diet in order to reduce the risk in later life of diabetes and heart disease.

Her diet was eating as a state of mind. For as far as the slender, feather-light Victoria was concerned, appearances really mattered. For her, it was not just diet but the whole package that had to be groomed and immaculate, a vision of perfection. 'Do I look fat in this?' was her constant refrain when she was trying on clothes. Control is the key to understanding Victoria. While she tried as best she could to control circumstances, be it the media, her image or her career, life was an unruly beast. What she could control was her body, whether it be her looks, her weight or her shape. She later confessed, 'I became obsessed with what I looked like. I would look in the mirror and check the size of my bottom, see if my double chin was getting smaller.'

Eating disorders specialist Dr Paul Flowers, a consultant psychiatrist who has treated numerous celebrities for eating-related problems, has observed that their public greed for publicity and recognition, and their desperation to be the centre of attention, hides a deep psychological hunger: 'They show all the signs of suffering from an eating disorder. These eating habits are phobic and extremely unhealthy. When you are losing weight it is because you are quite disturbed and depressed. After all, half the time you are in a state of complete starvation, but the hunger they have is as much psychological as physical. While many people are predisposed towards anorexia, it takes determination and discipline, qualities which she has in abundance, to succeed.'

It is no coincidence that many anorexics are adolescents, precisely because the illness is about avoiding issues of conflict and separation with parents and others. In short it's about growing up or rather not wanting to grow up. Having reached her mid-twenties, Victoria remained something of a Peter Pan figure, not yet secure in her own identity and not quite free of parental influence. The birth of Brooklyn perhaps unconsciously forced her to address those unresolved issues in her life.

As Dr Flowers commented, 'She is a needy and narcissistic individual who sees the baby in terms of herself, as a fashion accessory. But the child makes great demands of a carer and for Victoria it has been a turning point in her life that has put her in touch with her own neediness. So becoming a parent is a form of role reversal. "What about me?" is her cry. She wants to be the baby in the family, to be looked after and cared for.'

At the same time the Peter Pan syndrome produces an internal conflict: wanting to grow up but being terrified of doing so. By losing weight, he argued, a troubled young woman like Victoria was trying to expel the womanly, maternal side of her.

She had to be able to rationalize her distorted body shape as well, believing that it made her look good and distinctive. Hence Victoria's need to show herself off in public, be it at Elton John's lunchtime bash or on the catwalk during London Fashion Week. 'As an anorexic, you love the attention your condition has generated,' Dr Flowers observed.

For while the birth of Brooklyn brought much joy to David and Victoria and their respective parents, it unearthed qualities in themselves and their family relationships that may have remained hidden.

Victoria's own childhood gave clues to help explain her behaviour. The Adams' are the ultimate tight-knit, closed family who have deliberately set themselves apart from others, their independence bolstered by their reliance on one another. As youngsters Louise, Victoria and Christian were discouraged from leaving the family compound to play with other children. Victoria's own memories are of her father's long hours, the chaotic mealtimes and her own unpopularity at school. She was famously singled out as different when her father dropped her off in his Rolls-Royce.

Her school life was in complete contrast to her time at home. 'I was picked on a lot at school,' she has recalled. 'I was never particularly good at anything at school, but I had a lot of drive and ambition. I didn't have a nickname because nobody would talk to me.' When those outside were the enemy and equalled unhappiness, it is not hard to see where she inherited her chippy 'me against the world' attitude, as well as her seeming indifference to public opinion. 'I'm not that desperate to be liked,' she has said.

However there were other qualities that helped her on the path to fame and fortune. The tough-minded drive and business acumen that brought Tony and Jackie Adams to leafy suburbia from the streets of Tottenham in North London was echoed in the ambitions they harboured for their offspring. Jackie registered all three children with a modelling agency and for a time Louise was more successful than her elder sister.

Like anyone involved in the image business, Victoria naturally cared more about how she looked and appeared than perhaps her teenage contemporaries. As an erstwhile model and a drama student with dreams of a career as a dancer or singer, this merely served to emphasize her concerns about her poor skin and insecurity about her figure.

At the same time she has been refreshingly honest and open about her natural appearance, remarking, 'I look terrible most of the time. I'm not one of these people who can get out of bed and look great, like Natalie Imbruglia. I imagine that she looks great all the time, but I'm not like that.'

Yet when she found fame with the Spice Girls, looks counted for a lot. Her image as the pouting, classy flirt was carefully controlled by her manager, Simon Fuller. Again, like the other Spice Girls, she did not have complete control over was her body and her diet. As Mel C has said, the decision to break with Fuller was a 'huge release' as it enabled them to stop feeling guilty about what they ate and made them remember who they really were as individuals. 'I went completely teetotal and would never, ever eat anything naughty,' recalled Mel C. 'Now I am in control of my life, I've loosened up a bit and even have a drink now and then. Now it's like, so what?'

The underlying unhappiness she felt, even at the height of her success, meant that for Victoria, security and safety resided in her home life. Even though she left home after leaving school to attend theatre college, Victoria remained a self-confessed home bird. When she found fame with the Spice Girls, she was the one who was truly homesick on tour, endlessly phoning her mother and father for comfort and advice. It is easy to see why. Her father has always been very protective of her well-being, easily provoked to aggressive behaviour by the presence of paparazzi photographers when he is with her in public. Even though her mother is easy-going and welcoming on the surface, like her husband, she is as protective as a lioness looking after her cubs when it comes to her children. She has no hesitation in complaining to the media if she feels that they have unjustly criticized her daughter.

After the birth of Brooklyn, Victoria was a contrasting mixture of confident superstar and little girl who had yet to cut mummy's apron strings. The relationship was one of mutual dependence where both mother and daughter seemed to have moved on little since the days when Victoria was a schoolgirl. Victoria, who bought the house in Sawbridgeworth because it was near her parents, used to seem lost and alone when she was at the Alderley Edge apartment, and she visited her parents' house as often as possible. There is a certain symbolism in the fact that she would return to the same bedroom she had as a child. Her reluctance to fly the nest set her husband against his football manager because of his life as a long-distance commuter.

Victoria was more than happy to be cosseted by her mother, her every need and whim taken care of, whether it be looking after the baby, washing and ironing her clothes or taking care of day-to-day decisions. At the same time, both her mother and her younger sister Louise acted as her personal assistants, religiously saving every single picture and press cutting, making diary arrangements and sorting out the accounts.

While the other Spice Girls engaged the services of professionals, Victoria relied only on her immediate family. 'I'm the only person she can trust,' said Louise. While Victoria controlled the purse strings, it was all too easy to imagine how this must have altered the emotional dynamic inside the family, with mother and sister behaving rather like ladies-in-waiting, dancing attendance on a princess. They became used to her wildly varying moods: one minute equable, the next depressed and snappy.

While she boasted that she did not need a nanny for Brooklyn, the reality was rather different. 'I insist on being with him every step of the way,' she has said adamantly. 'I know people think it's weird that we don't have a nanny, but we insist on doing everything ourselves. People think it's funny, but we wouldn't have it any other way.'

The reality was that without the continual support of her husband and her extended family, as well as advice from friends like Mel B, whose child is a month older than Brooklyn, and mother of three Jill Hughes, the wife of former Manchester United striker Mark Hughes, she would have found it very difficult to be a Spice Girl and a Spice Mum. She is the type of individual who always needs someone around helping her in order to cope with daily life. Lacking confidence in her own abilities, she has tended to depend on others. Her reliance on her mother, mother-in-law, younger sister and husband inevitably led to tensions and difficulties. She has admitted that she is a domestic disaster, unable to switch on the washing machine or work the cooker. When she has tried her hand at washing, expensive clothes have shrunk, become discoloured or worse.

For a woman who likes to be in control, she is a notoriously untidy individual. 'Messiness must be my most annoying habit,' she has said, admitting that her behaviour has caused friction between her husband and herself. By contrast David, as self-reliant as he is self-possessed, used to take on the duties of house-husband, always ready to attend to Brooklyn so that Victoria could have a lie-in. For a long time they didn't employ a cleaner, so it was left to David to do the washing, ironing or vacuuming around their apartment in Alderley Edge. He would do the cooking, usually straightforward fare such as spaghetti bolognaise or lasagne, and when he wasn't there, his mother came to help out. Perhaps without her army of surrogate mothers, Victoria would have found it hard to cope with her son on her own, a little girl lost in a grown-up world. As commentator Allison Pearson noted, 'Have you noticed how it is nearly always Dad we see carrying Brooklyn and not Mum?'

Similar remarks were made when debate about Victoria, her weight and the difficulties of being a new mother was first mentioned. It was noted that she seemed lost, unsure of her place and her role in life, flailing around to find direction and meaning. It was the conflict between the mental image she carried of being a strong positive role model for youngsters and her psychological anxieties that was most revealing. Even the bold statement she made to startled writer Stuart Jeffries – 'I think I'm a pretty positive role model for kids. I'm not out getting pissed every night, shagging loads of different men, and if they slag me off at the end of the day I don't really give a shit' – contained the rather hysterical and depressingly vulgar defiance that is her trademark. This is the same woman who has spoken repeatedly and rather prissily about teaching her children the value of good manners and good behaviour.

By contrast, the arrival of Brooklyn was the making of David Beckham. He found a kind of fulfilment in his son. His birth brought out a nurturing, protective and publicly demonstrative love that has seen him hailed as a New Man, a model father for a new generation. Indeed psychologist Professor Anthony Clare argued that the football star was even more preferable as a role model than British Prime Minister Tony Blair, who became a father for the fourth time at the age of forty-six. 'Beckham is a better example because football is such a male environment,' said Professor Clare. 'The fact that he is prepared to be so involved with his baby really matters to all the young men who want to be affectionate to theirs, but have no role models.'

In public and private, David was the personification of the doting father, spending every minute he could with his first son. 'I love Brooklyn so much and I would do anything for him,' he enthused. 'I'd recommend fatherhood to anyone. If I've had a bad day or I'm getting stressed about something, it's wonderful to come home and see him. It just clears my mind and I forget about everything.'

He loved feeding him, watching him breathe, witnessing the almost daily changes in his appearance and even enjoyed changing his nappies. During the football season he took him to training at the

Carrington training centre, leaving him in the players' lounge where the toddler played happily with a toy dog, watched by doting canteen staff. Even on match days the youngster was never far from his thoughts. After the half-time team talk during home games at Old Trafford, David used to pop into the crèche to snatch a few moments with his son.

Once Brooklyn started walking, he was able to kick a miniature ball with his dad. When the Beckhams looked at Heath Mount, the £2,335 a term school in Hertfordshire proposed for Brooklyn, they were shown around by headmaster, the Reverend Harry Matthews. David was doubtless nonplussed to learn that the school only played rugby. However, having a superstar dad to teach the boys the tricks of the trade must have been a strong incentive to put football on the syllabus.

While he has worn golf shoes emblazoned with his son's name, perhaps his most public statement of affection was the guardian angel tattoo he had etched between his shoulder blades with 'Brooklyn' tattooed at the base of his spine. 'Brooklyn is beneath so it's like he's watching over him,' David said afterwards. The design, which was inspired by an album cover of his favourite rap artist Tupac Shakur, took two hours to etch in and the pain of the operation left the soccer star with tears in his eyes. Tattooist Louis Molloy, who spent two weeks researching the design based on David's initial sketch, observed, 'David did say that it hurt, but hats off to him. He stuck with it and took it.' Indeed it was so painful that David's friend Gary Neville, who had also considered having a tattoo, decided that it was not for him.

After the initial tattoo work, David and Victoria were said to have spent several evenings looking through a book of Latin quotations to find a suitable inscription to put under the outstretched arms of the guardian angel. In the end they chose '*Et Animus Liber*' (Free Spirit), but after the pain of the original tattoo, David decided to postpone having the Latin words added.

Less macho but more fun, David loved to take Brooklyn to the weekly meeting of Tumbletots, a playgroup for pre-school children. He joined in with the toddlers and their mothers singing nursery rhymes, and watched Brooklyn as he dived through hoops on the junior assault course or played in the 'pond' filled with plastic balls.

When the couple first arrived at the Old Masonic Hall in Macclesfield, the local Tumbletots venue, mothers were agog that the new royal family had deigned to join them. They had been told beforehand not to take photographs or ask for autographs and to treat them as they would any other newcomers. Tumbletots organizer Martin Lawson recalled at the time, 'Brooklyn is fabulous. No problems. A smashing little boy.'

As Brooklyn really enjoyed playing with the other children, the Beckhams decided to make it a regular event. At first David was rather embarrassed and self-conscious, not only because he was the only man there, but because his celebrity status had put him in the spotlight amidst the fifteen or so mothers who spent their time watching him when they thought he wasn't looking. For once Victoria was amused by their behaviour rather than jealous of it. 'He loves spending any time he can with him,' she said.

'That's what you do with kids – and we appreciate every second.'

David was so besotted with the youngster that when he came home late from a game or a night out, he often woke Brooklyn up to play with him, treasuring every moment of quality time they spent together. When he was little, their son appeared to accompany them everywhere; on one occasion, a diner at London's Ivy restaurant was surprised when Victoria lifted a sleeping Brooklyn out from under the table. He was likely to be taken out of his cot at all hours of the day or night for a long motorway commute or for a plane flight.

So David's adoration of his son helps explain why he gave the England fans an obscene one-fingered gesture when they taunted him after a match against Portugal during Euro 2000. They had shouted that his wife was a whore and hoped Brooklyn died of cancer. His gesture provoked a furore. Labour peer Lord Hattersley complained that Beckham was a 'national liability'. 'You don't beat yobbishness by being a yob,' he opined. However, the overwhelming majority of commentators and fans had sympathy for his plight. As the former England coach Kevin Keegan said, 'It is nothing to do with the game of football. It is something we all have to put up with at times and we do it quite well, but there is a point where every human reaches a limit and it has gone well beyond that. I can't understand why it happens.'

If Keegan had no obvious explanation for the fans' behaviour, British journalist Julie Burchill ascribed it to the homoerotic relationship between fans and their idols. 'Physical rather than cerebral, thoughtful rather than articulate, Beckham is not a neurotic career-obsessed salary man, but one who has his priorities completely sorted out at an impressively early age. Not a lad, but a real man. And it is for this – not for losing football matches – that so many of the inadequates currently rallying round the England flag hate him.'

While nasty comments about Brooklyn have made David see red, the child's arrival also exacerbated the simmering tensions between the two families. When David took Brooklyn, Victoria and his in-laws to a zoo in March 2000, for example, his own parents were conspicuous by their absence.

During the visit David stripped to the waist, and, clinging to the bars of the lions' cage, he flung lumps of red meat to the prowling big cats, while Brooklyn watched entranced. In the background, David's mother-in-law Jackie took pictures for the family scrapbook while Victoria, her father, her sister Louise and Louise's toddler Liberty looked on. Based in the grounds of the Paradise Wildlife Park in Broxbourne, near the Adams family home, the zoo had closed off the lion enclosure to give their celebrity visitors a chance to enjoy themselves in peace and privacy.

But once again David was away from his home base in Manchester, just before he and his teammates were due to fly to Italy for a match against Valencia in the European Cup, knowingly flouting club rules and risking the wrath of his manager. His parents were naturally worried for his career, but also dismayed that they had not been invited to see their grandson. They doted on Brooklyn, but felt that they did not see him often enough, and so they would no doubt have regarded the Sunday afternoon trip as another missed opportunity to spend time with him.

The day out with his in-laws will have been viewed as another example of the growing influence of Victoria's family on David. Indeed the birth of Brooklyn came to symbolize the conflict between two such close-knit, supportive, yet very different families. The Beckhams are a demonstrative and loving family, deeply protective and justly proud of their superstar son, and equally adoring of their grandson. 'What I really liked was that David was really close to his family,' said Victoria of her first encounter with the Beckham brood.

If there was a chance of seeing his grandson, Ted used to finish work early for the opportunity to spend time with him. Whenever Victoria and David were preoccupied with work matters, Sandra was only too happy to look after Brooklyn, feeding and playing with him, reading him books and going for walks in the local park. As a mother of three children and something of a surrogate mum, she naturally enjoyed her grandson's company, and she and her husband always looked forward to the time they spent with him. As David was nearby at the Adams' house at Goff's Oak so frequently, there was often a deep sense of disappointment when they missed seeing the youngster for whatever reason.

Ever since his marriage, David's parents constantly worried about the emotional and physical demands made of their son as he tried to reconcile his football career in Manchester with the showbiz lifestyle favoured by Victoria and her family. While Ted Beckham has hinted at the tensions, he has tried to smooth over talk of a rift. 'Of course we have differences, the same as anyone else,' he has said. 'I'm from a footballing background, they are from a music background, but we have a good relationship with them.'

Their fear that the Adams family was affecting David's performance on the pitch might have reflected a deeper concern that they would never be able to compete with the opulent and glamorous lifestyle of their high-profile in-laws. In private, Ted spoke to friends about the fact that David's personality and ideas seemed to be changing, not always for the better.

While Tony and Jackie Adams lived in a detached mock-Tudor mansion in leafy suburbia, and drove round in Rolls-Royces and Porsches, the Beckhams made do with a modest semi-detached house in Chingford, Essex. David's father worked long hours as a commercial kitchen fitter, partly so that he could earn enough to enable him and his wife, a part-time hairdresser, to watch their son play every week, be it home or abroad. Inevitably, though, they perhaps felt overshadowed by the Adams family, sensing that they were second-class citizens in the new world of Posh and Becks. Though they had gained a daughter-in-law, they might also felt that they were losing a son.

It was at the lavish wedding that the first cracks appeared between the two families. Although the bride's family is traditionally responsible for the wedding plans, it was natural that Ted and Sandra would have wanted to be involved in the organization of their son's wedding, but they were sidelined. Victoria and her mother decided the venue, the flowers, the caterers and the entertainment. Like many commentators, members of the Beckham family felt the celebration was extravagant and wildly over the top. David's uncle Peter, who was left off the guest list, observed, 'The lavish display didn't fit in with what I know of David. It's probably Victoria's influence not David's.'

Perhaps more hurtful was the impression left by David in his speech at the wedding, in which he seemed to spend more time praising his in-laws than his own family. Indeed this may help explain some of the difficulties facing the two families. According to marital etiquette, he was correct to behave in this way, but the Beckhams, feeling rather upstaged and marginalized, may have felt once again that they were being downgraded. From that time onwards slights, real or imagined, have dogged the relationship, particularly with Victoria.

The most public manifestation of this ill-feeling took place at the wedding of David's sister Lynne at a register office in Hornchurch, Essex, in October 1999. There was keen anticipation that Brooklyn would be present and so everyone felt let down when he was not brought along to the event. Victoria's absence was also significant. As onlookers shouted, 'Where's Posh?' newspaper commentators saw her lack of presence as a sign of a family rift.

While one spokesperson for Victoria said that she had been up with the baby all night, another said that she was recording in Sheffield. The bride and the rest of the Beckham family could be excused for feeling confused by these contradictory explanations.

As with many families, money is a point of division. When Victoria was a member of the Spice Girls she was earning three times more than David. That financial disparity was made apparent on a number of occasions when they splashed out on their respective families. So while Tony Adams celebrated his fifty-third birthday with a Porsche Boxster car, courtesy of Victoria and David, Ted Beckham received a Manchester United shirt with his son's name on the back. Again Victoria spent £500,000 on a house for her sister and brother next door to their parents compared with the more modest semi-detached home in Ilford, Essex, that David bought for his sister Lynne. When Lynne was given a new Ford Escort, Louise Adams received a more expensive A-class Mercedes and Victoria's brother got a new Golf GTI convertible. An exception to the inequality in their generosity was the gift of a Mercedes tied with a red bow that Ted received for Christmas. While David and Victoria have every right to spend their money exactly as they choose, it is entirely understandable if the Beckham clan felt somewhat aggrieved by the disparity.

If the arrival of Brooklyn caused tensions inside the family, the celebrity status of his parents meant that the normal events of childhood – a walk in the park, a day trip, even a birthday party – could no longer be taken for granted. Simple pleasures became complicated, with everything having to be orchestrated and organized. Spontaneity is always the first casualty in the world of super celebrity. So when they decided to take Brooklyn to Stockley working farm near Knutsford, Cheshire, in spring 2000, the farm manager was contacted and warned that the Beckhams were coming. With security staff in tow to keep away onlookers, the couple spent a happy few hours looking at the farm animals. Brooklyn, who loves dogs, was mesmerized by a giant sow, while Victoria enjoyed cuddling a newborn lamb. Farm manager Richard Furnace said afterwards, 'They were approachable, not at all aloof, and interacted with the animals.'

While visitors to the farm were delighted when the Beckhams signed autographs afterwards, it was a different story when they took Brooklyn to Chester Zoo on Victoria's twenty-sixth birthday in April 2000. Even though they requested a private day out, photographers were on hand to snap them as they strolled around in between heavy rain showers. Over-protective zoo staff then closed the monkey house and giraffe enclosure to the paying public so that their celebrity guests could enjoy a few minutes' privacy. It did not please the other visitors who were left out in the rain, and nor was the local chamber of commerce impressed. Secretary Bob Clough-Parker thought it was a 'bit rich' for a couple enjoying their celebrity status to complain of media attention.

While the Beckhams received a few media brickbats, that operation was literally a stroll in the park compared to the commotion surrounding Brooklyn's first birthday party. That really was a zoo as press and public converged on a Knutsford hotel, which Victoria had chosen to turn into a circus for a day. Before the clowns, the tumblers, stilt-walker and the face-paint artists arrived for the £10,000 party, the rooms were prepared as if for a high-powered political summit. Former soldiers-turned-security-men swept the place for bugs and hidden cameras before watching stony-faced as an array of guests, including Manchester United players and Spice Girls, arrived to join in the fun. They formed a phalanx of grey suits to stop photographers taking pictures of the activities inside, including the cutting of the birthday cake.

The event illustrated the mixed and confusing signals that David and Victoria would send out about their treasured son. It was an incongruous combination of protection and exhibitionism. While they feared for his life and privacy, shielding his head from photographers, for example, they also dressed him from top to toe in designer clothes, paraded him round like a trophy and sold family pictures. Just as her mother pushed Victoria into a modelling agency, so Victoria said that she wanted Brooklyn to have a modelling career, with his face appearing on the cover of glossy magazines like *Vogue*. 'He loves all the attention he gets. He's a real exhibitionist,' she has said, qualities obviously inherited from his mother. Victoria's role as mother is characterized by this ambivalent behaviour – on the one hand showing off about her son, and on the other being intensely protective of him.

Victoria truly discovered the drawbacks of celebrity when she and Brooklyn were virtual prisoners in their penthouse apartment in Alderley Edge. They didn't mix with the neighbours in their complex, rarely used the communal lawns or went out for a stroll to give the boy a breath of fresh air in the nearby parks. The couple's fear of stalkers was real enough. A mentally deranged woman bombarded David with love notes and sent items of clothing to his apartment. Then she took to sitting outside on a bench nearby watching for any sign of the soccer star. On one occasion she ran up to his car when he was waiting for the electronic gates to open and shouted, 'I love you, I love you.' Even a visit from the police failed to put a stop to the harassment. A few days after the police had seen her, she tried to enter the building to speak to the object of her fixation, but got no further than the ground floor. In the end the police were forced to detain her under the Mental Health Act.

In truth, Victoria never felt comfortable in their penthouse apartment in Alderley Edge. She reportedly never made the effort to get to know her neighbours in the communal Victorian house, ignoring them if they greeted her and she never attended meetings to discuss joint problems, impervious to complaint or criticism. 'They seem superior and they're not here most of the time,' one local complained.

Their neighbours became increasingly irritated by fans who hung around the gates and the fan mail that cluttered communal areas. Their two Rottweiler pets, Puffy and Snoop, lived in a makeshift kennel behind the communal garages, which became an unsightly and unpleasant mess.

Matters came to a head in summer 2000 when one neighbour, Cybil Davis-Brummell, a former aide to Princess Alexandra, reportedly took the trouble to start a petition to ask them to leave. She complained that she had been stopped from using the communal gardens by the Beckham's minders so that Brooklyn could play there in safety. Nor was she said to have been happy with Victoria's foul language during a dispute with a neighbour over car parking. 'Posh is really common. You can tell that when she opens her mouth,' she was quoted as saying, a comment that had academics musing how old money had always looked down on new money.

As a result, Victoria could not wait until their new home, a £2.5 million seven-bedroomed mansion in Hertfordshire, set in 24 acres of grounds, was ready for the family to move in, to give them some much needed peace and privacy. As mistress of the manor, Victoria was in control of the design and decoration, with the exception of David's snooker room, which he intended to make a shrine to sport, exhibiting not just his soccer memorabilia, but his collection of other sporting artefacts.

Victoria though had plans of her own. 'We've bought a huge house and I want to fill it with children,' she said.

Eight

Fast and Furious

David Beckham has had a love affair with cars and speed ever since he could drive. Cars are, as he has said, his 'pride and joy'. It would destroy him if he were unable to drive for any reason. He is like a Latin lover, falling for the curves and colours of one seductive sports car only to discard her for another a few months later.

On one occasion he saw a two-tone silver and blue TVR model on the forecourt of a dealership in Alderley Edge. Like a child in a sweet shop, it seemed he had to have it whatever the cost. As the trade-in price he was offered for his Porsche seemed less than generous, he was advised to go directly to the Blackpool-based manufacturers of the TVR. They hand-built the car in two weeks, fitting a special rear seat emblazoned with Brooklyn's name. But David soon discovered that the TVR was strictly for the enthusiast. The ride is hard and unforgiving, and after only a few hundred miles his love affair ended as abruptly as it had begun. And after all, why not? 'I like changing cars, and I suppose if I can afford to do it, I'll keep doing it,' said David, in justification of his passion. 'It isn't a crime to have a nice car.'

His first car was a humble Ford Escort, followed by a Volkswagen Golf. When he and other United youngsters such as Nicky Butt and Gary Neville were given Honda Preludes as their first club cars, Beckham apparently irritated his manager by having his fitted – at his own expense – with leather upholstery and customized wheels; always wanting to be different, always wanting to stand out from the crowd. Since then he has graduated to BMWs and Porsches, and at one point had an array of cars that included a Mercedes SLK, a Lincoln Navigator, a top-of-the-range Range Rover and a Ferrari 550, which Victoria had bought him for his twenty-fourth birthday.

Something of a boy racer, he talked about installing a quad-bike track in the grounds of his new home, and thoroughly enjoyed an afternoon's go-karting with the rest of the United team at a local indoor track.

Being contractually forbidden from indulging in hazardous activities such as riding motorbikes, David has only been able to express his enthusiam for biking through fashion. Thus when Victoria was filming a pop video, he sported a yellow and black biker jacket emblazoned with the name of champion rider Kevin Schwantz.

While bike-riding remains a fantasy, he has always loved to drive his cars, and as someone with superb reflexes he likes to drive fast, as his numerous speeding offences attest. In the old days, women and drinking were the status symbols of successful sportsmen. These days fast cars seem to be the trophy of choice, particularly among young footballers. On match days, Old Trafford has become a veritable showroom for customized sports cars. The only thing that can slow these racers down would seem to be the law; and even then the club, which protects players and staff vigorously, has done its best to shelter them.

In October 1999, manager Sir Alex Ferguson escaped a conviction when he convinced magistrates that he was driving on the hard shoulder of the M62 in his BMW 750 in order to avoid a traffic jam because he had a severe bout of diarrhoea and needed to reach the Old Trafford toilets. On another occasion, no one at the club would admit to driving a leased BMW 750 through a speed trap in Derbyshire. A charge against Sir Alex was dismissed, although the club was fined £650 with £35 costs for failing to name the driver.

In December 1999, it was David Beckham's turn. The previous July he had been caught exceeding the speed limit near his home in Alderley Edge, and now that his case was due to come before the magistrates, he was a worried man. While he dreaded losing his licence – he had already accumulated ten points for previous convictions – he and his advisers had already put into effect plans to hire a full-time chauffeur. However it soon became apparent that more was at stake here than a straightforward case of speeding. What happened that day in court, and the events that followed, shed a fierce light on to the nature of modern celebrity, the murky world of public relations and the way in which the media, the public and even the judiciary can be overawed by those who have enough fame and money. It was also an episode that revealed the true consequences for those who got on the wrong side of this modern aristocracy.

In early December, a few days before Beckham's court case, photographer Chris Neill and a fellow snapper were outside Old Trafford, waiting for United midfielder Roy Keane. The protracted contract negotiations in which Keane had been embroiled were about to be resolved, and the *Daily Express* had commissioned Neill to take a picture of the Irish international. Neill's white Fiesta and his colleague's blue Mondeo were parked on the forecourt. As they waited, David Beckham marched up to Neill and launched into a torrent of abuse, then turned on his heel and left. Both photographers were shocked and bemused by his unprovoked tirade.

Days later, on 9 December 1999, Beckham stood before the magistrates at Stockport, Cheshire, and explained why he had been caught by speed cameras driving at 76 m.p.h. on a 50 m.p.h. dual carriageway five months previously. He told the court that he had been 'intimidated and petrified' by an unidentified paparazzo photographer driving a white Ford Fiesta who had trailed him for ten miles. During thirty-five minutes of sworn evidence, Beckham related how he had noticed the white Fiesta when he reached the end of the drive of his Alderley Edge home. The photographer had taken a picture, and then the white car had followed him. 'It was very close and I felt uncomfortable,' he said, adding that during the pursuit, the photographer had almost caused a serious accident as he had tried to overtake his £150,000 Ferrari to snatch another shot. 'He was swerving, taking pictures. He was not in control,' said Beckham.

Concerned that his pursuer was more than simply an overzealous cameraman, the football star, who was on his way to join his teammates for a pre-season friendly, decided to get away from him to prevent a serious accident. 'I was petrified,' he told the court. 'I felt intimidated. He was driving very dangerously and that scared me.' After driving twice round a roundabout to shake off the other car, Beckham put his foot down as he drove along the A74, which was where the police speed camera had caught him. Such was his concern that within two minutes of being caught, Beckham had phoned Wilmslow police station, Greater Manchester police headquarters and the force's traffic unit to explain his behaviour.

Beckham's defence immediately conjured up memories of Princess Diana's fatal accident in Paris, where she and her lover Dodi Fayed had been followed by paparazzi, and the Mercedes in which they were travelling was involved in a collision with a mysterious white Fiat Uno. When magistrates viewed the police video, they did see a white Ford pass by the camera eight seconds after Beckham. The driver has never been traced. The magistrates, however, were not convinced by the player's story, saying that his actions were 'unreasonable', while Manchester police confirmed that they had no evidence that the driver of a white Fiesta was harassing him. Beckham was banned for eight months and fined £800, and immediately launched an appeal. So anxious was he about the ban that his solicitor Nicholas Freeman took the highly unusual step of going to a judge to ask for his client's licence back pending his appeal, which was set for the following Thursday, after the magistrates initially turned down the request.

As the media launched a hunt for the paparazzi photographer in the white Ford Fiesta, some people in Manchester guessed that the culprit had been Chris Neill, as he was one of only two freelance photographers who regularly snapped local football stars. Furthermore, he had a white Fiesta.

Soon his phone was ringing red-hot. Despite strenuously denying all knowledge of the alleged incident, Neill had become prime suspect. When the national newspapers began calling they took all his denials with a pinch of salt. A reporter from the *Daily Mail* asked him how much he had earned from the photos of Beckham and wondered whether it had been worth the risk of chasing the football superstar at such high speed. 'It was like being in the middle of a nightmare,' Neill recalled. 'I thought I would never work again unless I could prove where I was. Any moment I expected the police to come round and arrest me. It was a dreadful experience.'

Neill was desperate to clear his name. He, his friends, and his family all believed that he would end up being tarred with the same brush as the paparazzi on the night Diana died. Growing increasingly frantic, he looked in his diary to see what he had been doing on the day in question and suddenly realized that he had a cast-iron alibi. At the time that David Beckham had allegedly been chased by a paparazzo in a white Ford Fiesta, Chris Neill was 3,000 miles away, staying with a cousin at Niagara Falls in Canada with his five children. After this discovery he carried his passport with him to every job to prove to sceptics that he was not the culprit. He also decided to exchange his now notorious leased Fiesta for a red Mondeo. Looking back, he said, 'It was a terrible experience for my family and myself. If I hadn't been in Canada and hadn't had my passport stamped my life would have been ruined.'

As the photographer licked his wounds, the Beckhams and their son spent five hours Christmas shopping at Harrods. David once again hit the headlines with his eccentric choice of headgear, namely a knitted Tibetan peasant's hat complete with bobble and ear flaps. It was a second shopping trip to the same store later that week, just forty-eight hours before he was due before a judge to ask for his driving ban to be quashed, which provided a further twist to the saga.

As on the previous Saturday, when they left the store they faced a dozen or more photographers waiting for them to get into their car. The routine was the same. They lingered in the store foyer, put on baseball caps and determinedly put their heads down so that the photographers would get a poor or unusable shot. As usual Victoria went ahead while David, carrying Brooklyn, and their bodyguard Mark Niblett followed behind. There was the usual brief mêlée as they pushed past the waiting snappers, Victoria thrusting one of them out of the way as she got into the car. Then the party drove off.

Those to whom I have spoken who witnessed the scene were astounded to see the banner headline 'Posh Baby Grab Terror' splashed across the following morning's *Sun* newspaper. The article, billed as an exclusive by the deputy showbiz editor, revealed how 'brave' Posh Spice had knocked a crazed fan to the ground as he tried to grab her son. The incident, which was quickly followed up by others in the media, was confirmed by the couple's spokeswoman Caroline McAteer.

According to the story, the unidentified 'weirdo' had grabbed Brooklyn's arm and yelled, 'I just want a picture of me and Brooklyn together. Please, please let me.' Victoria was quoted as describing how she had pushed the man away from her 'like any mother'. The paper went on to say that the twenty-five-year-old singer admitted that she was scared and feared for her son's life: 'David and I were both shocked by the whole incident as any parent would be.'

Strangely, the incident was not captured on film either by the CCTV cameras outside Harrods or by the dozen or so photographers who had been within inches of their Mercedes car. A housewife who was quoted as a witness has proved untraceable. Strange, too, that the police, who had spent nearly a year investigating alleged death threats to the couple, were not immediately informed.

Could it have been a case of skilful spin-doctoring on the eve of David Beckham's appearance before a judge to win his licence back? As *The Guardian* newspaper noted: 'Headlines such as "Anger as Beckham escapes speeding by blaming snappers" melted into "How Posh stopped babysnatcher". Beckham and Victoria were transformed from spoilt celebrities into heroic parents.'

That same somewhat cynical stance was echoed by others who had been close to the scene. Harrods media relations officer Michael Mann said of the alleged assault, 'It was not caught on security cameras and we have very good coverage. No one saw it, not the doormen and not the photographers.

In my opinion it may not have happened and was possibly for the papers.' One photographer who was there described the incident as 'rubbish'. 'Nothing happened,' he explained. 'Before they came out they lingered in the foyer of door five. They looked at us. They came out with caps pulled down over their faces and heads down. A photographer got in the way; she pushed him. David Beckham had a court case at the time. He used the incident, spin-doctoring to get him off. There was no manic fan. Victoria Beckham hasn't got the strength to push anyone.'

Similar views were held by their former body-guard, who had been with them both inside and outside the store. 'We never even discussed it until the next day when it was in the paper,' he recalled. 'It was simply the fact that Victoria likes to get the boot in with photographers and give them a hard time. She hates the baby being photographed; it is her major concern. David had the baby and was just getting into the car . . . She was in one of her tempers and she lashed out at the photographers who were there. Nobody saw anything, I certainly didn't see anything and they didn't mention anything.'

The incident conformed to what the paparazzi had come to expect from the Beckhams. While Victoria has made her name and fortune through her music and image, she loathes the freelance photographers who make their living taking pictures of her. In the early days of the Spice Girls, photo-graphers remembered her as friendly and amenable, eager to help a snapper to get a good shot. After her engagement to David, she began to take a dim view of the paparazzi who dogged her on an almost daily trail of retail therapy in London's ritzy Knights-bridge, tailing her from Prada to Gucci, on to Dolce & Gabbana, over to Harrods and back to Prada again. And as they sat in pavement cafes, waiting for the next celebrity to walk into their web, the free-lance cameramen talked in equally disparaging terms about her, recalling the verbal and sometimes physical assaults they suffered when they dared to photograph the media's new princess. One experienced paparazzo who had followed her throughout her career said of her, 'Now she is morose and rude. It doesn't have to be like this. Other Spice Girls are still fine. Mel C, for example, is always co-operative. Fame doesn't seem to have changed her. Not Victoria.'

Her uncompromising attitude is not uncommon. There exists a 'celebrity syndrome' in which media stars become so used to being surrounded by yes-men and other fawning acolytes, so that when they come across those who treat them not as icons to be worshipped but as normal people, they find it difficult to handle. Dr Glenn Wilson, who has made a study of celebrity psychology, has observed that 'celebrities become so self-important they think that no one can cross them. There is an implicit feeling of arrogance that you can dress how you like, do what you like and treat people how you like. It is a sign of having made it. Photographers are frequent targets for this behaviour.'

As the nation pondered the latest threat to Brooklyn, described by one media wit as the most famous infant since the one born in Bethlehem 2,000 years ago, his father prepared to face Judge

Barry Woodward, himself a collector of classic cars, at Minshul Crown Court, Greater Manchester. During his sworn testimony, Beckham again argued that at the time of the offence he was being trailed by a paparazzo photographer. Curiously, as Beckham had to admit, none of the photographs supposedly taken by his alleged pursuer had ever been published, even though he agreed they would be worth a small fortune.

He was, however, quick to tell the court about the incident at Harrods. After informing the judge of another occasion, when he and Victoria had been followed by two carloads of photographers just before they were married, he went on to explain what had happened just days before as he left the Knightsbridge store. 'I was holding my baby boy and my wife was in front of me . . . as we walked out, someone lunged towards Brooklyn and me, and my wife pushed them off and then we got into the back of the car.'

Speaking of the Harrods incident, his solicitor told the judge, 'It's difficult for anyone to under-stand what it is like to be in David Beckham's shoes. It's like a mass hysteria. He is always followed, but in this instance it got out of hand. It was the straw that broke the camel's back.'

At the end of the five-hour hearing, Judge Woodward took pity on Beckham, whom he described as an 'honest and truthful' witness, and handed back his licence. In his judgement he said that the case must be considered on its own particular merits. 'In effect, a burst of speed with the purpose of putting distance between himself and his pursuer does constitute a special reason,' he said.

'Mr Beckham had a reasonable feeling that there could be a fifty miles-per-hour crash on a relatively busy road. He has had many incidents in which, by reason of his fame, he was pestered to such an extent he had cause to fear for his and his family's safety.' The decision caused outrage among motoring organizations.

Commentator Mark Lawson said in *The Guardian* immediately after the case: 'This feels like a landmark judgment. For the first time, the celebrity defence is enshrined in British law.'

The celebrity defence – which dictates that the famous are held to different legal standards – originated in American courts and achieved its ultimate judgement in the case of O. J. Simpson, the Hollywood star who was controversially cleared of murdering his estranged wife and her companion.

Did David Beckham sincerely believe that he was being followed by a photographer in a white Ford Fiesta? Were he and Victoria genuinely certain that a maniac had tried to harm their son? Few others agreed, it seems.

It is inevitable that a certain amount of hype and spin should be part of the day-to-day life of modern celebrities, especially those as much in the public eye as David and Victoria Beckham. They are by no means unique. The exaggerated quote, the elaborate photocall and the contrived story have all become part of the symbiotic relationship that exists between stars and the media. Bogus stories all add to the gaiety of nations, a surreal world where fact, fiction and fantasy collide. And yet the prevalence of spin in modern society, be it on behalf of politicians, royalty or pop singers, ultimately demonstrates a contempt for the public. Truth, however uncomfortable, becomes secondary to self-interest, however entertaining.

In an institution like the judiciary, where truth is the handmaiden to justice, spin-doctoring ultimately has a corrupting effect on the legal process. Ultimately it is all about control. The sociology of spin, the ability to control what people think about a celebrity, a politician or even a government policy, invariably reflects the psychology of fame. Since the early days of Hollywood and the growth of mass entertainment, celebrities have tried to control and doctor their image. It is a state of mind that breeds a certain narcissism, a belief that everything must reflect their image and conform to their desires. Often this need for control can take on absurd proportions. As Dr Glenn Wilson says, 'Stars become control freaks, hooked on publicity and power, manipulating the public for attention, but vindictive against those whom they feel have unjustly obstructed or humiliated them.'

An incident in March 2000, three months after the dust had settled on David Beckham's controversial court case, gives a revealing insight into this dark side of celebrity. When he was sensationally dropped by Alex Ferguson after missing training to be with his sick son, the spin doctors went into action, with the pro-Beckham media portraying the argument as a clash between a responsible new-age father on the one hand, and the unreasonable old-style dogma of the manager on the other.

Crucially, the debate featured pictures of the errant player being ordered off the club's Carrington training ground by his boss – pictures taken by Chris Neill. The publication of the photographs was beyond the control of either side, and embarrassed the club and the manager, and humiliated Beckham. A few weeks later Neill was waiting by traffic lights near the ground when David Beckham pulled up alongside him in his distinctive Lincoln Navigator. The football star wound down his window and hurled a handful of stones at the photographer's car, breaking his passenger window. Then he ran the red light and drove off.

In a world where image is everything, Chris Neill had broken rule number one: he had presented the unvarnished truth.

Nine

Brand it Like Beckham

It had been a light-hearted dinner party for the Princess of Wales; a glass of white wine, a plateful of Marks and Spencer's lasagne and the chance to chat with friends. As far as Diana was concerned the evening, hosted by her friend the newspaper heiress Kate Menzies, had given her an opportunity to escape her claustrophobic life at Kensington Palace. So it was a jolly Princess who emerged from the mews house where her detective Ken Wharfe was waiting for her. She was larking about with another of the guests, Major David Waterhouse of the Household Cavalry, trying to put a rubber balloon over his car exhaust. In a matter of minutes, though, her carefree laughter would turn to tears.

Lurking in the shadows was a young paparazzo photographer who captured the potentially embarrassing scene of the Princess having fun with a young man who was certainly not her husband. The photographer was spotted and Diana's detective swiftly moved into action, apparently removing the film from the camera. Brushing aside tears of anger and frustration, Diana confronted the young cameraman, telling him that he and his sort were making her life a misery. 'I've been working hard all week,' she told him. 'It's the only time I've been out . . . I've got so few friends left and this will only make things worse for me.'

When the story broke in the autumn of 1987, the photographer, twenty-two-year-old Jason Fraser, became that week's hate figure in the mass media. He was dubbed 'the man who made the fairy-tale princess cry'. While his exposure in the popular press disconcerted him, it did not deter him. Almost until the day she died, Fraser stalked the Princess, snapping her around London and on holiday. Of all the paparazzi, it was Jason Fraser whom she feared most – and with good reason. Charming, bilingual and articulate, Fraser does not conform to the public's image of a photographer 'stalker' of the stars. Over the last decade he and other paparazzi have built a tightly-knit group who target the playgrounds of the rich and famous. It was he who organized the selling and distribution of the now infamous pictures of Diana kissing her lover Dodi Fayed during her last holiday in the Mediterranean on board the *Jonikal*, the yacht owned by Dodi's father, Harrods boss Mohamed Fayed.

Ironically, since Diana's death, Fraser scored a major coup with grainy holiday shots of Camilla Parker Bowles, as well as other celebrities such as model Claudia Schiffer, and singer and actress Madonna. Like a modern-day, big-game hunter, this doyen of the paparazzi has boasted of the adrenalin rush he gets from each exclusive celebrity 'kill', in particular the buzz he experiences hanging out of helicopters with his long lens. Ruthless, well-connected and highly successful, Fraser does admit to having his own self-imposed code of ethics. 'I would never do to anybody what I wouldn't want done to myself,' he once said.

Fraser happened to fly back on the same plane as the Beckhams after their honeymoon in July 1999, sitting two rows behind them on their British Airways flight from Nice to Heathrow. He observed David feeding baby Brooklyn, changing his nappy, and soothing him when he cried. Later he watched as Brooklyn vomited over his father's blue linen shirt. Afterwards he said, somewhat disingenuously, 'Seeing Posh, Becks and Brooklyn was one of the most enchanting sights I have ever seen.' By a sublime twist of fate, the king of the paparazzi, the man who had made the life of Diana, Princess of Wales so difficult, was about to become the unofficial 'By Appointment' photographer to the new royal family.

This arrangement would add a further dimension to the dynamic that exists between celebrities, paparazzi and the public. Before Diana's death, the public, for all their gripes about the content of the tabloid press, nevertheless enjoyed the vicarious thrill of seeing stars 'off duty' and going about their private lives. While they may have criticized the underhand methods employed to catch celebrities off their guard, they loved the end result. Hence the rise in the circulation figures of those newspapers that published the infamous photos of Sarah, Duchess of York having her toes sucked by John

Bryant, or the no less invasive shots of Princess Diana with Dodi Fayed.

Since Diana's death, however, the role of the paparazzi has come under intense and hostile scrutiny. The British media have taken steps to clean up their act with a self-policed code of conduct. The use of intrusive pictures, particularly of children, has been widely condemned.

So what have the stars and their photographer stalkers done? Welcome to the world of the paparazzi photocall. As in the bad old days, this new generation of photographs looks for all the world like casual, unposed snaps of stars at play. The celebrity subjects seem oblivious to the presence of the camera, the settings seem impromptu, the pictures themselves invariably fresh and revealing. Unlike more formal arrangements, such as the annual photocall of the royal family enjoying themselves on the ski slopes, there seems to be nothing staged about these paparazzi pictures.

And yet far from being spontaneous, the paparazzi photo opportunity is as contrived an event as a first-night celebrity party. The paparazzi are contacted in advance by the stars or by their agents, a suitable deal is struck and photos are taken which make it appear that the subject has been caught unawares. Everyone is happy. The public think they are being given a secret, unauthorized glimpse into the private lives of the stars, and the magazines and newspapers are able to feed that illusion and increase their circulations as a result. The celebrities themselves profit either financially or through publicity or both, and the photographer takes informal pictures without the hassle of stalking an unwilling quarry. As one senior newspaper executive admitted: 'We get revealing pictures and the stars get publicity, a free holiday and a few grand in their back pockets.' In a way, it is a natural development of the notion of 'infotainment'; the meshing of fact and fantasy, entertainment and news, which is subsequently passed off as real life.

Few celebrities will admit to being willing participants in such an arrangement, and most resent any implication that they would be party to such collusion. Victoria is no exception. When she and her sister Louise were driving to the opening of a new Thai restaurant in Knightsbridge at the end of London Fashion Week in September 1999, several paparazzi received calls to tell them of their impending arrival. After they were photographed, Victoria complained to the restaurant, accusing them of tipping off the media. Suggestions made on the British news programme *Tonight With Trevor McDonald* alleging that she or Louise had engineered similar tip-offs were hotly denied by the singer. 'That really upsets me,' she stated. 'If my sister did that, you'd think they'd get something more juicy and accurate, wouldn't you?'

In a conversation with writer Mike Pattenden, David also disputed the notion that he had encouraged media interest by actively courting the press. He pointed out that their chat was only the fifth interview he had given in two years, and said that, apart from the famous £1 million wedding pictures sold to *OK!* magazine, he had never been paid for any press.

That interview took place at the end of March 2000, a few days after he had had his famous blond locks shaved off for a Number Two haircut costing

£300. His usual stylist Tyler had travelled to Goff's Oak from the Knightsbridge salon of Vidal Sassoon to give him that masculine, somewhat aggressive haircut. When word leaked out that the man once known as 'Pretty Boy' had changed his look so dramatically, fans scoured the dustbins in the hope of finding a lock of his shorn hair as a souvenir.

Nor was David the only one to get the chop. Brooklyn was given a similar skinhead cut, while Victoria had her hair coloured blonde by Yotis, the head colourist at Vidal Sassoon. Soon everyone was clamouring for pictures of the family's fresh, radical look, with sub-editors salivating at the prospect of writing the headline: 'Short Beck and Sides.' Unbeknown to the waiting photographers who were camped outside the house in Goff's Oak, the Beckhams had other ideas.

They had a meeting planned with their new paparazzo acquaintance Jason Fraser, and for it to be successful, they had to avoid the presence of other photographers. David religiously kept on his trade-mark baseball cap to hide his sharp new haircut from prying lenses. A call to the local constabulary ensured that the police were on hand to stop any tailing paparazzi, and the Beckhams made good their escape from Goff's Oak.

Nevertheless, a green Subaru filled with photographers slipped through the police cordon and set off in pursuit. When they reached Piccadilly in central London, a handy Securicor van driver was commandeered to help. As his van was in front of the photographers' car in a narrow one-way street, he was asked if he would stop to allow the Beckhams, who were in front of him, to lose them.

The impromptu plan worked perfectly. The driver stopped at the T-junction, successfully blocking the road and preventing the paparazzi from following any further.

A few minutes later the couple pulled into the NCP car park close to Harrods, where Jason Fraser was waiting. He needed only a moment to take the shots. As the light in the car park was poor, he asked them to cross the road outside with baby Brooklyn, and then to lose themselves inside Harrods for a few hours in order to give him time to sell the exclusive pictures. So the couple went through their paces, their unsmiling faces giving the impression of uncomfortable irritation at the presence of a photographer, and Fraser duly sold the snaps to *OK!* and *The Sun* newspaper. Rumours abounded in the tabloid world that on this and other occasions Fraser had paid them a substantial part of the money he received for these photos.

When the pictures were published the issue of money became a major talking point for quite another reason. David Beckham had famously signed a lucrative sponsorship deal with the makers of Brylcreem hair products, and some commentators were quick to condemn his lack of commercial sense, arguing that the loss of his longer hair would be certain to jeopardize his deal. Victoria took the trouble to phone a radio station to pour scorn on this idea. 'David has not lost any money from Brylcreem,' she told them. 'So when you said he has no brain for shaving off his hair because he would lose four million pounds, you were wrong. He has not lost a penny. I would go crazy if he lost four million pounds by having his hair cut.'

The couple's own spin on the haircut saga was that David had shaved his head because he was tired of fans imitating his look. In any event, financial analysts valued his Brylcreem deal at £200,000, a fraction of the reported figure. 'He's a professional sportsman, not a model,' a friend was quoted as saying, ironically just as David was posing in a range of designer gear for a men's glossy magazine.

Interestingly, his Brylcreem contract was due to be renegotiated shortly before he cut his hair. No less curious, in the Fraser photographs, he was seen in a £100 white Tommy Hilfiger T-shirt at a time when the trendy clothing company were considering a sponsorship deal with the Manchester United star.

The couple's next liaison with their favourite paparazzo came in May 2000, when David arranged a 'surprise' holiday for Victoria at a secluded villa in Tuscany. Only it was no surprise to Jason Fraser, who happily organized pictures of the couple for *OK!* and *The Sun,* as well as for foreign magazines. This time Victoria's agent, Alan Edwards of the Outside Organization, liaised with the photographer and the media.

And the media wanted more. *OK!* offered £100,000 for pictures of their trip to Los Angeles a few days later, where Victoria was due to team up with the well-known American songwriter Rhett Lawrence, who has written for Whitney Houston, Mel C and Christina Aguilera, to pen lyrics for her debut solo album.

Thus when the Beckhams boarded their Upper Class Virgin flight at Heathrow on Sunday May 7, Jason Fraser was sitting nearby. Just like real royalty, however, there was no question of fraternization with the media. This was business, not friendship. Victoria and David were deeply uncomfortable at the prospect of being discovered associating with the king of the paparazzi. Nor was the smooth-talking Fraser, who is widely admired for his intrepid skills at hiding in bushes or behind windbreaks, keen to be unmasked as going 'straight'. Both parties preferred to keep their dealings at a distance, the Beckhams' agent Alan Edwards or their bodyguard Mark Niblett acting as the buffer between them. Indeed, Victoria was irritated that Fraser had been on the same flight as they had and he also stayed in the same hotel, the five-star Peninsula in Beverly Hills. She insisted that any photo shoot be completed in the first couple of days of their holiday to give her time to relax.

Their plan ran into problems from the start. First they were snapped at LA Airport by a rival American photographer. Then, while the couple were walking around Bloomingdale's store at the Beverly Center mall with Fraser snapping away, a security guard, unaware that the whole enterprise was an elaborate set-up, threatened to throw the paparazzo out for harassing these celebrity shoppers. Besides, while pictures of Brooklyn taking packs of Ralph Lauren boxer shorts were all very well, Fraser wanted more intimate poses from the famously sulky couple. After some tetchy negotiations, they agreed to stage a photo call by the fountain outside their hotel.

It was a Royal Command Performance with a difference. The 'royal couple' posed at the direction of their tame paparazzo, kissing and cuddling by the fountain and kicking a football to toddler Brooklyn. When Victoria, wearing a white vest emblazoned with the words 'Rock Star', left them to join her songwriting team, David and his son, with bodyguard and photographer in tow, visited Disneyland.

Finally Fraser left them in peace. Before he returned to Britain to sell the shots, however, he asked the Beckhams to keep out of sight. He was particularly worried about David's plans to visit his favourite basketball team, the LA Lakers, fearing that if he was pictured attending the game it would dilute the exclusivity, and hence the price, of his own set of photographs. David chose to ignore the request, such is his passion for the sport and for his team, who were in the national play-off finals. He attended the match as planned, and was was thrilled to meet stars such as Dustin Hoffman, Jack Nicholson, and German soccer ace Jurgen Klinsmann.

Meanwhile Victoria was equally happy, inspired by the love songs that she had written, most of them concerning her relationship with her husband. To cap a successful week, their spokeswoman Caroline McAteer faxed to their hotel a copy of *The Sun* in which Fraser's pictures appeared, complete with the front-page headline 'Beck in the USA'.

Victoria has consistently emphasized how important it is to maintain her son's privacy. 'He is the one thing in our lives that is private,' she has said. 'That's why it is upsetting when people said I was planning to make money out of selling pictures of him. We have never intended to do that.' On another occasion she explained, 'Brooklyn won't do any pictures until he is big enough to decide what he wants to do or doesn't want to do. He's not a money-spinner. People were saying: "They left the hospital with their little asset", and that really hurt a lot.' However, despite these assertions, Fraser was once more helpfully on hand to record the couple's visit with Brooklyn to their local zoo in August 2000, pictures of which appeared in the Sunday papers days before the release of Victoria's first solo single. A far cry, some uncharitable critics would say, from their avowed intent to keep Brooklyn away from the cameras.

While Victoria should be admired for the skill with which she managed her fame and that of David and Brooklyn, their fans might have welcomed a little more honesty about their relationship with the press.

The couple have made plain their views on what they regard to be media harassment. Many people no doubt sympathized with David when he said, 'When the media intrudes into your private life and makes you have to change the way you live, I think the press has gone too far.' Certainly they have always had support from their celebrity friends. When pictures were taken of David and Victoria sunbathing by the pool at Elton John's villa in the south of France during their courtship, the singer made an official protest to the Press Complaints Commission. The PCC upheld his complaint, agreeing in their adjudication that the pictures, published in the *Daily Star*, had been intrusive.

Victoria's fellow Spice Girl Melanie Chisholm added her voice to those who believed that the nation was displaying an unhealthy interest in the Beckhams, maintaining that their private life had become the focus of an obsession equal to that of Diana, Princess of Wales and Dodi Fayed. 'We don't have Princess Diana to follow around any more, so people have picked on her [Victoria],' she said, which provoked Diana's mother, Frances Shand Kydd, to condemn the Spice Girl's remarks as 'hurtful' and 'insulting'. 'There is a great deal of difference between being a showbusiness personality and a princess,' she argued.

Ironically, Victoria has used the 'Diana' defence to justify her dealings with the press, arguing that in a world where pursuing paparazzi will go to such dangerous lengths to snatch 'that picture' of a celebrity, it is occasionally necessary to allow privileged access to selected snappers in order to safeguard their privacy and security the rest of the time.

What neither Victoria nor David have mentioned is whether the rumours that they have made money from these secret deals are correct, and whether there is any conflict between what they say in public and what they negotiate in private. Yet the apparent contradiction between their complaints about the press on the one hand and their willingness to use the media on the other does little to help the important debate which has been raging about public figures, namely their right to privacy and the limits of permissible intrusion. The government was considering legislation on this crucial issue, which came even more to the fore in the summer of 2000 when the British Prime Minister's own family became a media target, first with stories about his teenage son, Euan, and then with pictures of his baby Leo's christening.

Tony Blair, who had expressly asked for press discretion on this intimate family occasion, described the publication of the christening pictures as a gross invasion of privacy. When *Heat* magazine asked

Victoria to comment on Blair's distress, she was dismissive of his reaction, saying that she had had to put up with much worse, including one front-page photograph which had shown Brooklyn completely naked. 'He's only realized it's a bad thing now it's happened to him, but this sort of thing has been happening for years,' she said. 'Now that it's happened to his son, something might change at last. It's about time we had decent privacy laws in this country. I'm not complaining about the attention I get because I ask for that, but my family doesn't.'

Some might feel that her remark was as hypocritical as it was disingenuous, with her own role in organizing photocalls of herself, her husband and son and selling the pictures for six-figure sums to celebrity magazines only making it harder for others, be they pop stars or politicians, to insist on their privacy being respected by the mass media. In some ways it is easy to see Victoria's point of view. If pictures of her and her family sell newspapers, why should they not be the ones to take the lion's share of the money? If fame is a commodity, why should the paparazzi get pictures of them for free, when every snatched shot is 'stealing' a slice of that fame? But the Beckhams' actions are based on a double standard: they want to have their media cake and eat it. They complain about intrusion into their lives and that of their son, and yet when it suits them they engineer that very same intrusion, exploiting their own privacy for publicity and profit.

The issue of double standards aside, in many ways the couple, particularly Victoria, have become very clear-eyed and businesslike in trying to make the most of their commercial potential. She has recognized that they only have a short shelf life and she does not want to fritter away the slightest opportunity. Brought up at the feet of Simon Fuller, who saw everything as entertainment, she felt that as David was such a gifted player and a valuable asset to the club, then he deserved special treatment, earning money from his image on the shirts, for example, and other memorabilia that the club sold. This attitude ran counter to the ethos that flowed through Alex Ferguson's blood, however, that loyalty, team spirit and discipline are vital qualities for a soccer player. Unlike celebrities of yesterday who frittered away their talents or money and ended up with nothing, Victoria is one of a new breed of stars who want to control and merchandise every facet of their lives.

It irked her when United's then team captain Roy Keane landed a new contract worth £52,000 a week. Immediately she started agitating for her husband to negotiate a pay rise, publicly voicing her concerns during a radio interview when she pleaded for a new deal.

As far as Victoria was concerned, football was a commodity and she believed that her husband should exploit it to the full. If that meant going abroad, then so be it. Doubtless she had calculated that the time spent commuting between Stansted and Milan, for example, was only marginally greater than to Manchester. Previously AC Milan President Silvio Berlusconi had indicated that Beckham was on his shopping list and the astronomic sum of £50 million was mentioned.

Companies see them simply as marketing tools to sell their goods – so why shouldn't they do the same?

Better that they themselves should profit from their own fame than others should simply make money at their expense.

Since famously selling their wedding pictures to *OK!* magazine for £1 million, the Beckhams have cashed in regularly through their connection with the celebrity publication owned by Northern and Shell. The couple have also set up a company, based on the initials of Victoria and David Beckham – to manage a future licensing venture, and are following in the paths of American stars such as basketball player Michael Jordan, who have made millions from the value of their names. Such is the need to protect the Posh and Becks brand that when Northern and Shell discovered I was writing a book on the Beckhams, they sent threatening legal letters to myself and to employees at my British publishers, Michael O'Mara Books.

The couple are inundated with offers on an almost daily basis. One moment David is considering an approach to front the launch of a breakfast cereal, the next they are talking about appearing naked in *Playboy*. There seems to be no limit to the financial horizons for the Beckhams to explore. Much of the credit is due to Victoria, whose keen eye for a deal and ruthless exploitation of her status is matched only by her ambition for herself and her family. Never content with her social position, watchful and at times envious of the achievements of others, she is the commercial dynamo that drives the Posh and Becks machine.

As the music critic Ray Connolly has observed of her: 'Driven by ambition, she has a gift for marketing, a genius for selling herself. If she hadn't become a pop singer, she would almost certainly have found some other way to make her millions. She's a born entrepreneur, endlessly offering up some new product to the all-buying consumer.'

In 2000, the girl who was once on the dole was rather proud of the fact that in the league tables of richest young entertainers she stood out way in front with a fortune estimated at £24 million. It gave her quiet satisfaction to know that she was considered to be the most financially astute and marketable of the Spice Girls. She was particularly pleased that singer Geri Halliwell, formerly Ginger Spice, who had split from the all-girl band on the brink of a lucrative American tour, was valued at a mere £17.2 million.

Like many self-made millionaires, she displays a curiously contradictory attitude towards money. She is happy to spend £15,000 on clothes in a morning, but at the same time she will scrimp on a tip to the taxi driver. The daughter of a self-employed businessman, she describes herself as a 'tight arse' and with good reason. Not only is she careful with her millions, she is acutely aware that her name and status can help secure discounts with those who supply goods and services. She has said with obvious pride that one of the best things about being famous is that she gets a 30 per cent discount from Gucci. And just as Sarah, Duchess of York, notoriously haggled with traders when she was furnishing her new house, so Victoria Beckham has few qualms about negotiating deals.

British Airways found that she was no pushover when her luggage was stolen while returning from Miami to Manchester, after recording a Spice Girls album. Four Louis Vuitton suitcases containing toys, her song-lyric book – later returned – and numerous specially-made designer dresses went missing. Victoria was furious about the theft, all the more so as she arrived home with few other clothes to change into. 'I literally didn't have anything else to wear – not even a pair of knickers,' she claimed. 'All my favourite clothes were in those bags.' The airline paid a high price for upsetting the formidable Mrs Beckham.

Yet hard-headed as she may be when it comes to business, from time to time she has shown a softer, more sentimental side. On one occasion she and her sister Louise went shopping to Tesco supermarket and Marks and Spencer in Alderley Edge. During the trip the diamond from her £40,000 engagement ring fell out, possibly when she caught her hand on the metal mesh of her shopping trolley. Even though they were offered a £5,000 reward, security staff never found the missing stone. While she was deeply upset about the loss, she expressed the wish that a homeless person had found it and used the money to buy themselves a house. The plight of the homeless is constantly on her mind, especially when driving through central London, which at times resembles a refugee camp, such are the numbers and the variety of homeless people, particularly the young, sheltering in doorways. Before getting into her chauffeur-driven Mercedes she often gave a ten- or twenty-pound note to a homeless youngster if she saw one near the recording studio that the Spice Girls used in Whitfield Street in London's West End. In an exclusive interview with *The Big Issue*, the British street magazine sold by homeless people, she admitted that their problems struck a chord. 'I still feel quite guilty about spending [money],' she said. 'It's hard to justify spending five thousand pounds on a coat when there are people living rough on the streets.'

Neither is she quite the misery-guts she would like to pretend – even to the much-derided media. When she was being interviewed by one journalist at Alderley Edge, she offered the non-driving scribe a lift back to London in her chauffeur-driven car.

On her birthday it has become something of a ritual for her to visit local hospitals and hand out cake to youngsters in the children's ward. She finds a charitable use, too, for her unwanted designer clothes. After her sister and other members of her family have rummaged through them, they are put into black plastic bin-liners and sent to the local charity shop at Goff's Oak. 'She is very generous,' one charity worker said. 'People think she is stuck up, but they don't see the other side of her.'

Even though she was driven to school in a Rolls-Royce, Victoria knew both rejection and failure before she found fame with the Spice Girls, an experience which has made her all the more keenly aware of the pleasures of success. In contrast, while David is a working-class boy from a modest background, success has literally been at his feet throughout his teenage and adult life. Cocooned inside the Manchester United institution since he was sixteen, he consequently has very little concept of the true value of money. Ironically, the working-class boy made good behaves more like royalty than his wife as far as finances are concerned. For him, money is simply a prop in the theatre of life. While Victoria is calculating, he is carefree. 'It's the one thing David and I differ on,' says Victoria. 'He never looks at the price of anything.' He seems happy to let her apply the brakes to his spending, even when it relates to his passion for cars. 'If she doesn't want me to have it, she just phones [the suppliers] up and cancels it,' he has admitted.

Though they approach the notion of wealth by different paths, they have both arrived at the same location: the undisputed king and queen of conspicuous consumption. While the House of Windsor stands by the values of duty, a wider obligation to society, and a virtuous frugality, this new royal family worships at the altars of extravagance and indulgence. Gucci, Prada and Donna Karan are their gods.

Virtually every day they pay obeisance at their shrines to shopping: the Trafford Centre in Manchester, and Knightsbridge in London. They can spend in an hour what some people earn in a year, lavishing thousands on jewellery, clothes and cars. In 1999, David was known to spend around £66,000 a month on everything from private jets, first-class flights, watches and sports cars.

Like the aristocracy of a bygone age, they have always been eager to display their wealth. 'It's absolutely gorgeous,' boasted Victoria when she showed off the £50,000 black diamond ring that David bought her for their first anniversary. It neatly matched the £30,000 earrings he had surprised her with on her twenty-sixth birthday.

As psychologist Dr Glenn Wilson observes, 'Their endless shopping trips are a need to remind themselves that they have made it, that they are successful. For them, wealth is a new idea, and their addiction to consumption reveals a couple of limited scope and imagination. Quite simply they are doing what many people dream about if they won the lottery: big house, flash cars and everything money can buy.'

Since becoming a national institution, however, they have begun to move in the social stratosphere where money becomes secondary to status. Their holidays are an indication of the extent to which they have truly made it. Just as the young royals spend their vacations at the villa homes of their rich and famous friends, so the Beckhams are following in their wake. They have been frequent guests of Elton John's, while Lord Lloyd Webber invited them to stay at his villa during their honeymoon.

In summer 2000, they crowned their rise to the summit of the nation's *nouveaux riches* when the Harrods owner, Mohamed Fayed, invited them to his villa in the south of France. During their week-long stay they joined Fayed on board the same yacht on which he had entertained Princess Diana and his son Dodi in the summer of 1997, shortly before their deaths. A friend was quoted as saying, 'He is used to entertaining royalty at his home, and it's fair to say David and Victoria were treated like a prince and princess.'

For once no photographer was on hand to capture their enthronement.

Ten

What She Really, Really Wants

She didn't want to go, she really, really didn't want to go. In fact what she really, really wanted was to stay at home. That much was utterly clear. A clear sign of her nervousness was her language. Normally it was one colour. Blue. Today it was deep blue, her apprehension was mixed with real fear and resentment, resentment at the hidden stalker who had the one thing she hates to give up: control.

The horrible threats had unnerved her so much that ever-professional Victoria could have been excused for wanting to pull out of the annual Brit Awards where she and the remaining Spice Girls were due to be presented with a Lifetime Achievement award. In the days before the prestigious ceremony, held at London's Earls Court, she had been sent a sick letter containing a newspaper photograph of her, altered to show blood spurting from a bullet hole in her head and the chilling warning: 'You are going to get yours.' This latest threat, which was immediately sent to the police for forensic tests, contained the date, 3 March 2000 – the night of the Brit Awards. What Victoria didn't realize at the time was that former Spice Girl and her then arch-rival Geri Halliwell had received a similar threat.

Onlookers could have mistaken her edginess for stage fright or prima-donna behaviour when she joined the rest of the Spice Girls for several hours of rehearsals before that evening's gala event. Her reflex aggression, the usual sign that she is trying to disguise her nervousness, was apparent to those who had to deal with her. As she was walking off stage after the rehearsal, someone in the gantry shone a powerful red laser pen at her, the beam hitting her on the shoulder. For all Victoria knew it could have been an assassin armed with a rifle mounted with laser sights. She was absolutely terrified and was immediately hustled away by a mob of security guards and taken to her private dressing room. Senior police officers climbed the gantry in a vain search for the intruder, while back in her dressing room Victoria waited nervously.

As the girls were the last act to perform, Victoria had several long hours to fill, anxious minutes of worrying and waiting. By the time she and the other girls went on stage to collect the award from Hollywood actor Will Smith and sing a medley of their hits, Victoria was in pieces. Just before their entrance there was a commotion in the audience as Geri Halliwell made a dramatic exit, a phalanx of dark-suited minders clearing a path through the astonished audience. No one knew of the death threat to Geri and many must have thought her departure a direct snub to the other Spice Girls. She had already caused quite a stir, not only with an overt performance of her new single, 'Bag It Up', which offended Victoria with its pointed references to independent women and shopping trolleys, but also because she had refused to join the Spice Girls on stage to collect their award.

Victoria appeared not to notice Geri's exit as she, Mel C, Mel B and Emma went through their routine, and as the words of their final song 'Goodbye' echoed round the hall, many in the audience thought that this was their swansong. As they reached their finale, the stage was shaken with a series of explosions and the audience was treated to an unexpected fireworks display. It was too much for Victoria. It seemed she hadn't been told about the surprise ending and in her acute apprehensive state presumably thought a bomb had gone off nearby. The singer, her heart in her mouth, collapsed in tears and had to be helped off the stage by her colleagues. Members of the audience, thinking that she was overcome by the emotion of the evening, simply applauded her and the other girls all the louder. It was not the farewell Victoria would have wanted.

In truth, life with the Spice Girls hadn't been the same since the departure of Geri. The birth of Brooklyn, her wedding and the arrival of Mel B's daughter, Phoenix Chi, indicated that the days of the Spice Girls were drawing to a close. These brash young women who had taken Britain by storm in the mid-1990s were now mature, responsible adults, as concerned about changing nappies and feeding babies as going out clubbing and cutting loose.

On the surface things were still fine. In the autumn of 1999, when they were recording their third album in the famous Abbey Road studios in North London, the girls seemed to be having fun. Victoria, as usual, brought along bags of crisps and sweets for the girls and the recording crew as well as bottles of Asti Spumante, which the girls used to drink before they became famous. But this time she brought more than refreshments. She carried Brooklyn into the studios, leaving him sleeping with a similarly comatose Phoenix Chi in a makeshift crêche filled with toys that she had brought with her.

The girls met up with Rodney Jerkins, the US songwriter who was producing the album. It had been said that the hard-working American could be an intimidating character. Naturally the girls knew he was good and everyone wanted to do well. Victoria may have been more nervous than the others, aware that her voice was the weakest of the quartet. Doubtless she didn't want to let her fellow Spice Girls down, so she would have been delighted when he heaped fulsome praise on her and the others about their work. It really broke the ice and from then on the girls joshed Jerkins mercilessly about his diet – he apparently ate about six hamburgers a day – and his heavy gold jewellery, in fact anything they could think of. He and his team teased the girls right back and, much to the amusement of studio technicians, over the weeks a relationship of good-natured mockery and respect developed.

David spent as much time as he could spare in the recording studios, playing with Brooklyn and listening to the girls. After each recording session he was quick to bolster Victoria's confidence, telling her how good she was. His encouragement and support played a large part in convincing her to continue in the pop world after she had started to question her own abilities. As he said in an interview with *OK!* magazine, 'I think there was a period of self-doubt because she hadn't done anything for about six to eight months. Brooklyn had just been born, we'd got married, we'd done the family thing by being together – and people were starting to notice that the other girls were bringing out solo things and Victoria wasn't.'

The Spice Girls continue to support each other too. So they all went along to the Round House in London's Camden Town to support Mel B, who nervously paraded down the catwalk during a fashion show, and they all turned up for a concert in Sheffield when Mel C launched her first solo single.

Inevitably, though, tensions inside the group began to mount as they all tried to pursue their own solo careers while remaining loyal to the band. Mel C was first to break cover, revealing that there was some friction between the girls with the forthright admission: 'There are rows and ructions in the band every other day.' Perhaps the others in the band felt some resentment since Victoria had become the most photographed woman in Britain, and Mel C made it clear that she disapproved of her lavish lifestyle when she criticized the wedding as 'over the top'.

Inside the industry rumours were rife that a band, long past the normal sell-by date for pop groups, was on the verge of splitting up. When the group convened in London for a private meeting with record industry executives and their advisers to discuss the future of the Spice Girls, Mel C didn't turn up, and again when the girls were finishing off recording their third album in Miami, Mel C failed to join the others. She flew in after they had all left to lay down her vocals to songs that the rest of the band had already recorded. It was not long before the rumour mill had begun to churn out story after story, saying that the girls gone their separate ways.

At the same time, whatever their personal differences, they had contractual obligations to meet. An eight-concert tour in Manchester and London in December 1999 was a sell-out and they spent weeks rehearsing at Elstree Studios in Hertfordshire. Nothing seemed to go right for them and Victoria complained about everything from the choreography to the organization. While the concerts were well received, there wasn't the vitality or commitment of old. Critics noted Victoria's unwillingness to participate in the band's on-stage antics during their opening concert in Manchester in December 1999. It was felt that Victoria's heart might not be in it any more, her famous enigmatic aloofness making her look 'oddly detached' from the others. Now she was a wife and a mother, the Girl Power thing had worn thin.

At the end of each concert in Manchester, rather than stay for an after-show drink with the rest of the band and production crew, it was noticed that Victoria and Mel C left as soon as they had taken their bows on stage. It seemed that Victoria felt that she had grown up, moved away from the larking-about, acting-the-fool, all-girl band. Every performance it was the same story: last to arrive, first to leave.

Even their solid fan base seemed to be dwindling. Since their debut as complete unknowns at the Brits only three years before, they had racked up no less than eight UK number-one singles, two smash-hit platinum albums, selling 35 million albums and 24 million singles worldwide. But in the ephemeral world of pop that counts for nothing, the teenage readers of *Smash Hits* magazine still voted them the worst band in Britain that month.

While there was still talk of a European tour in the summer of 2000, it seemed apparent that the UK concerts would be their last. Victoria was so overcome with sadness that after their last concert at London's Earls Court she shed tears on stage, no doubt thinking of good times past and good times gone. Even more distressing was news of the death of a rigger, who fell as he was dismantling the band's stage set after their last Earls Court concert. The accident seemed a tragic epitaph for the death of the band. So when the girls unveiled statues of themselves in the Rock Café, they were just going through the motions – professional smiles, private distance.

So after they collected their Lifetime Achievement award at the Brits in March all the girls had begun to pursue independent ventures, though Victoria had a bit of catching up to do in pursuit of her solo career. Unsure of her singing ability, it was not at first certain that she would follow the same path as the four other girls and go solo. Instead, she tried television and film before going back to her singing roots.

While she turned down the chance to appear as a stand-in presenter for *The Big Breakfast* TV show, she did spend several weeks filming for her own TV documentary programme, *Victoria's Secrets*. Even so she was still keeping one eye on the film world, auditioning for numerous parts, including remakes of *Charlie's Angels* and *What's New Pussycat?*, and reading a number of scripts. She emphasized that far from being typecast in a glamorous role she would much prefer to try her abilities as a comedian, playing a 'wacky, dippy' role in a movie. Unfortunately, the only kind of parts on offer involved appearing nude or taking part in a love scene, which David would never allow. So it seemed Victoria's film career was going nowhere, and although her TV documentary *Victoria's Secrets* had garnered reasonable reviews, it was more of a curiosity than a career move.

She had meetings with various media movers and shakers in London and Los Angeles, including Hollywood director Oliver Stone, and took the time to have acting lessons with a coach in Primrose Hill, North London. 'They're a lot of fun,' she said. 'I'm taking my time on what to do outside the Spice Girls as I don't want to make any mistakes.'

Victoria was finding out the hard way that success as a pop singer might open doors, but does not guarantee success as an actress. Gamely, she had to come back from numerous disappointments. When she went to audition for the role of Lara Croft, she was really excited about the possibility of spending months filming in exotic locations and having martial arts lessons to be able to do the complex fighting moves herself. So she was doubtless bitterly disappointed not to get the part.

In a way she has Sir Alex Ferguson to thank for kick-starting her solo singing career. After his bust-up with David, Victoria realized that, whatever she might have wanted, she had to spend more time in the north for the sake of her husband's career. In order to make the best of a bad job, it was suggested that she link up with Take That singer Gary Barlow who lived nearby. At first, though, she was extremely reluctant. Barlow had endured a terrible roasting in the media since the band first split up, when his singing stardom was eclipsed by former colleague Robbie Williams, and Victoria may have been afraid that if the meetings were publicized they would be presented as a desperate attempt to shore up a failing career. But in fact their songwriting union worked well. She recorded several ballads with him, and was inspired enough to travel to Los Angeles to work with songwriter Rhett Lawrence for her first solo album.

A new career beckoned for Mrs Beckham.

Eleven

Tears, Tantrums and Tenderness

It had been a satisfying day for Victoria Beckham, her husband never far from her thoughts. For hours she and Take That singer-songwriter Gary Barlow had been writing and recording love songs for her solo album in the high-tech studios at his home in Cuddington, Cheshire. The lyrics for the ballads that they recorded all centred around her devotion and passion for David. By the end of the second long session she was feeling very pleased with herself, and anxious to tell her husband how the day had gone.

She knew they had nothing special planned for that night, but David had other ideas. It was May 2000, the end of a hectic soccer season. With the Premier League Championship title guaranteed, his manager Sir Alex Ferguson had given him a six-day break. He wanted to do something special for Victoria, the woman who had made his life so happy and fulfilled.

Ever the romantic, David's first thought had been to surprise her by flying her to an island she had always dreamed of visiting: Maui, near Hawaii, in the Pacific Ocean. But when he realized that it would take twenty-three hours' flying time to reach this idyllic spot, he had to think again. Phone calls were made, friends and acquaintances sounded out. A senior executive from Virgin Records, the Spice Girls' label, agreed to loan her secluded villa outside Florence in Tuscany, while another friend had a private jet standing by at Manchester airport to whisk the couple and their son away for their secret break in Italy.

All that remained was the packing. When Victoria left that morning for the thirty-five minute drive to Gary Barlow's mansion, David and her mother Jackie filled suitcases for the trip. Then David collected her from the singer's home, telling an unsuspecting Victoria that they had to drive to the airport to pick up a relative. It was only when she was about to board the flight to Tuscany that her husband revealed he was taking her on a second honeymoon.

Their relationship at this time was said to be intense and passionate. He considered his wife to be both his soulmate and his saviour, a partner who had helped to make him stronger and more self-aware. 'Victoria has given me so much confidence,' he has said. 'I'm quite a shy person, but she's brought a bit more out of me.' Indeed, theirs was an almost obsessive love affair where they only came alive in each other's company.

They regularly sent short love notes and cards to one another, spoke constantly on their mobile phones and bought each other small gifts. They were an intensely tactile couple, holding hands and cuddling each other in public. 'We love spending time together,' Victoria has revealed. 'We're both very affectionate and I've never really been like that with any other boyfriends.'

On anniversaries and birthdays, David in particular has been known to make an extra-special effort. On Valentine's Day 2000, he got up early and filled their apartment in Alderley Edge with balloons, streamers and bouquets of lilies, Victoria's favourite flowers. Another time he rang singer Elton John to ask his advice about a piano he wanted to buy his wife as a surprise present.

He is equally given to extravagant, almost foolhardy, gestures that speak volumes about his devotion to the object of his affection. When Victoria was in Los Angeles on business, he risked the wrath of his manager by flying halfway round the world to spend two days with her. After paying for flights for himself, Brooklyn, his friend David Gardner and Gardner's girlfriend, Victoria's sister Louise, he had little change out of £20,000. While David was well aware that he could face trouble from his club – the couple flew back on separate flights to avoid adverse publicity – his romantic gesture made it clear where his priorities lay.

On another occasion, returning from a soccer tournament in Tokyo, he did get permission from his boss to leave the rest of the team in order to surprise his new bride. Victoria was due to attend the Art of Barbie Ball with Elton John in support of the singer's Aids Foundation. David arranged with Savile Row tailors William Hunt to make him a suit in the style of Barbie's boyfriend, Ken, to match Victoria's pink Barbie dress. The outfit was made in double-quick time and biked to Goff's Oak to await his return.

As soon as he landed at Heathrow, David dashed to his in-laws' home, quickly washed and changed and drove to central London to be at his wife's side. 'It was a nice surprise to see David,' said Victoria, her matter-of-fact response revealing how much his thoughtful and romantic surprises had become an accepted part of their lives.

Yet it is also true that their love has not been without its emotional fireworks. Their union has drawn its strength from an explosive dynamic of opposing emotions and priorities; her needy, him giving; her withholding, him generous; his gentleness, her aggression; his passivity, her dynamism; his romantic nature, her matter-of-fact qualities.

Her boast about David being 'an animal in bed' and her belief that every woman in the world wants to snare her husband masked a deep and abiding insecurity. While her troubled soul may have been the engine that has driven her relentless ambition, conversely her very outspokenness and her reflex aggression have disguised a vulnerability which suggested that she was not able to find peace of mind with her partner, no matter how often David has reassured her or indeed how regularly she has proclaimed her love to the world.

She is aware of her emotional vulnerability, when surges of anger rise within her if she sees another woman daring to look at her man. 'It makes me want to smack them in the mouth,' she has admitted. Her jealousy was exacerbated by the frequent physical distance between them, so that she fretted and worried every time he was away on his own in Manchester, fulfilling his club commitments. But though Victoria has generally always been less than impressed when women have tried to chat up her husband, she has found it highly amusing when gay men have come on to him.

It was always worse when they were in Manchester. On one occasion the couple were window-shopping in the city's Trafford Centre when two young girls asked David for his autograph. The footballer, who was carrying Brooklyn, deposited his son in his buggy and cheerfully signed their books. When the youngsters began cooing over the baby, Brooklyn took this as his cue to burst into tears, which resulted in Victoria accusing David of being a bad father, and angrily asking him why he was signing autographs for those 'tarts' in the first place. As sales staff and customers in a nearby card shop looked on in amazement, the couple proceeded to have a heated exchange before marching out of the store to continue their verbal fisticuffs.

Over time, her extreme, often irrational reactions must have exasperated and bewildered her husband on occasions. Before he met Victoria, the soccer star had dated Julie Killelea, the daughter of a Lancashire construction millionaire, for two months. After they split up she started seeing David's friend and fellow Manchester United player, Phil Neville. When the couple decided to get married in December 1999, they organized a colour co-ordinated wedding. They asked all the men to wear red ties featuring the groom and bride's initials P and J, while the female guests were requested to wear a combination of the team's red, white and black colours. Everyone obliged, except for Victoria.

Determined to stand out on the bride's big day, Victoria stole the show in a strapless, low-cut, coffee-coloured, designer dress split revealingly to the thigh. As one commentator noted, 'Posh Spice upstaged the bride.' Her behaviour did not endear her to the Neville family, not least because her outfit was widely featured in the pages of *OK!* magazine, which had paid £100,000 for exclusive rights to publish the photos of Phil and Julie's big day. The wedding itself took place in the same week that Victoria had lost the stone from her own diamond ring while shopping. She was frantic to ensure that she had a copy of the original to wear on the big day, fearing that if she appeared in public without her ring it would start tongues wagging. She seemed to be so wound up about the wedding of her husband's former girlfriend that it must have been something of a relief when a bomb scare at the reception, held at the Midland Hotel in Manchester, enabled her, David and Brooklyn to depart the wedding throng for a while before the all-clear was announced.

Often one of their spats would be prolonged because of the distance between them. A tiff that ordinarily would have blown over in a matter of hours continued for days because one or the other had to go away on business. Invariably, during these emotional altercations, it was Victoria's mother who acted as the diplomat, soothing David out of a sulk or her daughter from an angry mood.

Nor was the jealousy and insecurity one-way traffic. David would happily have confronted her former boyfriend, Mark Wood, when the latter was also present at the Brit Awards at Earls Court where the Spice Girls received their Lifetime Achievement award.

Such has been David's possessiveness that, after Brooklyn's birth, if Victoria had to go out alone to a showbiz event, her husband bridled if she wore one of her many skimpy, if glamorous, outfits. He hated the idea of other men ogling her, and there have been words between the couple about her fashion choices. From her point of view, she felt that she could do and wear what she liked, particularly as it was that same glamorous look that had attracted him to her in the first place. Meanwhile, David worried about her revealing outfits, feeling that since marrying and starting a family, the flirty image that was so successful with the Spice Girls was no longer appropriate. As she remarked in 2000, 'I like short skirts, but David says I can't do that now I've got a baby.'

Not that David should ever have had cause for concern. For all the raunchy dance routines and the sexy outfits, Victoria has always been a traditional, one-man woman who takes a dim view of those in her showbiz or soccer circle who stray from their partners. So she was shocked when a well-known TV personality tried to chat her up at a celebrity lunch, complaining primly afterwards about his behaviour.

Just as their mutual jealousy has revealed how much they love and care for each other, so their wardrobes give an insight into the closeness of the bond that unites them. Both are performers who love the limelight, enjoying the adulation and acclaim. Their private selves are reflected in this public display, feeding the innate narcissism in their characters: Victoria, the childhood show-off who loved to strike a pose; David, the little boy who always liked to stand out and be different. 'I take pride in my appearance,' he has said. Even as a child he had firm views on his image: once when he was a pageboy at a wedding, he chose to wear maroon velvet knickerbockers, long white socks and ballet shoes, even though his mother Sandra thought that he looked 'silly'.

David's dandyism has come to full flower since he met Victoria, sealing his reputation as a fashion icon and a gay pin-up. While she has always been credited with shaping his style, it owes as much to his own theatrical instincts. Perhaps there is also a touch of rebellion against the old-fashioned values of his father Ted, who would mock him when he saw pictures in the media showing David (or Camp David as he became known) in his famous sarong or wearing a silk bandana. As far as his father is concerned, football comes first, second and last in life; fashion is an effeminate distraction. He reportedly told a friend: 'Just look at him . . . it's not the David I know.'

From the moment David saw Victoria dressed head to toe in PVC for a pop video and she spotted the Manchester United player in the pages of a glossy magazine, they hunted each other out as assiduously as any big-game trophy-hunter. Once captured, these two young people saw in each other a reflection of themselves, their vanity and self-absorption perfectly matched. As the relationship has developed they have become almost interchangeable; their mannerisms, their body language and particularly their clothes have become remarkably similar.

It started with the famous matching purple outfits for their wedding in Ireland and soon became a signature that defined the couple. So for a Gucci party they wore identical leather outfits, for a night out at the trendy Sugar Reef restaurant they were in matching denim, while for a film première they were in similar brown gear. Hailed as style icons, there was an androgynous sexuality about their behaviour, a quality that might explain their popularity with the gay community.

However, there is a danger inherent in an existence where Posh and Becks as a couple are seen as a brand, an institution and a lifestyle. As marriage guidance counsellor Lucy Selleck of British relationship charity Relate warned, 'If people's identities are too linked into "the couple" rather than themselves, that could be a problem. We call such couples "Babes in the Wood". They cling to each other in an unhealthy way and can't function properly.'

Like the real royal family, there has been an 'us against the world' quality about their behaviour, each giving the other mutual support during some of the very public traumas in their lives. When David was sent off during the World Cup, it was Victoria to whom he turned for comfort and consolation. In a neat role reversal, it was she who told him he looked 'lovely' in an outfit because, for all his pin-up good looks, he is often unconfident about his appearance.

Again it is she who went out and publicly defended him against critics who suggested that he was 'thick', with a voice like a vacant little boy. She has always been most concerned to set the record straight on his behalf. Crucially, while it rankles with her what the rest of the world thinks, he has professed not to care. 'Victoria gets more annoyed than I do about people saying I'm thick and that I sound stupid. I just get on with it,' he has said.

When one of his childhood friends committed suicide, David was devastated by his tragic death. As youngsters they had played football together and David had kept in touch with him when he left to play in Manchester. Victoria, knowing that it was the first time her husband had attended the funeral of a close friend, showed a maturity few would credit, mothering him solicitously through his ordeal.

Equally, David has shown the same intense concern for Victoria. Before a Manchester United game, if he knew she was in the crowd, he always scanned the stadium to make sure she was all right. Only then could he relax and play soccer. Sometimes he took his support for her to extremes. During the last Spice Girls tour, he sat in the front row night after night even though he knew that the first five rows would be drenched in fake snow which always showered that part of the audience. After a few nights, most fans brought umbrellas, but not David. He insisted on sitting in the same seats without protection.

Indeed she has been so reliant on his support that once they had a disagreement when he failed to ring her soon enough after she had sashayed down the catwalk during her first attempt as a model in February 2000. It was a short-lived tantrum, for they were soon billing and cooing over each other, but it showed just how much she needed his reassurance.

The episode illustrates an essential difference between the couple. He seems content to be who he is, secure in his skin, a talented footballer doing what he has always wanted. On the other hand,

Victoria is driven by the demons within; a woman who is at once dauntless, intrepid and dynamic, and yet insecure, vulnerable and needy.

Certainly the question of talent is an issue. David has innate ability, while Victoria made her fame and fortune through hard work, determination, drive – and a large slice of luck. 'He gets more respect because he is more talented,' she has noted, a view that reflects the common belief that she was the weakest singer in the Spice Girls, the one known for her looks rather than her voice. In the ephemeral world of showbiz, that knowledge breeds its own insecurity. As consultant psychiatrist Dr Paul Flowers has observed, 'While she has a lot of acclaim, she feels that she is a bit of a fraud, famous for being famous. So when she is with her contemporaries and peer group, that is, other singers and showbiz types, she may feel that she is something of a failure. Fame is a hollow achievement and having struggled and strived for success, once she has attained that goal she may feel more, not less, insecure.'

So while Posh and Becks are both vain and self-absorbed, almost inevitable qualities in lives performed so publicly, it is Victoria whose constant craving for attention has led her to the wilder shores of excess. She is a past master at producing the outrageous remark. The constant need to make headlines means there is never a question, however personal, that she will not answer, a statement she will not make.

She previously announced on her official website, for instance, that she 'crouched to avoid contact' when it came to toilet hygiene. She has also boldly revealed that 'I've weed in front of David right from the beginning, but then we've always been more like friends.' She was forthright about motherhood – 'I've given up breast-feeding now,' she said, explaining how 'Brooklyn was getting too hungry, so I'm feeding him bottles. My nipples didn't get sore or anything. I just wasn't giving him enough.' – and when asked by the men's magazine *GQ* if she had ever been totally sexually satisfied she said, 'Yes, recently. That's important if you want to spend the rest of your life with someone – if not, you start to look elsewhere.'

Nor was this an isolated comment. As she enthusiastically told showbiz writer Dominic Mohan after Brooklyn's birth, 'I want another [baby], that's for sure, but we are both so busy. That's not to say our sex life isn't great though.' Then she added, some might say over-defensively, 'It's fantastic and always has been, thank you very much.' As the novelist Shyama Perera noted, 'It's as if she thinks a constant public acknowledgement of their union will provide the spiritual underpinning for their love.'

Her frankness about their personal life contrasts with David's demeanour, a man who treads warily when he is on parade, saying little in public and giving away less. Of course it must be remembered that as an international footballer David's name makes the sports headlines on an almost daily basis, whereas Victoria has to work harder to grab the spotlight. Nowhere was this better expressed than during Channel 4's *The Big Breakfast*, when she remarked that her husband had worn her thong underwear, a seemingly throwaway line that was nonetheless guaranteed to make headlines in the tabloids.

Interestingly, it was Victoria herself who later underlined the absurdity of anyone taking this story seriously in an interview with London *Evening Standard* columnist Zoe Williams. 'I mean, how's he going to fit into one of my thongs?' she pointed out.

A perfectionist, Victoria has known from an early age that she would have to try harder and work harder in order to reach the top. With little God-given talent, it is her determination and ferocious self-belief that has sustained her. She is a born leader who commands respect, and at times fear, from those who cross her. Victoria has often said that she is the 'bitch' while David is the 'pussycat'. The celebrity photographer Annie Leibovitz captured the essence of her dominance and his docility during a photo shoot in a Scottish baronial mansion, where she had the couple striking rather smouldering if self-conscious poses, as the mistress of the manor and the sensual servant.

Victoria is the business brains of the partnership, the one who thinks up schemes and organizes deals, exploiting their celebrity to the full. Dynamic and aggressively ambitious, no doubt she becomes frustrated by her husband's seemingly more laidback, easy-going nature. It is something of an illusion. Her restless energy has pointed to deep-seated anxieties, tensions manifested in her eating habits and the very public debate about her weight loss. The woman who can make David Beckham laugh one minute and cry the next is much more troubled than she or her circle would like to admit.

Not for nothing did she name her company Moody Productions.

In the early hours of a Sunday morning in August 2000 at the Astoria Theatre in London's West End,

Victoria Beckham launched her first single, 'Out Of Your Mind', with Dane Bowers and Truesteppers.

It was G.A.Y. club night at the venue, packed with 1,500 people, mostly young men, dancing together and having a good time before the arrival of the main attraction. Over the thumping dance music, the tension was slowly building. The boys have always loved the Spice Girls since the heady days when they launched their career under the auspices of the same club night, singing 'Wannabe', the single that made their name and their millions. As club promoter Jeremy Joseph remarked, 'There's a lot of nostalgia for them.'

Finally, it was time for Victoria to make her entrance. As the lights went down and the smoke machines were pumped up, dancers wearing miners' helmets surrounded a very slim, gold-clad figure centre stage. It was Posh. She performed, or rather mimed, her single while she and the dancers went through a very tight, obviously well-rehearsed dance routine including funky, well-manicured hand movements. The crowd cheered, wanting more. And they got it. David Beckham was beamed up on the screen behind the stage saying some kind words about his wife, which were drowned out by the noise of the enthusiastic crowd. She nearly drove them wild when she cried out, 'Do you think David's an animal in bed?' To ear-splitting whistles being blown by most of the crowd, Victoria graciously came back on stage for an action replay of her new song, going through the same motions all over again. Clearly not a huge repertoire yet.

Round the back, at the stage door, there was a small but well-behaved scrum of gay boys and a few teenage girls who had obviously been loyal Spice Girls fans since the good old days. They crowded round the door hoping for autographs. Victoria smiled and signed a few posters for her handful of fans before being swept away down the alley into the night.

Her frantic endeavours to ensure that her first single hit the number-one spot said much about her life and her character. With the gradual decline of the Spice Girls, she had perhaps the most difficult journey of all the group members. As the other girls brought out solo singles and albums, Victoria had stayed in the musical background. It would have been all too easy to slip into the shadow of her husband, to become a famous mother who used to sing and dance. There would have been no disgrace in that route.

But that would be to underestimate her drive and energy. Although she is no more ambitious than the others, she is perhaps without Mel C's natural talent or Geri's individualism. Victoria showed a lot of guts to take the plunge and go it alone. 'I'm not the best singer or the best dancer in the world, but I work hard,' she said.

When her single was released in August, it was hard to avoid Victoria Beckham as she careered around the country on a promotional tour like a woman possessed. In a week she travelled an estimated 8,000 miles, signing her single in stores around the country as well as flying to Ibiza for a gig. When she and David appeared at Woolworths in Oldham, Greater Manchester, to promote her efforts, *The Sun* newspaper described her in a banner headline as 'Desperate'. There was glee too when it was revealed that her friend, *OK!* magazine owner Richard Desmond, had given his staff cash to buy copies of the single in various stores, and yet further amusement when a mystery woman bought thirty-four copies of the single at a Woolworths branch near Victoria's home. While her mother denied accusations that she had attempted to rig the charts, the impression was left that Victoria would do and say anything to win the battle for number one. In spite of her efforts, however, she failed by a whisker. Her rival Spiller took the number-one slot, so Victoria had to make do with silver.

'It's made us feel great that Posh Spice felt so threatened that she had to pull out so many tricks to get publicity,' said her Spiller rival, Sophie Ellis-Bextor, who added insult to injury by wearing a T-shirt that read 'Peckham'.

Though Victoria may have lost the battle, she seemed to win the war inside herself, for the first time proving that she could perform on her own and could attract the crowds on her own merits. In Oldham, for example, police horses were called in to control the estimated 6,000 fans who had gathered to see her and her husband. 'Usually if I'm with the Spice Girls, I think all the crowds are there to see Emma or Melanie,' she admitted, 'but for the first time, people are there to see me and it's really flattering.'

A newly-confident Victoria Beckham was about to embark on possibly the most exciting phase of an exhilarating career. Now that is what she really, really wanted.

Twelve

The Stamp
of Success

The Victoria and David Beckham phenomenon
has defied all the laws of celebrity. Unlike other
famous people whose stars glowed and then
quickly faded, the popularity of the Beckhams went
from strength to strength during the early winter
months of 2001.

Although Victoria's single with Dane Bowers and
garage outfit Truesteppers had failed to reach the
coveted number-one slot, 'Out Of Your Mind' was
revealed to be the bestselling number-two single of
2000, with an impressive 180,584 copies sold.
Meanwhile, aside from publishing an autobiograph-
ical book, being the subject of an ITV documentary,
giving countless interviews, and featuring in a
documentary film about Manchester United, David
reached a new milestone in his career when, at the
age of twenty-five, he was honoured with the
England captaincy. Could there be any greater accolade for the talented footballer?

At the end of 2000, the Beckhams had not only been voted the most stylish and popular couple in Britain, but were ranked 59th in a *Guardian* poll of the most influential individuals in the country, ahead of the Prince of Wales, and just behind the then Tory leader William Hague. Recognizing the new millennium's preference for media icons, and one media couple in particular, Peter Jennings, Fellow of the Royal Philatelic Society, even suggested that images of Posh and Becks should appear on British postage stamps.

Others continued to pay homage to the couple – or at least to their pulling power. Lynton Hemsley, inspired by an eighteenth-century painting, depicted them as characters from classical mythology, portraying David as the god Jupiter and Victoria as his semi-naked, adoring wife. The painting was auctioned on the Internet to raise money for British children's charity, the NSPCC. Similarly, artist Adrian Luty created a huge collage of the Beckhams from thousands of newspaper and magazine clippings about them, which was put up for auction in aid of the Meningitis Research Foundation, a charity with which Victoria has become closely involved.

The couple also sportingly faced spoof rapper Ali G for an interview televised on the BBC's *Comic Relief* charity night in March 2001. While along with other celebrities, David contributed directly to a children's book in aid of Kosovan orphans, and also handed over a cheque for $25,000 to the United Nation's Children Fund, on behalf of his club and Excite UK Ltd, to promote Manchester United's partnership with the charity – United for Unicef.

While the Posh-and-Becks machine continued apace, there appeared to be a significant shift in the dynamic of the couple's relationship. Both seemed at pains to dispel the generally held perception that Victoria was the one in the driving seat, suggesting that David should be seen as his own man. 'Matey-boy over there is very dominating, but people don't see that. I need someone to keep me in line,' said Victoria, in the autumn 2000 TV documentary *The David Beckham Story*. Similarly, David made it very clear that although he loved his wife, he would not be moving to Madrid or Milan merely because she preferred the shops there. Rather he would be making up his own mind when to move on from Manchester United. 'People say that Victoria is pulling me away from the club, which she has never done. At the end of the day it's a family decision, but it will be my decision whether I stay at Man United or not,' he told MUTV.

Could it be that Beckham was acting upon undoubtedly chauvinistic advice from the likes of Sir Alex Ferguson and former football manager Brian Clough? In the January 2001 edition of *Match of the Day* magazine, Clough revealed in his column his worries for Beckham's career once Sir Alex left his position as United's manager, advising that David 'should sign a new, long contract with United' and, 'persuade his missus to have a few more bairns'. 'I used to like my players to marry young,' Clough continued, 'but . . . it was up to my players to control their wives. Alex Ferguson is just as old-fashioned as I am about that.'

Though there were rumours that Victoria was expecting a brother or sister for Brooklyn, David strongly denied that she was pregnant. Certainly, when the 2000–1 football season began, David spent more time in Manchester than he had done in the past. The fact that he was not travelling to and from Goff's Oak – still Victoria's preferred home while their Hertfordshire mansion underwent an extensive and costly refit – seemed initially to help his game, and he embarked upon what promised to be one of his finest seasons with the club. Ferguson had demanded that Beckham 'get forward more' and had set him a fifteen-goal target for the season. David thought this 'realistic', and by the end of December, about halfway through the season, he had duly scored eight times. However, he could only manage a single goal for the rest of the season, and thus fell well short of fulfilling his manager's hopes.

Another ambition spurring Beckham on was his last chance to score at Wembley before the destruction of the existing stadium. Having managed to score only one goal in the shadow of the twin towers in the 1996 Charity Shield game against Newcastle United, in October 2000 he hoped to help the national side win three valuable points in the World Cup qualifier against Germany. 'It would be a good way to finish at Wembley . . .' he said. 'I've got some great memories of the place. My dad used to take me to England Schoolboys games all the time when I was ten and eleven, and even then I dreamed of playing at Wembley for England and Manchester United.'

David was also looking to improve his game at international level, having scored only one goal in thirty-four internationals with England. In the event, neither ambition was realized. Although England had triumphed against Germany in Euro 2000 for the first time in more than three decades, Germany upheld their run of Wembley victories with a 1–0 win, to the disbelief of the entire English nation. Furthermore, a knee injury not only forced Beckham to leave the pitch early, but also meant that he missed the World Cup qualifying match against Finland four days later.

Away from the soccer scene, David engaged in a whirlwind round of interviews and signings to promote his new book, *David Beckham: My World*, a handsome production filled with glossy pictures of the star. Thousands of fans queued to buy signed copies of the book, making it a bestseller, and David emerged from promotional interviews in a far better light than in the past. Although always nervous of interviews and, unlike Victoria, reluctant to discuss his personal life in any detail, he came across as a quietly confident young man with a self-deprecating sense of humour. When, for example, he was asked about his latest tattoo – his wife's name spelt in Hindi – he admitted that he had first intended it to be in Chinese and had tried to copy the letters from a menu in his local restaurant. 'It probably said "fried rice" instead of "Victoria",' he quipped.

It was perhaps fortunate that he could joke about it, because despite the fact that tattoo artist Louis Molloy had consulted carefully with the Manchester Buddhist Centre to ensure that the new tattoo would not cause offence, *The Guardian* newspaper reported that Hindi experts declared that the six-inch-long design on the inside of David's left arm actually spelled 'Vihctoria'.

The most daunting interview for David was a much-hyped appearance on the BBC's *Parkinson* show in October 2000. He admitted nervously beforehand that he was worried that Michael Parkinson might ask him questions with long words that he wouldn't understand, no doubt fearing a resurgence of the 'nice-but-dim' taunts that had all too often come his way. Only a couple of months earlier, Victoria had lashed out at such criticisms of her husband, saying – not entirely complimentarily – that he chose not to use long words in interviews because he was a sportsman, not a TV host. In the past, David had always been content to let Victoria do the talking for both of them, yet in the event, when he was faced with the legendary television chat-show host, he tackled every question with aplomb, and even chided his wife for saying too much in public. Afterwards, one sports columnist noted that the universal reaction to the interview was that David was 'very nice'. If not the highest praise, at least there was not a whiff of 'dim'.

Beckham further proved just how much he was an object of interest to the nation when he became the subject of two prime-time documentaries in autumn 2000. Indeed, it took him fifteen minutes to wade through the crowd of fans when he arrived at the October première of a fly-on-the-wall documentary about his football club, shown at the Trafford Centre in Manchester. A month later, more than 10 million people – nearly half that night's television audience – tuned in to ITV's documentary *The David Beckham Story*. Disappointingly, especially after the success of the Parkinson interview, the soccer star came across as not terribly interesting. Viewers were offered an insight into what can only be described as bland, cosy domesticity. They were treated to David shaving before a photo shoot, dropping off his wife at the airport and talking about his love of shopping, fast cars and fast food. It was all undeniably mundane, as was his reflection in the programme on the price of fame: 'You have to take the rough with the smooth. If you like the good stuff, you have to take the bad stuff.'

Unsurprisingly, the critics bemoaned the show's lack of substance and the football star's failure to illuminate his life. Even the producer was moved to complain that the reason why the show was boring was because Beckham's life was boring. It was clear that the mutual love-hate relationship between the Beckhams and the media was not to be easily resolved. As David tellingly commented in an interview with MUTV about the appointment of new England manager Sven-Göran Eriksson, 'I think he's got to be given a chance by everyone. Media wise, they can make or break you, really.'

One publication with which the Beckhams do hold some sway is *OK!* – a magazine that has unfailingly portrayed them in a positive light. Thus when Richard Desmond, the owner of *OK!*, acquired Express Newspapers in November 2000, one of his first acts was to order his staff to ensure that Victoria and David were referred to by their proper Christian names. The couple were given a VIP tour of the *Express* offices, during which David reportedly rebuked the sports journalists for 'turning him over' in their pages. 'You won't be doing that any more,' he told them, presumably hinting that his good relations with their new boss should encourage more positive reporting from the sports desks.

While Victoria has always shown herself to be extremely sensitive to criticism, David has tried hard to ignore the flak that has come his way, whether from the press or from abusive fans who still enjoy taunting him about his wife and family. During the local derby in November 2000, Manchester City fans tried to put him off his game by hurling coins at him, forcing him to cover his head and move away from the touchline. David has admitted that he has found the insults hard to stomach, particularly where Brooklyn is concerned. In an interview with *OK!* he revealed that he keeps a 'little book' containing references to everyone who has criticized him. 'I've written down the names of those people who upset me the most,' he was quoted as saying. 'I don't want to name them because I want it to be a surprise when I get them back. I know I will get them some day.'

Despite his efforts to stay cool, he once again displayed the regrettable loss of temper that infamously caused him to be sent off during the World Cup. A spitting incident in September 2000, occurring after German referee Markus Merk booked him for dissent during Manchester United's Champions League defeat against PSV Eindhoven, earned him a UEFA fine of almost £4,000. Although the incident showed that Beckham could still lose control on occasions, this did not dissuade acting England coach Peter Taylor from giving him the captain's armband in November, albeit for a friendly against Italy. 'He has good experience, is playing well and deserves it,' observed Taylor. 'I have no worries about his temperament. I have been impressed with him since the World Cup in 1998. He took a lot of stick after being sent off, but handled it very well.'

Many were surprised by the appointment, not least because Beckham's reputation was as a shy, silent character who let his right foot do the talking for him. 'I have to admit that I never saw him as captain,' said former England and Arsenal captain Tony Adams. 'But then nor did Sir Alex Ferguson. It was a surprise to me when Peter Taylor chose him.'

David, naturally enough, was delighted. 'I can't believe it,' he said. 'Even if it's just for one game, it's still amazing that I've made it at twenty-five.' He was so overwhelmed, apparently, that he forgot to pack his famous silver Predator boots – he likes to wear a fresh pair for each game – which meant that football officials had to fly out a pair to the team's camp in northern Italy. In fact, the urgency was as much commercial as sporting: Beckham has a multi-million-pound sponsorship deal with adidas, a company that would not have been pleased to miss its moment of glory.

Sponsorship deals have become an increasingly valuable source of income for David Beckham. According to a *Sunday Times* poll in 2001, his annual earnings were an estimated £5.2 million, his regular salary with United boosted by such deals as a £1-million, two-year contract with Police sunglasses. But even though his income had grown enough to exceed that of his wife, it still trailed behind such players as Luis Figo of Real Madrid.

* * *

While David's career and future potential were the subjects of considerable discussion at this time, Victoria's were receiving rather less attention. While hard at work on both an autobiography and her first solo album, she also intended to host a TV show, *An Evening with Victoria Beckham*, in spring 2001, singing tracks from the new album and answering questions posed by her audience, but the programme was never made.

The release of her album was always destined to be a testing time for Victoria. If it was not well-received by fans and critics, it would probably signal the demise of a singing career that already had a big question mark hanging over it. Undoubtedly she had to bear many disappointments. Not only had she lost to Sophie Ellis-Bextor in the race to number one in August 2000, but the stress and hard work surrounding her solo release seemed to take their toll on her fragile frame, and in early September she was struck low with viral meningitis. Two months later, she duly joined her fellow Spice Girls to promote the release of their third album, *Forever*. Yet, in spite of the hype, the album only briefly hit the Top Ten before rapidly falling down the charts, and it barely registered at all in the American charts. While their single 'Holler' did make it to number one, music critics loudly sounded the group's death knell. 'It is obvious the band are on their last legs,' noted music writer Rick Sky. 'They don't seem to enjoy it any more or need to do it.'

The Spice fan base seemed to be moving away from them as well. In a teen magazine the band topped the categories for the worst album, worst single, worst video and worst group, while unhappily for Victoria she was voted a 'sad loser' along with Liam Gallagher of Oasis. The girls made a valiant attempt to maintain control of their image, arguing that while they had solo careers they would still come together from time to time, but the cracks were all too obvious. Emma Bunton admitted that the band would not be touring in the near future and Victoria's comment, 'At the moment, we're just having a bit of a rest from Spice,' gave no assurances that the Spice Girls would be back. It was widely felt that the time had come for them to retire with grace and make way for a new sensation.

Meanwhile, Victoria was clinging on. Her expressed desire to work with the controversial singer Eminem could have been because she genuinely admired the popular rapper, whose music was more likely to appeal to David, or perhaps it was because she simply felt the need to be associated with stars of the moment. Without the Spice Girl tag and the Posh persona, however, and with the press producing statements such as 'She could soon find that she is just a has-been', Victoria faced an uncertain future under the glare of the media spotlight.

Away from the music scene, Victoria's ever-changing image began to gain her most attention – as well as the cost of maintaining it. Several of the tabloids noted that she had sported nine new looks in as many months, one report claiming that she spent £50,000 a year on her hair.

In January 2001, her lifestyle was placed under mocking scrutiny when she appeared at Isleworth Crown Court to give evidence against twenty-year-old Mark Oliver, who was accused of stealing her luggage after a transatlantic flight from Miami the previous year. The press had a field-day picking over the contents of her bags, and their high cost. She was pilloried for not only being a designer-label junkie, but also for the sheer volume of clothes she appeared to need for a short trip. When she initially handed a list to the police about the missing contents of her Louis Vuitton suitcases, it contained more than a hundred items of designer clothing. The overall effect of this exposure was an unhappy one. While Oliver was without doubt the villain of the piece, and had caused Victoria considerable distress over her missing song lyrics and sentimental items such as photos and a baby book containing a lock of Brooklyn's hair, the court case turned into a trial as much about her conspicuous consumption as a criminal case in which she was the victim. A male writer in *The Times* letters page caught the mood when he ironically observed, 'I have suggested to my partner that if Posh Spice can manage with these few things then surely she can too.'

In the meantime, David's England career was boosted further in February 2001 when new coach Sven-Göran Eriksson retained him as captain of the national side in the friendly against Spain that month, which resulted in a 3–0 win to England. David had been sad to see the departure of Kevin Keegan after the catastrophic defeat against Germany the previous October, and had defended Keegan's decision to resign, telling MUTV that the players must take responsibility for trying to revive the national team's lack of form: 'At the end of the day it's all the English players who have got to go out and play well and get some points, not just for the fans and the manager, but ourselves.' He welcomed Eriksson's appointment, however, and was eager to excel under his experienced leadership, particularly because with every England game he played he was clearly growing in stature. As England defender Rio Ferdinand later commented, 'Becks has been brilliant as captain. He turns a lot of negatives into positives.'

A high point in his England career came in March 2001, during England's World Cup qualifier against Finland at Anfield, home of Manchester United's fiercest rivals, Liverpool. After scoring the winning goal in the 2–1 victory, he savoured the moment when 40,000 fans sang, 'There's only one David Beckham.'

'The most rewarding thing for me is that I have won people over with my football,' he said. 'I could have done interview after interview explaining myself, but I did it on the pitch with the football.'

Thirteen

Wounded Hero

From 1998 to 2003, David Beckham went from zero to hero. Ironically, it was the dignified manner he handled the worst moment of his career – when he was sent off during the Argentina game in 1998 – that proved to be the springboard for his rehabilitation. 'It definitely made me grow up a bit,' he has since remarked. 'You can either go home and cry – which I felt like doing at times because it was so upsetting – or you come out fighting. I had people round me who made me come out and fight and prove that I deserved to be out there, no matter what people were saying.'

Though England memorably beat Germany 5–1 in Munich in September 2001, the national side stuttered towards qualification for the 2002 World Cup. It was only a trademark Beckham free kick deep in injury time that secured a nail-biting 2–2 draw with Greece a month later, which ensured that England topped their group and enabled them to book their passage to play in Japan and South Korea, the joint hosts of the tournment. Such was the tension that even the British Prime Minister was caught up in the moment, apparently punching the roof of his official car when the England captain scored. 'On the Friday I'd hit a lot of balls and they'd all gone in,' said Beckham, who ran nearly 10 miles during the match to drag his team virtually single-handedly into the finals. 'I knew this was the last chance.'

When England were seeded along with Argentina, Nigeria and Sweden in the so-called 'group of death', all eyes and hopes focused on Beckham. If soccer is war by other means then the draw ensured a continuation of the feud between England and the South American nation who fought a bloody conflict over the Falkland Islands in 1982 and have continued the fight on the soccer pitch ever since. Nobody had forgotten how Diego Maradona cheated England in the 1986 World Cup in Mexico with his infamous 'Hand of God' goal. This was to be a fixture with form. 'It's a great chance to lay the ghost of France '98,' said Beckham simply, his sporting stature growing despite his club side's failure to beat Arsenal to top spot in the Premier League championship. Indeed when he was voted BBC Sports Personality of the Year in December 2001, it was public recognition that the prodigal son had returned, his sins forgiven if not forgotten.

Given the inevitable hype surrounding the World Cup, there was national consternation when, in April 2002, just weeks before the team flew east to prepare for the tournament, Beckham broke a small bone in his left foot during a Champions League quarter-final match with Spanish side Deportivo La Coruña. As a further affront to national pride, the perpetrator was Argentine defender Aldo Pedro

Duscher. While Duscher was demonized, the nation mulled mournfully over the captain's broken metatarsal bone. With England's first game only fifty days away, the clock was ticking on how quickly the 'devastated' star could recover from an injury that normally takes between eight and ten weeks to heal. 'I'll be gutted if I don't make it,' Beckham announced.

The tabloid press was less phlegmatic. The *Daily Mirror* yelled, 'The Foot: A Nation Holds Its Breath,' while a rival tabloid screamed, 'Horror Tackle. The Moment The Dream Died.' The Anglican bishops of Blackburn, Birmingham and Manchester called for prayers, while the leader of Britain's white witches, Kevin Carlyon, announced that he was going to work on a remedial spell. Just so that nothing was left to chance, *The Sun* newspaper printed a full-size picture of Beckham's foot on the front page, and asked readers to place their hands on it so that their healing energy could be transferred to the stricken star. Even the Queen was drawn into the debate, suggesting that her granddaughter Zara Phillips, who had recently qualified as a physiotherapist, could help find a rapid cure.

When the footballer was involved in a minor car accident later that same month, driving his Mercedes 500 with his leg in plaster, it dominated the headlines; the British Prime Minister even told his Cabinet that 'nothing was more important' to England's World Cup hopes than the state of the captain's foot. For a time it seemed that England's preparations were jinxed, especially after Beckham's best friend and England teammate, Gary Neville, suffered precisely the same injury two weeks later in the first leg of the Champions League semi-final against Bayer Leverkusen, a cruel blow that ruled him out of the tournament.

While a parade of experts gave their opinions on Beckham's chances of recovery, the superstar rested at home; his wife, then five months' pregnant with their second child, bustled around him, making cups of tea and even feeding him grapes, many sent by well-wishers. For a time he forswore the marital bed for a specially installed oxygen tent, used by long-distance runners such as Paula Radcliffe, which helped maintain his fitness while his injury healed.

Against all the odds, the England captain managed to recover sufficiently to join the national squad for light training during their preparations in Dubai for the opening match against Sweden in early June. Before he left his pregnant wife behind, she gave him one piece of advice: 'Please, don't take any penalties.'

While he was prevented by the England doctor John Crane from using his precious left foot in tackles and hard kicking, Beckham was nearly as relieved as the nation at his return to the game he loves. 'The most important thing to me is my family, but without my football I'm a lost man,' he admitted. 'I've been lost for the last seven weeks because I haven't been able to do anything and it's nice to be involved again.' Such was his enthusiasm to pull on an England shirt again that he often trained into the early hours to get fully fit. 'I could walk past the treatment room after midnight and I would still be able to hear the quiet pounding of feet on the running machine,' remarked coach Eriksson. 'Often it would be David.'

His obvious desire to lead his country contrasted markedly with the way his Manchester United colleague and Ireland captain Roy Keane stormed out of the national side following a vicious confrontation with coach Mick McCarthy. While the brooding Irish midfielder watched the World Cup on TV at his home in Cheshire, David Beckham led the England team out for the crucial opening match with Sweden in Saitama. His appearance answered the prayers not just of the nation, but also the money men who had invested millions of pounds in the man dubbed 'Goldenballs' to give his Midas touch to their products, be they sunglasses or football boots. In a land where the Emperor is imbued with god-like status, there was no doubting the reverence with which Beckham was held. His spiky Mohican hairstyle was endlessly emulated.

Where once his wife's decision to fly over his personal hairdresser Aidan Phelan from England to restyle his hair would have attracted ridicule, now it was treated almost as a necessity. Thousands of awestruck locals followed him wherever he went; a simple shopping trip and a meal in a local restaurant in Kobe turned into a spectacle involving a cast of thousands, including police to control the excited crowds.

For the watching millions, however, the game itself was not the feast of football they had dreamed of. Beckham lasted less than an hour of a dour contest with Sweden that ended in a depressing, if all too familiar, 1–1 draw. 'I thought he tired badly in the first game and I never thought that would ever happen with Becks,' said Sir Alex Ferguson, who later criticized the England management for insisting that the captain join the national squad before, in his manager's opinion, he was fit to travel.

Whatever the thoughts of the Manchester United boss, as far as Beckham was concerned he had a date with destiny – the looming grudge match with the pre-tournament favourites, Argentina. This would be more than a test of his recovering left foot. It was a chance to exorcise the ghosts that had haunted him for the last four years.

When England won a penalty and the captain bravely decided to take it, Beckham knew that the ensuing script was entirely in his hands. As he gulped in air, the nation held its breath knowing that its sporting prospects lay at his feet. Would he be cast as hero or villain? As he later recalled of that agonizing moment: 'I stood there looking at the ball. I have never felt pressure like that before. I had flashbacks in my mind from the last four years . . . as soon as I hit the ball, my mind went blank. It was the release of everything that had gone on.' His shot flew low and hard past the flailing goalkeeper, ensuring a happy ending. It was a moment of sheer catharsis relished by captain and country, as England clung on valiantly to their 1–0 advantage until the final whistle. As writer Rick Broadbent opined, 'For heart-wrenching, phone-a-friend, lump-in-the-throat reactions, that visceral moment was the pick of the sporting year.'

That night Beckham phoned his wife and family who, like millions of fans, old and new, were in awe of the guts he had shown in taking responsibility for such an important life-changing penalty. 'Good goal, daddy,' was the first thing Brooklyn said.

Sadly, this football fairy tale did not have an entirely happy ending. While Beckham was able to rid himself of his personal demons, England could not overcome the inconsistencies that had afflicted the national side. Although they managed a workmanlike draw against Nigeria and professionally disposed of Denmark, the surprising conquerors of France, they were no match for the silky skills and sharp finishing of the Brazilians, who went on to win the tournament. When the dust and disappointment had settled, it was clear that while Beckham had proved an inspirational figurehead, his lack of match fitness due to his recent injury had been a burden. 'I don't think he was on the ball enough,' his club manager complained in a sideswipe at Eriksson's tactics. 'You just saw bits of him here and there, but he wasn't the dominant part of the team. It was maybe the way England played. I don't know.'

No matter. Beckham had earned himself a place on the pantheon of Britain's sporting heroes, the moment making the man. It is doubtful if anything in his future football career will come close to matching the Argentina game as an example of both searing test of character and a true life odyssey.

Former England captain Tony Adams has grown to admire the man who has followed in his footsteps as skipper of the national team. 'The dedication to the game and the knowledge that he is part of a team make him a balanced individual,' said Adams. 'It is probably also why he appears to cope so well with the excess of publicity he attracts as a celebrity. He has the priorities right; family and football, and the rest is froth.'

The very public nature of Beckham's life, though, continued to expose the weaknesses in the relationships between himself and his manager, his club and his country. While saying little in public, his mantle of unassuming diffidence was misleading. Cast in the same mould as soccer legends like Paul Gascoigne, Eric Cantona, his hero, and George Best, he is a natural crowd-pleaser, a showman who is never happier than when strutting his stuff on the international stage. Like other sporting superstars, he thrives on the big occasion, the tension and attention bringing out his talent to the full. His ability as a dead-ball specialist merely serves to emphasize his qualities as a solo performer. His goals tend toward the spectacular, ensuring that the cameras and the watching fans are focused only on Beckham. Even at club football level it seems that he steps up a gear against the bigger clubs. Manchester United's match programmes noted that Beckham had scored twice as many goals when playing against London sides, usually more glamorous games, than other teams.

As a result there was a suspicion, particularly among some Manchester United fans, that he seemed more industrious and creative playing for England than his club team. According to Michael Crick, lifelong United supporter and Sir Alex Ferguson's unofficial biographer, this helped explain why the manager seemed more comfortable praising unassuming but talented players like Paul Scholes and Nicky Butt, while paying lip service to the contribution of his number seven. 'Beckham always seems to put more effort in for his country than his club,' argues Crick, a feature of his play that undoubtedly rankled with the United boss, who was notoriously grudging in his relations with the national team, particularly during Eriksson's tenure. In a newspaper interview, for example, he suggested that the United midfielder was only made captain of the national side because of pressure from the media.

The debate clearly demonstrated the fact that every feature of Beckham's professional and personal life was under the microscope in a way that would have been unthinkable just a few years before. His career and popularity now dramatically eclipsed that of his wife. A sign of the seesaw in their fortunes was shown by the fact that when this book was first proposed in May 2000, the working title was 'Posh'. At the time, David Beckham was simply a good-looking England midfielder, while she was an international superstar. Yet in a 2003 poll of 1,000 youngsters it was David who earned the 'coolest person in Britain' accolade, while his wife was named the least cool. As Victoria herself observed, 'When I first met David he wasn't what he is now. He was the same person, but he wasn't a pin-up.'

It was his growing status as a sex symbol, particularly among other female celebrities, that had begun to cause her anxiety. Victoria, who in her autobiography admitted to punching David, and contemplating suicide after newspaper claims he had an affair while she was pregnant, was unamused when singer Dannii Minogue discussed her fantasy encounter with her footballer husband. She was merely the latest in a string of celebrity women, including Janet Jackson and Kylie Minogue, who had admitted their lust for Beckham – and who caught the sharp edge of Victoria's tongue as a result. When British actress Tamzin Outhwaite talked about her fantasy of a one-night-stand with him, Victoria responded tartly, 'Firstly, I wouldn't say that about a married man, and second, as if, love.'

As a woman notorious for wearing her heart on her sleeve, her feeling of insecurity was further made manifest during discussions about who would be the ghost writer for David's second autobiography. She vetoed the suggestion of using a woman – Alison Kervin, the chief sports feature writer on *The Times*, was one candidate – insisting on a male author. As psychologist Oliver James observes, 'For a woman who has famously craved fame and all its trappings, who wants to be loved by the public, the rise and rise of her husband, at a time when her own celebrity seems to be waning, must be hard to bear.'

This view was endorsed by Head of Entertainment at London Weekend TV, Stewart Morris, who was executive producer on her fly-on-the-wall documentary, *Being Victoria Beckham*, broadcast in March 2002. 'It is amazing that in three short years she has gone from Posh Spice to Mrs Beckham,' says Morris. It was while filming the show, made with her co-operation, that he watched Victoria's dawning awareness that she was no longer the central figure in their very public double act.

During filming there was some doubt surrounding David's involvement in the programme. When he finally agreed to take part it was the equivalent of an A-list Hollywood actor agreeing to a role in a middle-of-the-road film. It made the movie. 'I got the impression that Victoria felt that the show should just be about Victoria Beckham,' recalls Morris. 'She was very conscious that her career was in decline and he was now the dominant celebrity.'

Certainly at first glance Victoria had enjoyed limited success since 2001. After her first single release was beaten to the top slot by Sophie Ellis-Bextor, the sales of her singles and album went into freefall. Her first genuine solo release in September 2001, 'Not Such An Innocent Girl', sold just over 80,000 copies. A contrived and much-hyped battle for the top slot between her single and Kylie Minogue's 'Can't Get You Out Of My Head' soon faded, the Australian singer outselling her by a ratio of ten to one. Her next effort, 'Mind Of Its Own', released in February 2002, was even weaker, selling just 66,000. Similarly her self-titled album, which cost an estimated £5 million, notched up just under 50,000 sales and fell out of the Top Fifty within a fortnight.

With the guillotine poised over the musical career of the aspiring, solo pop queen, the watching media harpies gleefully sharpened their knitting needles. Columnist Carole Ann Rice commented, 'From her hair extensions to her manufactured new bad-girl image, she is what she is: a pop-puppet, pocket-money snatcher who has had her day, and no amount of dieting, reinventing will recreate the hallowed glow of fame in its heyday.' In the *Scottish Daily Record*, columnist Joan Burnie anticipated the falling blade: 'She's harmless, but as a solo act she's a dud, and musically way past her sell-by date. It is only really the connection with Beckham which keeps her on the A-list.' It was left, however, to feminist champion Germaine Greer to deliver the *coup de grâce*, advising the one-time advocate of Girl Power to 'Keep quiet, have some babies, and put on some weight.'

Perhaps the low point of her solo career was when disgruntled fans at a concert in Leicester pelted her with onions and apples. Not only she was miming her song, but she was also quite clearly out of sync as well. It followed a similar debacle where she was booed by some of the audience in the 50,000 crowd at Birmingham's 'Party in the Park' concert in August 2001. Ironically, it wasn't her singing that caused the most controversy, but the fact that she was wearing a lip ring, a stunt that was even reported by ITV's *News at Ten*. Initially, she gave the impression that she had just been pierced, but then confessed it was, like her tattoos and hair extensions, just a fake. Comparisons with the lip ring and her singing made her an easy target, to the extent that the former Spice Girl even suffered the indignity of a verbal attack by topless model Jordan for being a poor role model, as the lip piercing might provoke copycat behaviour by impressionable youngsters.

Years of contrived showbiz stories – in fairness the stock in trade of every music PR worth his or her salt – came back to haunt her when she and her family found themselves at the centre of a real-life drama. In November 2002, a gang of Eastern Europeans allegedly planned to kidnap Victoria and her children, and hold them for a £5 million ransom. However, given the endless hype surrounding the Beckhams, the alleged plot, first revealed by the *News of the World*, was treated with scepticism in some quarters. As one observer asked at the time, 'Is she releasing a new single?'

The disappointing sales figures for her records were genuine, however, and inevitably she parted company with her manager John Glover and her record company Virgin. Like Emma Bunton and Mel B before her, Victoria Beckham had found it was not going to be easy to carve out a solo career. 'It's very difficult for someone like her as it's a case of style above substance,' observed *The Sun* showbiz editor Dominic Mohan. 'Record companies are starting to learn that if their artists are plastered over *OK!* magazine week in, week out, people will start to get tired.' Thus, when the Spice Girls enjoyed a reunion at Beckingham Palace in February 2003, a meeting that naturally sparked rumours of a musical reunion, one tabloid newspaper ran a campaign urging them to leave the past behind.

Nonetheless, in 2002 Victoria signed a new record deal with Telstar for a reported £1.5 million – though this figure was dismissed by industry veterans. With a new album planned for later in 2003, she was making a valiant attempt to kick-start her solo musical career. Industry executives though remained deeply sceptical. 'Her pop career is over. She should concentrate on her other strengths,' a senior music chief observed. 'I very much doubt that Telstar will make any money from her. She is now a celebrity, not a pop singer.'

When the work on her Hertfordshire home was finally completed, she duly sold exclusive picture rights to a weekly glossy magazine for a reported five-figure sum, in which she was happy to reveal her adoration of the actress Audrey Hepburn, which was expressed in a bathroom designed and dedicated to her memory. This, though, was not enough. In a financially inventive move, she and her then record company Virgin launched a website that included a virtual reality tour of her new palace. It included hide-and-seek competitions, a football game and space invaders, which were clearly aimed at her younger fans. While she complained in a web-cam interview about the invasion of her privacy, she saw nothing untoward about exploiting her son Brooklyn on her site, though she had previously scorned such an idea.

Even the demure BBC baulked at her artless hypocrisy. 'It is distasteful enough to be invited into a mock-up of Brooklyn's bedroom, but then we also learn that his favourite clothes are Gap Kid and Armani Kids,' complained reporter Emma Saunders. 'This may all sound like harmless fun, but it is hardly fair to put your toddler in the spotlight when he is too young to make a choice. It's a shame, since it takes the edge off what would otherwise be just a fun and comprehensive pop website.'

Certainly the fun was missing when some of those visiting her website left a string of abusive messages as well as unflattering comments about her voice and figure. In the end she decided to shut down her Internet chatroom, after her father-in-law Ted complained about the hostile remarks.

Indeed the last few years have seen Victoria use the law to make something of an ass of herself. She found herself on the losing side when she tried to ban a documentary about the early days of the Spice Girls, which was broadcast in March 2001. For Posh Spice, one of the more mortifying moments of the TV documentary, called *Raw Spice*, was the revelation that Victoria had once had a crush on Manchester United soccer star Ryan Giggs and had even kept a poster of him on her wall. A year later she found herself fighting a £500,000 damages bill for slander when she accused the owners of a memorabilia shop of selling fake autographs of her husband. The

McManus family, who ran the store at the Bluewater shopping mall in Kent, argued that as a consequence of the resulting publicity their business had suffered dramatically. In a court judgement, in March 2003, Victoria faced the humiliation of paying £55,000 to the company, as well as huge legal costs, issuing a public apology and agreeing to give some of her husband's memorabilia to the store in an act of goodwill.

Perhaps, though, the legal case that made her the focus of most derision was her bizarre attempt to prevent football club Peterborough United from officially registering its long-time 'Posh' nickname. She claimed that the name was now synonymous with her rather than the Second Division team, despite the fact that the soccer side had been known as 'Posh' since the 1920s. Chief executive Geoff Davey vowed to fight her action, launched in November 2002, arguing that the club had a prior and stronger claim to the name. In the end she dropped her suit.

While psychologist Oliver James saw in her behaviour further evidence of her deep-seated need for control, media pundits mused on other potential targets for her wrath – William Shakespeare and his play *Romeo and Juliet*, and the borough of Brooklyn in New York, were two obvious candidates. 'Posh should get a life and drop the whole thing,' opined a *Guardian* leader. 'She should stick to what she does best – whatever that is exactly these days – and leave the word where it belongs, in the dictionary, the property of us all.'

On the surface, and certainly as far as the media were concerned, Victoria Beckham had become a celebrity on the ropes, a convenient and easy punch-bag for critics looking to take a cheap shot. She seemed to have become the living embodiment of novelist John Updike's comment about fame: 'Celebrity is a mask that eats into your face.' While her gnawing need for the limelight betrayed the insecurity at the heart of her character, a moth eternally circling the fickle flame of celebrity, there was still no denying her continued appeal or her popularity with her true fans. Her fly-on-the-wall documentary *Being Victoria Beckham* attracted an audience of 8 million, which, apart from the soaps, was one of the highest rating shows of the year. She may only have sold a few thousand copies of her albums, but when she appeared on Michael Parkinson's chat show, millions of viewers tuned in.

Even when pregnant with her second child Romeo, who was born on 1 September 2002, she was still the most written about celebrity of the year, pipping Jennifer Lopez, Britney Spears and Kylie Minogue to the post. A sign of her enduring appeal was further demonstrated when she teamed up with former England football star Gary Lineker for a tongue-in-cheek commercial to promote a brand of potato crisps. The advertisement, which portrayed Victoria as a fairy-tale royal arriving at a palace in a coach and four horses, was so successful that supplies of the snack ran out and the commercial had to be withdrawn to give retailers time to stock up. Again, in a private poll about popularity commissioned by a major advertising company who asked not to be named, Victoria Beckham was the only celebrity who was identified by every single person who participated in the poll, proving herself to be more popular than such stars as Geri Halliwell, Kylie

Minogue, Cameron Diaz and *Friends* actress Jennifer Aniston.

When her memoir *Learning To Fly* was first published in September 2001, it was snubbed by the critics, yet it was a runaway bestseller. Apart from the reported £1 million advance that Victoria received, she also raked in a hefty proportion of the estimated £750,000 serialization rights from a Sunday tabloid newspaper. It was good business all round. Excerpts from the book added 170,000 to the newspaper's circulation.

One of the major talking points was her admission that she had previously suffered from an eating disorder, even though she had vehemently denied any problems during earlier interviews, most famously during her TV chat with Michael Parkinson. Bizarrely, she blamed her fellow Spice Girl Geri Halliwell for encouraging her behaviour, even though she admitted suffering from a morbid preoccupation with dieting and her appearance since attending stage school as a teenager. Not that the fans were concerned about the contradictions in her rather unreflective and self-indulgent rags-to-riches tale. During her book-signing tour, hundreds of fans queued for hours to see her. Admirer Stephen Burke was typical. 'I have waited for this moment for six years,' he said when she arrived in Dublin. 'She is so beautiful and has so much time for her fans.'

The adulatory response that Victoria Beckham elicited from her fans goes to the heart of the conundrum of celebrity. She is the celebration of the ordinary, the triumph of the common woman, the girl-next-door sprinkled with stardust. As TV executive Stewart Morris has noted, 'The question which is so hard to answer is why is Victoria Beckham still so popular? Since the Spice Girls split up she has consistently underachieved. She is not successful in her chosen career nor is she especially good-looking. Yet when you go out with her heads turn, people stare and people love her. We spend most of the time slagging off celebrities, but in truth we didn't meet many people who wanted to bad-mouth her. I have been sucked into the belief that she is an amazing person. Certainly there are a lot worse role models.'

It was a belief shared by the great and the good in the world of showbiz and sport. In May 2002, when the Beckhams threw open the doors of their lavish home – a former children's home converted at an estimated cost of £5 million – in a charity fundraiser for the NSPCC, a host of stars, including Joan Collins, Sir Elton John and George Best, enjoyed their generous hospitality. For these days their appeal goes way beyond their working-class roots; the Beckham name is as ubiquitous as it is classless. They went to the ballet at Covent Garden; they were invited to attend a dinner at London's Guildhall to celebrate the fiftieth anniversary of the Nobel prize-winning discovery of DNA; and they even featured prominently in *Tatler* magazine, house journal of the snobbish Sloane Ranger set.

However, their awesome fame had exacted a high price. Since the alleged plot to kidnap Victoria and her two sons – the case against the five suspected conspirators collapsed at Middlesex Guildhall Crown Court in June 2003 after it was revealed that the prosecution's key witness had received money from the *News of the World* for his story, and he was therefore declared unreliable by the Crown Prosecution Service – the couple were forced to hire former SAS-trained bodyguards. They even invited Ken Wharfe, former bodyguard to Diana, Princess of Wales, to advise them on beefing up security at Beckingham Palace, and were prepared to buy armour-plated BMW cars for added protection. 'The first role of a father and husband is to keep his family safe,' said the shocked England captain. Even the Queen expressed her sympathy when she met the soccer star and the rest of the England team at Buckingham Palace in November 2002, a few days after the plot was exposed. 'We spoke about increased security and how it would change our lives,' said Beckham. 'It definitely will change things, but it's just something that has to be done.'

It was left to Victoria's father Tony to oversee additional security measures. Their Hertfordshire home, which already bristled with infra-red sensors, pressure alarms and CCTV cameras, was further fortified by a team of SAS-trained bodyguards. To underline how seriously the Beckhams took the threat, they even discussed employing a night-time dog patrol. When they left their countryside redoubt, a posse of minders were conspicuously present. Even though David Beckham had been reckoned to be spending around £1 million a year on security, other professionals were not overly impressed. 'It seems that they are working on the principle that the darker the sunglasses, the better the bodyguard,' one security expert told me. 'Quite frankly, they have a very poor set-up. I would only rate it seven out of ten.'

While security professionals had misgivings about the way the Beckhams had increased their protection, there was no doubt that the alleged kidnapping plot had deeply shocked the couple. Victoria, whose reaction to previous kidnap scares verged on the hysterical, seemed most affected, and in her traumatized state she was comforted by Sir Elton John and her mother Jackie. 'Obviously it is not something someone can get over very easily,' said Jackie.

For days afterwards Victoria refused to leave her house, needing the constant attention of her mother to soothe her frazzled nerves. When she was seen out, the singer was visibly shrunken and nervous, observers speculating that the loss of a small patch of hair on her head was a result of the stresses and strains surrounding the alleged kidnap plot. Equally distressing were the anonymous letters and notes the Beckhams had received, saying that she deserved to be kidnapped or killed. 'What have David and Victoria done to deserve this?' wailed her mother.

For Victoria Beckham it seemed that there was the dawning and deeply uncomfortable realization that in her relentless pursuit of fame she had made a pact with the devil. With a public hungry for the vicarious intimacy of celebrity, she had exchanged her privacy for cash, her life experiences becoming just another commodity for sale. Perhaps she was beginning to realize that all the money in the world could not buy her peace of mind nor the safety and security she craved. For a woman so desperate to be in control of every aspect of her life, from her body to her media image, the thought of total strangers manipulating her life doubtless struck a very raw nerve.

There was no respite. No sooner had the singer begun to come to terms with the fact that she was a potential kidnap target, than she and her husband were the subject of an untrue rumour that swept around the world via the Internet. The story, which first surfaced in the gossip website 'Popbitch' in November 2002, concerned allegations about David's private life. According to the *News of the World*, the false gossip was based on the contents of a number of e-mails in general circulation. While Beckham took prompt legal action to force the site to remove the false allegations, it underscored the fact that in the global village, the Internet was the twenty-first century equivalent of the parish pump, the place where rumour, innuendo and gossip about the high and mighty is exchanged.

Other stories, as interesting if more benign, merely reflected and burnished the mythology surrounding him. While writing this chapter I was told on several occasions about a story, quoted as fact, that David Beckham had contacted a young man who was due to marry in the spring of 2003. The bridegroom had hired the banqueting suite of a five-star hotel – depending on the storyteller it was in the New Forest or Middlesex – for his wedding reception. It was also Beckham's favourite hotel and he was desperate to hire the venue on the same date for the christening of his second son, Romeo. Consequently he wrote out a cheque for £150,000 to pay off the bridegroom's mortgage as compensation for relinquishing the booking for his wedding reception. The story spread like wildfire, and the hotels concerned had to deal with endless calls from inquisitive journalists. In fact a similar apocryphal story generated considerable speculation when Beckham hired a castle in Ireland for his own wedding. In the world of David and Victoria Beckham, myth merged seamlessly into reality.

It was the shot, or rather miskick, that rang around the world in February 2003. From Sarajevo to Santiago, Madrid and back to Manchester, the moment when a furious Sir Alex Ferguson lashed out at football boot lying on the dressing-room floor at Old Trafford became the stuff of soccer legend.

The boot went flying and hit David Beckham above his left eye, leaving the face of United's number seven bloodied and his ego battered. In a typically blunt and blue Ferguson tirade, the England captain and United midfielder was accused of 'cocking up as a footballer' for his part in the 2–0 home defeat by arch-rivals Arsenal in the fifth round of the FA Cup. In Ferguson's eyes, Beckham hadn't been paying sufficient attention to his dressing down and so apparently the manager kicked the boot in his general direction – to bloody effect. According to at least one report, later denied, the footballer then spat at the man who had guided his career since the age of fourteen, his venom landing on Ferguson's jacket lapel.

Fellow teammates pulled the two men apart before tempers cooled sufficiently for David to be examined and patched up by the club doctor Mike Stone. Then he stalked out of the dressing room and joined Victoria and his two children, four-year-old Brooklyn, and his new baby son Romeo.

The importance of the spat with his famously curmudgeonly boss was signified by the fact that it generated more media coverage than any other event in the Beckhams' soap-opera lifestyle, dominating TV and newspaper schedules. In reality, it wasn't so much soap opera as knockabout pantomime, with Fergie effortlessly playing the role of Big Bad Wolf opposite Beckham's shy and retiring Little Red Riding Hood. For once sympathy lay entirely with the footballer.

This was a result of the astonishing change in his public image, from national villain to adored hero. He had transcended mere sporting achievements, and come to be regarded with the same kind of indulgent affection as others who have been awarded the unofficial accolade of 'National Treasure'. So when Fergie hit him with a boot, the shockwaves reverberated beyond the boundaries of soccer.

Yet the way he behaved after his bust-up with his boss gave a telling insight into the character of the most talked-about man in sport, revealing the remarkable transition of David Beckham, man and modern icon. Throughout his life he has been surrounded by strong, dominating characters, be it his father Ted, his surrogate father Ferguson, or his wife Victoria. Where possible he has always avoided confrontation, except on the pitch. As one former business associate observed, 'He hates conflict, he really shies away from it. He is very much a pussycat.'

His adult life, though dominated by conformity – a wife, children and a strong family – has also been punctuated by acts of occasional rebellion and individualism, invariably on the fashion front. While he has weathered the clash of the generations with his father, whom he described in his autobiography as 'quite hard-faced and sarcastic', he has found it much more difficult to defy his soccer 'dad' who famously kept him on a tight leash, determined to ensure that his showbiz lifestyle did not affect his work on the pitch. From forcing him to curtail his honeymoon to ordering him to drive from his home in the south to join the team bus up in Manchester only to drive south again to catch a flight at London's Heathrow airport to play in the World Club soccer tournament, Ferguson has bent Beckham to his will. For a time, he even banned him from having his hair cut in his now memorable Mohican style. Nor did it escape notice, particularly by Victoria's mother, that when the Beckham family were trying to come to terms with an alleged £5 million plot to kidnap Victoria and her children in November 2002, the United midfielder was ordered to attend training as usual.

This time, after the episode of the flying boot, it was very different. While Victoria, who described Ferguson as 'vindictive' in her autobiography *Learning to Fly*, offered to sort out her husband's boss, David had different ideas and staged a protest of silent reproach. The following day, when he left his home in Alderley Edge, he was happy for photographers to focus on his injury. He eschewed his normal garb of a woolly hat for an Alice band, so that his flowing blond locks would not rub his wound, and to make sure that waiting cameramen – and the world – got the message. Then, as he arrived at the training ground at Carrington, he raised the sun visor of his car to guarantee that everyone got another look.

His body language, scowling, frowning but resolutely silent, made clear that much more than his eye had been wounded. Certainly it rankled that Sir Alex had tried to make light of the incident, shrugging off calls for an apology and dismissing the injury as a graze that had not needed stitches. 'The only reaction to the publicity this has created is that it was an incident that was freakish,' Ferguson maintained. 'If I tried it a hundred times or a million times it could not happen again. If it could I would have carried on playing.'

The £90,000-a-week soccer star, who feared that the flying boot could have blinded him and ended his career, begged to differ. A statement released from his management company, SFX, indicated that the injury was more serious than Ferguson claimed: 'David did not want stitches at first, but two hours after the game, blood was still dripping from the wound and the club doctor visited David's house and fixed two Steri strips to stop the bleeding.' That a statement was issued at all was a signal of the antagonism between the two men.

Nor was Beckham's glowering mood lifted when, later that week, the *Daily Mail* reported that towards the end of 2000, Fergie had secretly visited World Player of the Year, Luis Figo, and his agent, with a view to bringing the Portuguese superstar to Old Trafford and selling Beckham to Barcelona, Figo's former club. The *Daily Mail* alleged that Fergie considered making the £37 million swoop in the winter of 2000 after dropping Beckham from the side when, concerned about Brooklyn's health, he had provoked his manager's wrath by missing training.

Several commentators suggested that the footballer was parading his injuries like a badge of honour. Others noted the similarities with the late

Diana, Princess of Wales, who used the photo opportunity to devastating effect during her long battle with Prince Charles and Buckingham Palace. She was never more eloquent than when she allowed her body language to do the talking. Examples abound. When their marriage was unravelling, she sat alone at the Taj Mahal in India, and later deliberately missed her husband's cheek when she went to kiss him after a polo match. On the night the Prince made his TV confession of adultery with Camilla Parker Bowles, Diana appeared at gallery opening in a stunning little black dress that stole the show.

In his silent struggle with Ferguson, Beckham, who like Diana has a love affair with the camera, used the silent iconography of protest to telling effect, the incident representing much more than a run-of-the-mill dressing-room argument. 'It was the wilful desecration of beauty,' commented feminist writer Bea Campbell.

Diana's style and behaviour were a striking cultural counterpoint to that of the rest of the royal family, characterized by the trembling lower lip versus the stiff upper lip. The division between Fergie and Beckham represented the struggle between Old Man and New Man; the traditional macho soccer culture versus the changing model of masculinity, the modern gentle man. In this regard Beckham is unique both as a contemporary icon and as a role model. As media pundit Marcelle d'Argy Smith has observed, 'Beckham is so twenty-first century.'

In the past, it was the flamboyant style of continental imports, stars such as Frenchmen David Ginola and Eric Cantona, whose flair and pin-up appeal captured the headlines. As foreigners, and therefore outsiders, it was easy to dismiss them as preening peacocks, effeminate if colourful. Their heyday coincided with the appearance of the last British soccer icon, Paul Gascoigne, a man both celebrated and condemned for the way he wasted his talent and life through drink and boisterous revelry. Yet, as Bea Campbell argues, Gazza was but a larger-than-life product of a crude and resolutely macho football culture. Darling of the terraces, he was the laddish clown prince of soccer, a grinning reprobate who was a constant thorn in the side of his long-suffering managers and the football authorities.

So for an Essex boy and an England captain to be as comfortable with his role as devoted family man, as his status as a gay icon and fashion leader, was and is a significant departure from the traditional attitudes that prevail in footballing circles. Here is a man who chooses his tattoos, his jewellery and nail varnish with the same relish as he flights in a cross to the penalty box. There was even talk that he had applied make-up to his cut eye. 'David cares more about his clothes than almost anyone I've ever met,' says Elton John's partner David Furnish, a growing influence in defining Beckham as a rather playful dandy. He is, in short, a man very much aware of and in tune with his feminine side, adored by women for his diffident beauty and admired by men for his soccer skills. As psychologist Oliver James, author of *Britain on the Couch*, observes, 'Beckham is unique in showing heterosexual males that there is a future for men inside less constrained and more relaxed models of masculinity without thinking that they are gay.'

By contrast, when Ferguson was asked in an interview if he was in touch with his feminine side, the

David and Victoria celebrate their son Brooklyn's second birthday at a Cheshire hotel.

Above: David reclines on the practice pitch, revealing the tattoo of his first-born's name, Brooklyn, inscribed at the base of his spine. Concealed beneath his shirt is a guardian angel tattoo he had etched between his shoulder blades. 'Brooklyn is beneath so it's like he's watching over him,' David explained.

Below: The soccer star has also had Brooklyn's name printed on his golf shoes.

Above: David's parents, Ted and Sandra Beckham, who have supported their son throughout his illustrious career and more recently become willing, hands-on grandparents.

Right: Victoria's father and mother, Tony and Jackie Adams. The couple have encouraged their daughter in every aspect of her life and career.

Left: David parted company with his beloved Manchester United when he signed for Spanish champions Real Madrid in summer 2003.

Below: David's Spanish interpreter Rebecca Loos (*left*) stands alongside Victoria and Romeo watching David settle into his new career at Real.

In November 2003, David was rewarded for his services to football when he received the OBE from Queen Elizabeth II at Buckingham Palace.

Left: Though David scored the winning goal against Ecuador to take England through to the World Cup quarter-finals in 2006, the team's performance throughout the tournament fell far short of expectations.

Below: Romeo Beckham clearly entered into the spirit of the World Cup, showing keen support for his father.

Right: Victoria attends a Paris fashion party in the company of her close friend Katie Holmes.

Below: After signing a five-year deal with LA Galaxy, David gives a press conference via live satellite from Madrid for the US media.

Living in America: what lies in store for the Beckhams as they prepare to take the USA by storm?

soccer knight was as bewildered by the question as he is by the changing nature of modern man. 'There's a need to be recognized, a need to be known,' he told *The Times* journalist Robert Crampton. 'You see that with earrings, tattoos, the way that dress sense and hairstyles change every six months.' He is not alone in his perplexity. On one occasion in 2003, the then Newcastle United manager Sir Bobby Robson shook his head in disbelief when the team coach had to return to the ground because his midfield dynamo Kieron Dyer had left a valuable earring in the dressing room.

It was no coincidence that in 2003 Ferguson's favourite 'son' was club captain Roy Keane, who was cast in the same sergeant-major mould as himself: flinty, uncompromising, taciturn, a loyal and obdurate disciple of the rough-hewn male hierarchy of football. No coincidence either that Beckham and Keane, two of the most famous faces in British football, have had their differences, representing as they do opposite ends of the spectrum of masculinity. As Professor Ellis Cashmore of Staffordshire University, who has written an academic study of Beckham, explains, 'If Beckham presents us with an agreeable emblem of gender confusion, Keane expresses an unambiguous reassertion of old-style masculine values.'

Confused or not, Beckham effortlessly won the battle for the public's hearts and minds, his star status confounding the accepted wisdom, certainly that of Sir Alex, that the club is always bigger than the player. Following the exposure of the rift between manager and player, shares in the club fell nearly 2 per cent, arising from fears that the club's biggest asset could leave. When Beckham became the first man to appear on the cover of the women's magazine *Marie Claire*, editor Marie O'Riordan drooled, 'He represents something for every woman: father, husband, footballer, icon. In a word, he's the ultimate hero.'

Despite his hero status, Manchester United's failure to win a trophy during the 2001–2 season, and Beckham's own stuttering performance during 2002–3, suggested that his career at the club had run its course, and that the fresh challenge of a new club was what he needed to maintain his momentum in top-flight football. As the soccer showman said himself, 'I want people to look back at me and say, "He was one of the best in the world." That's what I'm aiming for.'

When Victoria Beckham visited Milan during fashion week in March 2003, there were rumours, strenuously denied, that she had met with Inter Milan's president Massimo Moratti to discuss her husband's career. This speculation was given even greater weight when Beckham was left on the bench for the championship 'face-off' between United and Arsenal at Highbury, which ended in a 2–2 draw. Ferguson's decision to leave him out of the side, together with the way Real Madrid's full-back Roberto Carlos had exposed his shortcomings during United's 3–1 defeat by the Spanish club in the first leg of their European Cup quarter-final match in April 2003, ensured that the debate about his future continued apace. 'For years Beckham has been lauded, lavished with superlatives and showered with sarongs; now he has finally succumbed to his own hype and stagnated as a player,' was one fan's view expressed in *The Times*, an opinion shared, it seemed, by many.

There was no doubt though that the old order in his life, both personally and professionally, had changed. Since 2001 there had been subtle and not so subtle shifts in the foundation stones of David's life. Not only had his relationship with Alex Ferguson changed, perhaps irrevocably, but he had also to cope with the acrimonious divorce of his parents, Ted and Sandra, after thirty-two years of marriage. They went their separate ways in February 2003, much to the dismay of their three children. More than anyone Beckham realized the debt he owed them and the burden his fame had placed on their marriage. All his life his parents, fanatical United fans, have supported him at every game, a sheet anchor of common sense amidst the celebrity froth. Their respect for and admiration of Sir Alex Ferguson ensured that in times of trouble, particularly in the early months of his marriage, their son deferred to the will of his manager, often against the wishes of his wife.

At the same time his tight-knit group of friends had been gripped by the kind of bed-hopping, sexual intrigue that is almost a parody of the raunchy British TV series, *Footballers' Wives*, itself an ironic take on the lives of Premiership soccer stars and their families. In a kind of 'Changing Grooms' scenario, two of Beckham's best friends, United winger Ryan Giggs and soccer agent Dave Gardner, ended up engaged to girls they had both previously dated, and consequently found themselves under the media spotlight on account of their complicated and interwoven love lives.

During the 2002–3 football season, disquiet surrounding Ryan Giggs' personal life seemed to spill over into the dressing room with talk of a rift between Giggs and other players, including Beckham. At one point it was claimed that Sir Alex Ferguson – whose son Jason worked with Gardner – intervened to urge his players to leave their private lives out of the dressing room. Ever the team player, Phil Neville valiantly tried to cool the rumour mill, telling reporters, 'We are all best of friends and for people to suggest any of us have fallen out is a big insult to all the players here.'

It seemed that everything involving David Beckham, however tangentially, increased the gossip factor. It was merely another manifestation of his exalted status in the global village. He had become the modern-day equivalent to the local squire. With the waning economic and cultural influence of Britain's aristocracy, including the royal family, Beckham was indeed a prominent member of the emerging celebrity elite. Unlike the aristocracy, whose membership is defined by birth, class and privilege, the celebrity elite is a rather more fluid and democratic entity. Entry is international and open to anyone, but it is as hierarchical as any caste system. An 'A-list' celebrity like Victoria Beckham would never dream of rubbing shoulders with some 'D-list' wannabe such as a *Big Brother* contestant.

In many ways David Beckham is the living embodiment of the values of this new type of elite. Not only is he a role model for a new breed of man, he is an unashamed gay icon and has also been described as 'the most famous black man in Britain'. According to a Channel 4 documentary, *Black Like Beckham*, he has borrowed so much from urban black culture that, thanks to his taste in extravagant clothes and jewellery, penchant for rap music and his flash lifestyle, the blond footballer should be considered an honorary black man. While the proposition did not meet with universal approval, Michael Eboda, editor of the black British newspaper *New Nation*, conceded that there was a serious point behind this tongue-in-cheek analysis: 'Britain is a multi-cultural country and Beckham epitomizes that. He has absorbed aspects of black culture in the way he dresses.'

In fact his appeal is not just to blacks and whites, but crosses all racial and cultural boundaries. For example, the Beckham family was celebrated as gods for a major exhibition of Indian-influenced art for the Commonwealth Games in Manchester in June 2002. While David was depicted on a throne in a crown and robes as the Hindu deity Shiva, Victoria was the goddess Parvati and Brooklyn was the elephant god Ganesh. The artists, sisters Amrit and Rabindra Singh, described their painting as a 'light-hearted' view of fame. The fact that his name and persona was chosen by Asian film-maker Gurinder Chadha for her feel-good movie *Bend it Like Beckham* is further testimony to his cross-cultural appeal. Before the film was released in America to widespread critical acclaim, it made more than £30 million in Britain, becoming one of the biggest British-financed films ever.

Even at the highest level of British society, David Beckham's talents and achievements have not been overlooked, for in the Queen's Birthday Honours List, in June 2003, he was awarded an OBE (Order of the British Empire) for services to football. In response to the announcement, he said, 'I am honoured and privileged to receive this award; it's not just for me but for Manchester United, England, all of my teammates and my family.'

Fourteen

Adiós Manchester, Hola Madrid

It was the sporting event of the year watched by millions around the world. When David Beckham pulled on his white number 23 shirt for Real Madrid and ran out on to the legendary turf at the Bernabéu stadium for the first time, it marked the end of an era and the promise of a new beginning.

For the soccer superstar it was the next significant step in a career already studded with superlatives. It was a measure of his personal and sporting ambition that he had chosen to leave the comparative security of Manchester United, a club that had nurtured him since his teenage years, for a foreign land to play in a team that comprised the finest footballers in the world. If he wished to reign in Spain, Beckham would have to stand tall against the likes of Ronaldo,

Luis Figo and Zinedine Zidane, the *galácticos* of the modern game.

For despite the hyperbole and controversy surrounding his £25 million departure from Manchester for the Spanish capital in July 2003, there was no disguising or hiding from the fact that this was a mighty challenge for a showman who had proved much in the past, but who now had to match himself against a team of footballing giants, the soccer equivalent of the Harlem Globetrotters.

While he was adding considerably to his bank account, in both salary and endorsements, the twenty-eight-year-old multimillionaire was fully aware of the enormous risk he was taking. His new team-mate Zinedine Zidane, arguably the most gifted footballer on the planet, acknowledged that Beckham's professional gamble was as much a test of character as football ability: 'He is a winner and he will bring his special character to Madrid. It is the character of a proven champion, and that has been a deciding factor in the success of Manchester United and England. Now I imagine he will add new facets to his game and become a more complete player.'

That was Beckham's gamble. Would he follow in the footsteps of the likes of Gary Lineker and David Platt, and become a better footballer as a result of his continental journey, or would he, like Paul Gascoigne, who joined Italian Serie A side Lazio, fail to adapt to the rarified atmosphere and head home, his tail between his legs?

In some ways the choice had been made for Beckham months before. From the moment Sir Alex Ferguson decided to leave him on the bench for crucial games against title contenders Arsenal and then, ironically, against Real Madrid in the quarter-final of the European Cup, Beckham perhaps knew in his heart that his days as a United player were numbered. Even though he came on a substitute and scored two goals against the Spanish club, including one of his trademark free kicks, it was not enough to win over his manager.

Ultimately it was his failure to score goals and beat men in open play, combined with the fact that Ferguson's tactics had developed more towards a reliance on roaming attackers than those skilled at crossing the ball – Beckham's forte – that contributed to his demise at Old Trafford. At 25 per cent, the bald statistic that represented his proportion of completed crosses, which was the poorest of his teammates, did not go unnoticed either.

Not that footballing considerations were prominent in the cascade of speculation when Beckham was being quietly hawked around Europe by his agents and his club. Once again the player maintained the façade of injured innocence, pundits ignoring the fact that his reluctance to enter into negotiations for a new contract had forced Manchester United to take action. Rumours had already started to circulate in the spring regarding David's likely move to Madrid for the start of the following season.

In May, just days after Beckham had celebrated his sixth title win with his club, United's chief executive Peter Kenyon met with Beckham's agent Tony Stephens to discuss his future. Already word had got about that Real Madrid, AC Milan and Barcelona were interested in signing United's number seven.

Such was Real's interest that their shirt sponsor, adidas, had drawn up two possible deals with the Spanish champions – one with and another without Beckham in the side.

While the money men haggled, Beckham got on with his job, leading the national side on a goodwill tour of South Africa. Such was his celebrity that even former South African President Nelson Mandela found himself eclipsed. As *The Guardian* newspaper commented laconically: 'The President of South Africa was yesterday lucky enough to meet one of the world's most gifted footballers.'

On his return home, nursing a broken bone in his wrist as a result of the friendly against the African side, speculation surrounding Beckham reached fever pitch. No sooner had it been announced that he had been awarded the OBE, than it was revealed that Manchester United had negotiated a reported £30 million deal with Joan Laporta, an unfancied candidate for the presidency of Barcelona, to sell Beckham to the struggling Spanish club, which had performed so badly in La Liga the previous season that it had even failed to qualify for the UEFA Cup.

For Beckham, at the time on a promotional tour of America to try to win over a nation where soccer was principally played by women, this was a slap in the face. The England captain indicated his disappointment by saying that he felt that he was being used as a 'political pawn'. While he struggled to charm the media in the States, despite dining with Anna Wintour of *Vogue* magazine and presenting an MTV award, he dominated the front pages and TV news bulletins in Spain and Britain.

It soon became clear that the decision to make public the proposed deal with Barcelona was also a ruse to flush out other bidders, notably Real Madrid. Club chairman Florentino Perez had been playing a typically canny game in April 2003, stating emphatically, 'Nobody at Real Madrid has ever spoken about Beckham.' While a few weeks later, in early June, executives from United and Madrid were photographed at a secret meeting in Sardinia.

Following days of intense haggling, Beckham finally made the decision to join Real Madrid after a late-night phone call from his agent Tony Stephen to his Beckingham Palace home. That the Real deal, in United's terms, was so much less than the money on offer from Barcelona was an indication both of Beckham's desire and power. Fear, too. As David acknowledged to his father, he was concerned that, because of his deteriorating relationship with Sir Alex Ferguson, he could have been left to rot in the reserves like former striker Dwight Yorke if he had stayed at United.

Even though Manchester United emerged from the deal somewhat short-changed, it was Beckham, whose £90,000-a-week salary remained roughly the same after the transfer, who received sympathy from fellow superstars for his treatment. Former United manager Tommy Docherty reportedly described the manner of the transfer – Beckham initially learned he had been 'sold to Barcelona' from a journalist during his America tour – as 'abysmal', while United legend George Best fumed at what he considered a 'monumental mistake' by Ferguson. 'In the long term, screaming and shouting is a bad way to run a team,' said Best. 'The best talents won't be lured to a club where they will have to endure that kind of behaviour.' It was a prescient warning as targets on Fergie's hit list, notably Leeds United's Harry Kewell and Brazilian striker Ronaldinho, turned down the chance to pursue their careers at Old Trafford, and instead signed for Liverpool and Barcelona respectively.

The response from United fans was more muted, however, as a snap poll of listeners to a Manchester radio station showed that 70 per cent were pleased to say *adiós* to Beckham. Nevertheless, there was no fall in demand for Beckham merchandise at Old Trafford, even though the goods were destined to become memorabilia. When his departure became inevitable, the central characters in the drama, player and manager, played their parts with suitable dignity. 'I've known David since he was eleven years of age, and it's been a pleasure to see him grow and develop into the player he has become,' said Ferguson, openly wishing him well for the future. The departing hero was no less conciliatory. 'I would like to publicly thank Sir Alex Ferguson for making me the player I am today.' It was a profound parting of the ways, a dissolution of a soccer marriage that had lasted fourteen years.

For Beckham it seemed that the whole world, with perhaps the exception of America, was his field of gold. The transfer completed, he and Victoria left for a promotional tour of the Far East, selling everything from motor oil, beauty clinics and chocolates to second-hand cars. Indeed it was Beckham's appeal in the Far East that seemed to have clinched the deal for Real Madrid's money men. While the club has considerable commercial exposure in

South America and the Arab world thanks to Ronaldo and Zidane, their worldwide portfolio was completed courtesy of Beckham's pop star appeal in the Far East. A pre-season tour of Beijing, Tokyo, Hong Kong and Singapore in July and August effortlessly proved the financial point. Tickets to watch Real Madrid sold out in minutes and the club stood to earn £9 million for appearance fees and merchandising – a substantial proportion of Beckham's original fee. According to the adidas regional sales manager, his arrival in the team added 30 to 40 per cent in extra shirt sales alone.

Back in Spain, even before he had kicked a ball in anger, Beckham's name had sold 8,000 replica shirts at the Bernabéu stadium. When he arrived in the nation's capital it was as though Beatle-mania had hit the city, as 520 journalists – more than the number who cover the Oscars – and thousands of fans tried to catch a glimpse of the latest star in the Real Madrid galaxy. Such was the insatiable appetite for the player that several British tabloids appointed their own David Beckham correspondents to follow his every move in the capital.

With so much at stake, it was inevitable that the man voted second only to Brad Pitt as the top sexual fantasy of Spanish women, quickly captured the heart of the capital. 'The city can feel a kind of Beckham-mania in its skin,' commented one Spanish newspaper, while *Marca*, Spain's leading sports newspaper, said simply, 'Beckham: The Madness Arrives.'

The first sign that this was not so much a soccer transfer as a media circus was when Beckham's medical check was televised, and the club charged outside TV companies to buy rights for the sight of the new player's naked torso undergoing a series of routine tests. Even the clinic where the medical took place reportedly paid £250,000 for the privilege, but was well compensated by Beckham's brief pose by the logo bearing the owners' name. Not surprisingly he passed the examinations with flying colours, the club's head of medical services Alfonso del Corral proclaiming him 'healthy and strong as a bull'.

He was regarded as a nice guy too, for as he signed his first autographs as a Real Madrid player for clinic staff, a nurse commented, 'I never thought he would be so humble and down to earth.' The nice-guy routine continued when he was formally introduced to the Real Madrid faithful at a carefully orchestrated press conference, in early July, at the Raimundo Sapporta basketball stadium and training ground, near Real's Bernabéu home turf. Against a huge 14 metre by 8 metre photo backdrop of himself, he was officially handed the number 23 shirt by honorary president and soccer legend Alfredo Di Stefano. Beckham's first words in Spanish, *gracias* (thank you) and *hala Madrid* (up with Madrid), were considered perfect. As he freely admitted, 'It will be important for me to express myself in Spanish as soon as possible. I'll make a real effort because it will help me integrate.'

After club chairman Florentino Perez had waxed lyrical about his latest signing, Beckham went onto the pitch. In a final touch a bare-chested young boy, eleven-year-old Alfonso Lopez, ran towards the soccer star as he approached the waiting Real fans. Beckham picked up a spare shirt and dressed the youngster in his strip. The fact that the same stunt and the same boy were used when Ronaldo signed last year was lost in the click of camera shutters.

'I haven't come here to be a great star,' Beckham later told Real Madrid television. 'I'm part of a team full of great players who are stars. We haven't talked about my position. The first thing I'll have to do is battle to win a place. All the players have to fight to be in the starting line-up; that's what makes the team so great and helps them win so many titles.'

If he needed a reminder of how high the stakes were, he was joining a club where a successful manager, Vicente Del Bosque, and club captain Fernando Hierro (a team member for fourteen seasons), had both just been sacked, even though Real Madrid had won yet another Spanish championship. A sign that sentiment had no place in the Bernabéu was shown in the manner of Del Bosque's dismissal: he was told his contract would not be renewed during a late-night conversation in a corridor at the stadium with the club's sports director, Jorge Valdano. 'I felt badly treated . . . a little warmth is not a bad thing,' he said afterwards.

While Del Bosque's departure cast a shadow over the championship celebrations, for Beckham it proved a good omen. His new manager Carlos Queiroz had worked with him at Old Trafford when he was Ferguson's right-hand man and he was full of admiration for his abilities. 'The thing I have learned about David is that he could easily have been a professional athlete. He has tremendous resistance to fatigue,' said Queiroz. 'David is born to run, a footballer who never tires of working to make himself stronger and fitter, and I love that ethos.'

He was quick too to still speculation that Beckham's arrival would jeopardize the position of the Portuguese winger Luis Figo. 'People ask me if Beckham and Figo can play in the same team and my answer is one of them would only be on the bench if he is injured or out of form,' Queiroz confirmed. 'Admittedly, they more or less play in the same position, but they are very different players technically and tactically. I view the two of them as great – footballers who go down as legendary in the modern era.'

As Beckham started his first season in the white shirt of one of the world's most famous clubs, he was well aware of the expectations placed on his slim shoulders. A natural showman, he felt that he was able to meet the incredible demands placed on him. 'Signing for Real Madrid is a challenge in family as well as footballing terms,' he explained to Real TV. 'It's a new life for me, my wife and children; new schools, new customs. I'm looking forward to it.'

Several weeks later, though, as he sat in his lonely hotel bedroom at the luxury Santa Mauro hotel in Madrid, idly flicking through Spanish TV channels, it appeared that the reality of playing for the most glamorous team in the world was not exactly living up to expectations.

Hurt by his wife's continued refusal to join him in Spain, David found himself struggling to understand his teammates, let alone the locals, and for a man who loved his weekly fix of McDonald's hamburgers, he found that Spanish food not entirely to his liking. Evenings were most difficult. The highlight was saying goodnight to his boys and chatting to Victoria about his day, but doubtless this nightly routine also served as a painful reminder of what he was missing.

For a self-confessed family man who had always been something of a homebody, his only friend in Madrid was his new dog, a Shar Pei called Carlos.

Isolated and alone, David began to loathe the four walls of his hotel suite. Even when he ventured outside he felt trapped in his new surroundings, being forced to run the gauntlet of aggressive paparazzi and well-meaning fans. For a young man who had lived much of his life being told what to do by others – be it his father Ted, his Manchester United boss Sir Alex Ferguson and his ambitious wife – his new-found freedom was disconcerting. Obsessed by order and symmetry, he suddenly found life increasingly chaotic, and it wasn't long before those first few testing months in Spain had begun to take their toll on his personal life.

When David first arrived in Madrid, his sports management company SFX assigned him a linguistic go-between in the shape of Rebecca Loos, the attractive daughter of a Dutch diplomat. Bilingual and cosmopolitan, Rebecca became David's link to the outside world, helping him in conversations with teammates, fans and even restaurant owners. As Victoria had given Rebecca the once-over during her first flying visit to the Spanish capital, it seems unlikely that she detected any warning signs, otherwise she would surely have taken immediate action.

Thrown together by circumstance, David had been away from home, hearth and family for just two months when he apparently succumbed to the seductive charms of the twenty-six-year-old. Such behaviour seemed very much out of character for the England captain, especially as David had always maintained his reputation as a clean-cut professional who steered clear of the playboy lifestyles enjoyed by other soccer stars. But in September 2003, one fateful evening of free-flowing champagne and sexy conversation would change all that.

When he and Rebecca joined four other SFX colleagues for dinner at an exclusive Thai restaurant, David was determined to let his hair down. Homesick and glad of a night spent away from his five-star 'jail', he was in the mood to forget all his cares and have a good time. As the empty bottles of champagne stacked up, the tipsy group played a risqué game of truth or dare, at which point the conversation quickly became sexually suggestive. Stunned SFX employees could scarcely believe their ears when David claimed to be a member of the mile-high club, implying that he had had sex during a commercial flight. He then challenged Rebecca to walk back to the table from the bathroom with toilet paper dangling from the back of her trousers. She accepted his unusual dare, much to the amusement of their fellow revellers.

Perhaps David found Rebecca's smiling confidence, sense of fun and curvaceous good looks a refreshing change from the nervy moodiness of his size zero wife, for the chemistry between the couple became even more apparent when the boisterous group later moved on to the exclusive Madrid nightclub Andana. It would seem that David became increasingly amorous as the night worn on; Rebecca later recalled that his attentions made her feel like a million dollars.

According to Rebecca, it wasn't long before David was suggesting to her that they returned to his hotel suite. Stunned, she thought he was joking, and replied with a flirty oath. However it soon became clear to her that David's request was deadly serious. Her pulse quickened as she followed him to his chauffeur-driven car and they drove back to his hotel. In a moment of sheer recklessness he didn't seem to care that he was kissing her in full view of his waiting chauffeur and bodyguards.

The next day, the SFX office was buzzing with rumours. It did not take long before one concerned member of staff apparently decided to phone Victoria and warn her about possible trouble on the horizon. Victoria, who once said she would 'die of a broken heart' if her husband ever had an affair, was naturally devastated. In a jealous rage, she called Rebecca and told her bluntly, 'It's not your job to go out clubbing with my husband. Back off!' After making quick work of her apparent rival, she made a second call to her husband to ask him for an explanation. After receiving an inevitable tongue-lashing from his furious wife, the first person David confided in was Rebecca.

Instead of cooling their friendship, however, David allegedly warned her that his wife knew what was going on and so they had been be more careful in future. Such a defiant reaction seemed to show that he did not fully appreciate the potential effect his behaviour would have, not only on his wife and family, but also on the England team and his all-important brand image.

Predictably, it was not long before rumours of marital disunity between the Beckhams began to appear in the British media. One tabloid told of furious rows between the couple, while another pointedly printed a picture of Rebecca and David together outside the nightclub where the affair had allegedly begun. In time-honoured fashion the Beckhams hit back by issuing an uncompromising statement about the state of their marriage: 'Contrary to newspaper reports, our marriage is not in crisis. We are extremely happy together as a family. Our only difficulty has been finding a house in Madrid that suits our needs. Since we first met, our careers have always meant that we've spent time apart. This is no reflection on the strength of our marriage and we are very much enjoying our new life in Spain.'

In private, though, all was far from well. Just a few days after issuing their statement, David was out partying again on his own. This time he was attending the £100,000 bash thrown by his Real Madrid teammate Ronaldo in honour of his twenty-seventh birthday. Rebecca was also at the party, although other revellers noticed that she and David barely spoke to one other. Instead it seemed that David only had eyes for Spanish supermodel Esther Cañadas that evening. Rebecca later claimed that she saw him disappearing upstairs with the twenty-six-year-old blonde, but whatever she felt about his interest in the leggy model, she had few qualms about joining him later at his hotel suite after receiving a text message inviting her over.

It appeared that David's newfound friendship with Cañadas carried on after the birthday party. Several days later he was spotted by neighbours in the basement garage of the model's exclusive apartment block in Arturo Soria, a district of Madrid. He reportedly sent Cañadas sexy text messages, including one that read: 'Have a safe flight baby and I really wish we was in your bed now.' In spite of a

£100,000 offer to talk about her friendship with Beckham, Esther Cañadas has always maintained a discreet silence.

Whatever his feelings toward the Spanish model, it seemed Rebecca was never far from his thoughts – or his phone. Besides asking for advice and support, he allegedly sent her a stream of X-rated text messages, including: 'I want to hear you scream.' As far as Rebecca was concerned, though, their relationship was more than sex; effectively she was a 'surrogate wife'. She later alleged that he had slept with her in the same hotel bed he had shared with his wife, that she had used one of Victoria's hair clips to tie her hair back, and had also been invited by David into his family home. This last point had made her uncomfortable, she claimed, as she felt it was clear that David had wanted to have sex with her.

By December 2003, Rebecca was beginning to sense that their relationship was drawing to a close. Although David reportedly instigated another meeting with his assistant just before a Real Madrid home game, she noticed that his behaviour had changed. The generous lovemaking and attentiveness she had previously experienced was no longer apparent. Consequently Rebecca simply felt used. Worse was to follow. A few days later David terminated his contract with SFX in favour of employing his old friend and former England masseur Terry Byrne. With David's unexpected departure, Rebecca was surplus to company requirements and lost her job.

Perhaps David had decided to cut all ties with SFX in an effort to draw a line under his relationship with Rebecca. Certainly it was his wife and children who became the sole focus of his attention over Christmas. It was also the first time in ten years as a professional footballer that he was able to enjoy a proper holiday break, and not surprisingly, he wanted to make the most of it.

The Beckhams spent a magical few days in Lapland, where a delighted Brooklyn and Romeo met Father Christmas, before returning to Beckingham Palace, their family home in England. As he put a mince pie and a tangerine in the hearth before bedtime with his sons, and arranged presents around the tree with Victoria, David felt happier than he had in months. After a Christmas surrounded by their close-knit family, both David and Victoria returned to Madrid, welcoming the New Year in style with a five-star party at the Ritz with David's mother and Victoria's parents. As he drew his wife to him for a midnight kiss, David made a quiet resolution to put the past year behind him.

While David enjoyed Christmas present, however, the ghost of his past was about to come back to haunt him. The now jobless Rebecca Loos had decided to tout her story to the highest bidder, using the notorious tabloid Mr Fix-it, Max Clifford, to broker a reported £500,000 deal with a Sunday newspaper. David's worst nightmare was about to come true.

On Sunday 4 April 2004, the Beckhams woke up to see lurid details of David's alleged affair with Rebecca splashed across the British tabloids. '90 Minutes After This Picture Was Taken, They Made Love For The First Time' blazed the headline on the front page of the *News of the World*, which showed Rebecca and David together on their evening out at the Andana nightclub seven months previously. Rebecca had spared no detail of their sexy romance, giving a blow-by-blow account of the events surrounding their liaisons.

The next few days and weeks were a nightmare for the Beckhams, particularly Victoria who helplessly swung from tantrums to tears. According to her friend and confidante at the time, Abbie Gibson (who was also nanny to Brooklyn and Romeo), one moment Victoria was sobbing that she felt fat and unattractive, the next she was engaged in vicious slanging matches with her husband. The rows went on late into the night, and on one occasion Victoria is reported to have slapped her husband, screaming repeatedly that she was going to leave him. As far as Gibson was concerned, it was only the intervention of her mother that made her take stock and rethink her actions.

While Victoria shed tears in private, in public she was all smiles, realizing that in addition to her marriage, she also had a brand to save: Brand Beckham. As she struggled to come to terms with her husband's alleged betrayal, she looked to America's former First Lady for guidance by reading the parts of Hillary Clinton's autobiography that dealt with the Monica Lewinsky scandal. Victoria admired how Hillary used the media to her advantage, leaking candid shots of her and Bill strolling on the beach and dancing together. At the time of the scandal, the Clintons posed for celebrity photographer Annie Leibovitz, sending out a clear message that their marriage was strong and resolute.

But when Victoria called on her favoured

paparazzo Jason Fraser to capture the Beckham family frolicking in the snow at the exclusive French ski resort of Courcheval, this time the publicity stunt backfired. Ironically, despite being the wronged party, it was Victoria who bore the brunt of the criticism, condemned by the media as 'calculated and manipulative' for her attempt to present a united front. The fact that she had chosen not to join her husband in Spain gave the tabloids the opportunity to describe her as unsupportive. Even the couple's friend Sir Elton John agreed with the consensus, saying that Victoria should have moved to Madrid for the good of their marriage.

Rebecca Loos fared little better. Dubbed the 'sleazy señorita', her racy bisexual past was explored in graphic detail. As for David, he was merely painted as the hapless love fool, manipulated into bed by a charming gold digger after his wife had left him to fend for himself in a strange country. It also appeared that the current media revelations might just have been the tip of the iceberg. A few days after the Loos scandal broke, former glamour model Sarah Marbeck claimed to have had a nine-month affair with Beckham, which, she alleged, began in July 2001.

In a newspaper interview with a British Sunday tabloid, the slim brunette confessed that not only had she had enjoyed a night of passion with David during his soccer tour of the Far East, but she had had a second romantic tryst following an England game in March 2002, when Victoria was pregnant with the couple's second child. Like Loos, Sarah Marbeck claimed that the England captain had sent her a stream of explicit text messages; his pet name for her was 'Tinker Bell', while he was 'Peter Pan' and Victoria was plain 'Wendy'.

The children's storybook names seemed highly appropriate because, like the Loos affair, David appeared to display a childlike indifference to the consequences of his alleged actions. He reportedly contacted Sarah to inform her that Victoria had scrolled through some texts on his mobile phone and become suspicious. Yet he did not call things off, and continued to send Sarah messages.

As far as Victoria was concerned it was David's alleged criticism of her physical appearance that hurt her the most, when reports emerged that Loos claimed he hated Victoria's 'stick-like' figure, and now loved her more like a sister than a wife. Little wonder, then, that Victoria's thirtieth birthday was far from happy. She spent it with her parents and children in the Swiss ski resort of Verbier – with David away on soccer duty. Onlookers described her as 'looking drawn and miserable' as she picked at a plate of steamed vegetables in a restaurant.

As with the Loos allegations, Victoria faced her public with a tight defiant smile when she took her sons to watch their dad play football in Madrid. She looked glamorous, polished and composed, even though pitch-side screens around the stadium displayed adverts for a Spanish gossip magazine that read: 'Sarah Marbeck – Beckham's Malaysian affair.' Her ordeal continued on the evening that she and David appeared at a glamorous red-carpet event to celebrate nineteen years of their management company – Simon Fuller's 19 Management – for it was on the same day that a Rebecca Loos TV interview was broadcast on a British primetime talk show. It was no coincidence that Victoria flaunted the £1 million pink diamond ring that David had bought for her when he signed for Real Madrid, or indeed that she performed at the bash from the throne the couple had had specially made for their extravagant wedding.

It was now David's turn to face scrutiny within the public arena. In his own life story he dismissed the stream of allegations as 'a sorry procession of spiteful stories', and noted that his marriage was stronger than ever. Victoria was philosophical, later admitting to writer Richard Simpson that the couple had had a 'fair amount of crap ' thrown at them. ' I think we are a very strong family,' she said. 'It's easy to give up and a lot of people do. We love each other to pieces. You work things out if you really love someone.'

The message from the Beckham camp was clear: Brand Beckham was here to stay. Certainly tales of David's alleged affairs had not disillusioned advertisers if his lucrative £40 million deal with razor-blade company Gillette was anything to go by. Indeed advertising expert Trevor Beattie observed that Beckham's behaviour had added a new dimension to the star: 'Before he was a perfect role model – great dad, good bloke, brilliant footballer and husband. Now we have seen he is human and can be flawed.' Nor was public opinion unduly shaken. Thousands flocked to London's National Portrait Gallery to see *David*, a video installation by artist Sam Taylor-Wood that featured the soccer star asleep in bed. It was undoubtedly the most popular exhibit in the entire gallery.

In May 2004, with all the insouciance of a royal announcement, the couple issued a bulletin stating that Victoria would move to Spain to be with her husband, and their son Brooklyn would start at Runnymede private school in Madrid in September. Later that month Victoria took an opportunity to show her motherly side with a charity trip to the slums of Peru. The visit, part of a documentary to help raise funds for the British charity Sport Relief, saw the star spending several days with poor families in a district of the capital Lima. After witnessing children scavenging through rubbish dumps to find scraps to live on, she handed out footballs and toys to youngsters, and spent time chatting about her own family to different groups of children. She also sang for them, and even showed off her tattoos and belly-button piercing.

While cynics dubbed her 'Mother Victoria', accusing her of trying to redefine her spendaholic reputation, slum dwellers who met her seemed truly touched by her kindness. Mother of five, Bertha Cueva Zavaleta, described how a little boy proudly cradled an England football given to him by Victoria, while a group of children spent hours making a poster for the star. 'Everyone was laughing and crying – there was a lot of joy,' she said. 'We all thought we had been forgotten by the world – our Government doesn't help us. It made us all feel good that somebody loves us, somebody cares.'

While David and Victoria seemed to be redressing the balance of their private lives, professionally the soccer star's first season with Real Madrid had fizzled out in disappointment, the team having ended the season without a single item of silverware for the trophy cabinet. As David had gone to Spain for glory as well as a fresh challenge, it was something of an anticlimax. 'One trophy, never mind three, would have been the right way to say "gracias" to the fans, but we failed to give them anything after promising so much,' he observed at the end of the season.

He was hopeful that England's campaign in the upcoming European Championships in June would be more successful. The mood among the players and fans was optimistic, as they truly believed that they could be the champions of Europe. While the nation prayed for a successful tournament campaign, David was spending sleepless nights at the England team's training camp in Sardinia. The cause of his anxiety was not due to pre-match jitters, however, but rather the prospect of having to face his tormentors, the British media. As team captain he had an obligation to appear in front of the cameras, but he was all too well aware that he would also have to cope with a barrage of questions about his personal life.

He arrived at his first press conference on a rickety golf cart, and immediately took a swing at the waiting media. The statement he read out made his feelings abundantly clear: 'The way I and my family have been treated is an absolute disgrace. At the end of the day, I'm a nice person and loving husband and father. I've been called a bad father, I've been called a bad husband and my wife has been called a bad mother. Things always hurt that are said about my family, and for people to call my wife a bad mother is unbelievable. I'm a strong person, I'm a strong family man, I'm a strong husband and a strong father.'

With that ordeal behind him, he could now focus completely on the task ahead. The first game saw

England take on the reigning champions, France. Despite scoring first, they ended up losing 2–1 thanks to the brilliance of David's Real Madrid teammate Zinedine Zidane, who scored twice in injury time. While they won the next match against lowly Switzerland, the England captain was not happy with his game. Not only had the emotional demands of the past few months taken their toll, but a new gym routine had left him 14 lb heavier in muscle and consequently less mobile on the pitch. Nevertheless, a 4–2 victory over Croatia ensured that his team would face tournament hosts Portugal in the quarter-final.

The closely fought game ended in a 2–2 draw, which meant that the result would be decided in the cruellest way possible – a penalty shootout. The captain bravely stepped up to take the first penalty. As he ran to strike the ball, all England held its breath in anticipation, but just before his foot made contact David felt the pitch slip away. There was a collective groan from the England supporters as the ball sailed over the crossbar. As he walked sadly back to the halfway line, a surge of dread swept over him. Memories of being turned into a national villain after being sent off in the World Cup match against Argentina in 1998 came flooding back. He knew he couldn't go through that again, not just for himself but for the sake of his family. In the end it was Portugal who emerged victorious and once again a defeated English team trudged despondently back to the dressing room, denied victory on penalties once again.

This latest tournament exit was a disappointing end to a season that had begun with such promise and hope. A crestfallen David turned to Victoria for comfort and support. She had watched every game of the championship, and for the first time in his playing career she had begun to take a real interest in his form. As they sat in the hotel bar after the game, he poured out his feelings. She felt his self-doubt and insecurity keenly as he questioned the price he was paying as England captain, fearing the media backlash would target not only him, but her as well. Her response was emphatic: 'You've lost and we're going home. But you're England captain. Do you know how many people would give their right arm to be able to say that? All that matters now is that you get this out of your system and get on with the next one.'

In many ways the troubles of the last few months had served to bring the couple closer together. It was time to focus on their future, make a break with the past and rediscover their marriage, but being the Beckhams, they were going to do it in style. They marked their five-year anniversary with a holiday at the secluded luxury holiday resort of Amanjena, on the outskirts of Marrakech, to spend some time alone, before joining their sons for a family holiday aboard a stunning private yacht in the south of France. Having ridden out the storm of recent times, their commitment to one another seemed assured when, in August 2004, Victoria announced that she was two months' pregnant, which proved that at least some good had come out of the European Championships in June. As they prepared for the birth of their third child, the couple finally put down roots in Madrid, buying a new home complete with tennis courts, outdoor pool and two acres of woodland.

At the start of the 2004–5 season, their relationship was reminiscent of old times. During their courtship, David was often rebuked by his Manchester United manager for calling Victoria endlessly on his mobile phone, and now the new Real Madrid coach José Antonio Camacho had banned him from contacting her while the team was in training.

However, the couple still faced choppy waters as Victoria was still finding it difficult to adjust to life in Madrid. After all, despite her seemingly stylish sophistication, she had got used to living next door to her sister and seeing her parents every day while her boys had breakfast with their cousins each morning. Now, even though she had a private jet at her disposal, her family was three hours' away. She could not speak Spanish, and had no career with which to occupy herself. Newly pregnant, she found the Madrid summer heat oppressive and watched her expanding waistline with misgivings, perhaps fearing that David might look elsewhere. 'I hate Spain. I want to go home,' she sobbed to her sons' nanny, Abbie Gibson, unaware that worse was to follow.

Four months into her pregnancy, her trusted friend and beautician Danielle Heath sold her story to a British tabloid for several thousand pounds, alleging that she too had had an affair with David. Moreover she also revealed that they had had a sexual encounter at the family house in Madrid the day after Victoria's pregnancy announcement, while the former Spice Girl was hosting her youngest son's birthday party back in Britain.

Once again, the Beckhams were forced into public relations overdrive. They threatened legal action against Danielle and the offending tabloid, and issued an emphatic press statement declaring that they were 'sick and tired of people trying to make money out of our family'. In an attempt to give the impression of business as usual, the couple were photographed attending prenatal checks in London's Harley Street and having a romantic lunch together in a Chelsea restaurant. One diner was quoted as saying, 'They looked really happy. David kept leaning over and whispering in Victoria's ear, and then she would start giggling. It was very sweet.'

In private, though, the atmosphere was far from calm. According to Gibson, pregnant Victoria felt deeply betrayed, and as she sobbed and screamed at her husband, she tried to get him to confess his alleged infidelity. A close family friend is reported to have grown increasingly concerned for Victoria's wellbeing as she witnessed her shaking, crying and pulling out clumps of her hair. David was less sympathetic, storming out of the house at the first sign of conflict and staying away for hours at a time. Whenever he thought storm clouds were looming he deliberately left his mobile switched off.

The next few months were miserable for Victoria. Her condition prevented her from adhering to the stringent dietary regime that maintained her polished looks, while her skin began to suffer after she succumbed to cravings for French fries. At the same time, she confided to Abbie Gibson that she was horrified by her 'fat' pregnant shape, fretting that David would leave her for someone younger and more attractive.

Coming home each night to a tearful and insecure wife meant that he could no longer escape his domestic problems when he ran out on to the soccer pitch. His team was stuttering and spluttering – the highly-paid *galácticos* seemingly failing to live up to their superstar billing. To make matters worse, he was forced to watch from the sidelines for six weeks after suffering broken ribs in an England World Cup qualifying game against Wales in October.

Just before Christmas, the couple staged an elaborate and extravagant show of family togetherness when they threw a £500,000 christening party for their sons, Brooklyn and Romeo. The proud parents had a chapel specially built for the occasion, complete with mock ruins to echo the ancient church where they married in 1999. The boys' godfathers Elton John and David Furnish, design duo Domenico Dolce and Stefano Gabbana, and the former Spice Girls all featured on the guest list, which included a galaxy of showbiz and soccer stars. In the run-up to the event, Victoria, now six months pregnant, feared being upstaged and demanded 'modest dress' for female attendants. So she was rather put out when her friend Liz Hurley swept in wearing a revealing ivory satin gown and white fur shawl.

However, all Victoria's fears and worries seemed to fall away when her husband stood up before the assembled guests, looked into her eyes and paid an emotional tribute to her 'love and support' during their extremely difficult year. As she toasted her sons and her family, she doubtless hoped that he truly meant it.

Fifteen

A Cross to Bear

The birth of their third son on Sunday 20 February 2005 signalled renewed hope and the chance of a fresh start for the Beckhams. As Victoria contentedly cradled her newborn in a private ward of Madrid's Ruber Internacional hospital, her husband seemed to sense a change. He whispered a prayer for the infant's life and with tears in his eyes told his wife, 'I can't believe I nearly lost all of this.'

As with most things Beckham, the arrival of the 7 lb infant, who was born by Caesarean section, was not without controversy. The main source of the problem was the issue of his name. David's family had lobbied for a traditional English forename such as Robert or David. 'Something normal for once,' according to one of the Beckham clan. But Victoria felt she knew best, insisting that it should be unusual, like Brooklyn and Romeo. The couple duly chose the name 'Cruz', Spanish for 'cross'. It held a special meaning for Victoria, who hoped that the child, borne out of such difficult circumstances, would be guarded by the cross throughout his life.

Not everyone was convinced, however, as critics pointed out that not only was the name normally used for girls, but that the full translation meant 'cross to bear'. Two days later, David let his feet do the talking in Real Madrid's Champions' League home game against Juventus, when he set up his side's winning goal with a devastating free kick.

Already guaranteed a life of luxury, the new arrival's financial future was further secured when his parents signed a lucrative £5 million deal with beauty emporium Coty. They joined luminaries such as actor and singer Jennifer Lopez and fashion guru Vivienne Westwood with a specially designed 'his' and 'hers' fragrance to be released in autumn 2006. Not that little Cruz was aware of this as he lay gurgling in a designer babygro in his custom-built cot in the nursery at his Madrid home.

The start of the year had certainly heralded a number of new enterprises for the Beckhams. David had always seen his future introducing other youngsters to the sport he loved and couldn't wait until he could teach Cruz to take his first kick at a football. In the meantime, he had put his money where mouth was and shelled out the lion's share of the costs towards building the first David Beckham Academy in Greenwich, London. At the opening in March 2005, he outlined his feelings for the sport – and his own future: 'Working with children is one of the most important experiences you can have as a footballer. This is the most important thing in my life and is what I want to do after I finish playing football.'

Sponsors were naturally quick to recognize the financial potential of a string of Beckham academies, and plans were already underway to launch a sister academy in Los Angeles at the Home Depot Center, the home of the LA Galaxy soccer team.

While David was looking to the future, his wife was redefining the direction of her professional life. Her modelling and singing career now behind her, Victoria was deliberately marketing herself as a fashion icon and a style guru. For once it was a career move she felt comfortable with, as it gave her a tremendous surge of self-confidence.

A key decision in her lucrative journey of self-renewal was to switch publicists, allying herself with Henry's House who focused on fashion, rather than Simon Fuller's 19 Management. The fact that she had a fragrance and clothing line meant it was a logical move, and marked the moment of her making the steady transition from 'Queen of Bling' to sophisticated fashion icon.

Yet her transition came at a price. Just a month after the birth of Cruz, Victoria was very publicly photographed in skintight jeans and clingy top, cheering on her husband at the Bernabéu Stadium. Even though she looked good, her rapid weight loss after Cruz's birth had taken its toll. 'I've got so much saggy skin on my stomach,' she complained later, confessing that her rigorous dieting had left her 'with no bum at all'.

Then there were her three boys to think about. She may have been an aspiring fashion icon, but first and foremost she was a mother who felt a driving need to protect her brood. While she accepted that she was the natural prey of the paparazzi who dogged her every dainty footstep, she was infuriated by the way Spanish photographers would also treat her boys as fair game. While baby Cruz was blissfully unaware of the photographers who had snapped his first few moments in the world, his brothers were now old enough to notice their intrusive behaviour. Even without his parents' presence, Brooklyn, now six, was considered a celebrity. An innocent soccer game with his friends at school became tabloid fodder when the match was ambushed by some paparazzi, leaving the youngster startled and bemused. On another occasion his little brother Romeo, just two, was left sobbing and terrified when photographers took pictures of him while he played at a Madrid nursery.

Naturally the couple were desperately concerned. David took the opportunity to speak his mind before a crucial World Cup qualifier against Northern Ireland. 'There have been a couple of incidents in the last two weeks which have made me think seriously about how it affects my sons,' he said. 'When my children go to school or nursery, they should be left alone. But they're not being left alone and that's becoming a problem . . . I'm now at the point where I don't know what to do. Victoria and I have always accepted we're in the limelight and that people want to take photos of us. But my children?'

The behaviour of the Spanish media gave Victoria the perfect excuse to explore the option of returning home to Britain. While she quietly viewed £5 million homes in central London, it was rumoured that David was considering a move to the capital to play for either Arsenal or Chelsea. The couple's plans to build a £100,000 tree house for their sons in the grounds of Beckingham Palace added further intrigue to speculation about their future plans.

However, the move was not to be. At least, not yet.

After talking about it at length, the couple decided that, in spite of the paparazzi intrusion, their sons were now settled in Spain and it would not be fair to disrupt their routine. More than that, David was enjoying his soccer, and playing well for both club and country. He confirmed the couple's decision to make their home permanently in Spain. 'I've played for Manchester United, captained England and now I'm playing for Real Madrid. That would be the best way of ending my career . . .' he said. 'My family are very happy in Madrid, my house is lovely, the children are very happy and my wife is very happy.'

Game over. Certainly David did his best to soothe his wife's restless spirit, organizing a lavish thirty-first birthday trip to Paris for her in April. Even she was impressed when she stepped aboard the luxurious private jet that David had had specially painted with a 'V', and walked down the aisle on a carpet of fresh rose petals, her favourite flower. As the champagne flowed, it seemed that her husband had taken care of every detail of the £50,000 trip. Not only had he reserved the Coco Chanel suite, Victoria's fashion idol, at the Ritz Hotel in Paris, but he had also organized private visits to a succession of fashion salons and jewellers. She even had her own butler on hand to look after her pretty packages.

Having spent much of the past few months of her pregnancy longing for her husband's attention, Victoria returned to Spain feeling like his princess again. Unfortunately, the feeling wouldn't last, though David was not to blame on this occasion. Only days after returning to Spain, she discovered that her nanny Abbie Gibson, who had been her friend and confidante for two years, had sold her story to a British Sunday tabloid for a reported six-figure sum.

After yet another betrayal, Victoria was naturally devastated, and encouraged her husband to seek legal advice. Their lawyers' attempt to gag the former nanny was not wholly successful, as Gibson merely undertook not to disclose any new confidential details about the Beckhams' private life, while still being allowed to repeat the claims made in the original tabloid story. David and Victoria, now so cautious about whom they could depend upon that they flew the same team of trusted builders around the world and relied on their family members to handle their financial affairs, were distraught.

In the newspaper article, Gibson confirmed rumours of marital problems, and disclosed details of their late-night rows. She also revealed that she had read messages on David's mobile phone and found a string of sexy texts to a Spanish number. As their private lives became the subject of yet more tabloid fodder, David was quick to express their indignation. 'I find it amazing, quite unbelievable,' he said. 'When you've let someone into your home to look after your children, which are Victoria and my most prized possessions, you begin to trust that person . . . We are normal people despite what people might think of us. Of course we have arguments like any other couple, but I love my wife.'

Though the Beckhams threatened further legal action, it soon became clear that such proceedings would only prolong their public agony. Instead Victoria fought fire with fire, using the paparazzi to show that it was marital business as usual as she was photographed while shopping for a thirtieth birthday gift for David, with her son Romeo. With his mother's help, he picked out a £500,000 ring from the exclusive Madrid jewellers Suarez for the celebration in May.

While Victoria could manage to put on a brave face in public, in private she struggled to keep her insecurities in check. When a British tabloid revealed that the apparent recipient of the text messages was Spanish model Esther Cañadas – whom David first met at Ronaldo's birthday party two years earlier – she found it hard to remain philosophical, yet she managed. 'If it doesn't kill you, it makes you stronger,' she would say of the alleged affair.

A sign of her indefatigable spirit was clear for all to see as, once again, she smiled for the cameras as she and David strolled hand-in-hand through the narrow streets of Venice where they spent his thirtieth birthday. Flanked by fans and photographers, they cuddled up for a romantic gondolier ride and drank champagne at the legendary Harry's Bar before returning to the stunning £1.5 million Venetian palazzo of close friend Sir Elton John. Whatever was said behind closed doors, Victoria was determined to stand by her man, and the couple returned home to Madrid where she had organized a sensational party at the city's exclusive Buddha Bar. While rose petals had been scattered on the floor – echoing David's own romantic gesture on their Paris trip – the evening was far from a bed of roses.

According to newspaper reports, stunned revellers looked on in amazement as Victoria's father Tony was involved in heated exchanges with David's father Ted, whom he was upbraiding about his son's behaviour. He was heard shouting that Ted needed to 'sort his son out', blaming the soccer star for leaving Victoria 'all over the place'. The altercation, which was viewed as typical of the two families' mutual suspicion of one another, only ended after the intervention of one of David's relatives.

If the respective fathers were 'off message', David and Victoria were certainly right behind Brand Beckham, and ready to take on their biggest challenge to date – conquering America. Shortly after his birthday, the couple flew to New York where David began a promotional tour on behalf of adidas. As he pushed his way into the Manhattan sports store through the scrum of fans and paparazzi, it seemed they had succeeded beyond their wildest dreams. The buzz on the streets was matched by his media appeal. When he appeared on NBC's *Today Show*, his shy smile and chiselled features caught the attention of millions of soccer moms across the country. Ironically, his arrival in the USA caused much more of a stir than the appearance of the England soccer team, who had flown to Chicago to promote the 2006 World Cup. Embarrassingly, England coach Sven-Göran Eriksson was asked more questions about the absent team captain than the rest of the squad.

Beckham's charismatic star quality was further in evidence on the West Coast when, in early June, he opened his eponymous soccer academy at the Home Depot Center, home to Major League Soccer team LA Galaxy. Watched by hundreds of fans and dozens of photographers, he spent two hours meeting and greeting starstruck youngsters.

Watching the 'Beckham Effect' in action was Tim Leiweke, the multimillionaire president of LA

Galaxy. Amid the excitement of the England captain's arrival, Leiweke saw dollar signs and a golden future, and talked animatedly about the possibility of the LA Galaxy team becoming world-renowned if David ever decided to move West. 'All I can do is dream,' he said. 'It would be huge, but I'm not going to get too far ahead of myself. So we'll take this one step at a time.'

Certainly his words would have whetted the appetite of the other half of Brand Beckham. As her husband posed and preened on the soccer pitch, Victoria was far from idle, brokering deals to supply her VB Rock and Republic jeans to trendy LA stores such as Kitson and Fred Segal. She was clearly thrilled about how well she had been received in the US, and could really see a future for herself and her family in Hollywood.

That night, as David and Victoria unwound with a dinner at the home of their new celebrity friends Tom Cruise and Katie Holmes, she confided in the young actress about her hopes for the future. Revealing that fashion was her true forte, she explained to Katie that she wanted to succeed in fashion far more that she had ever wished for a number-one single. She had loved dressing up as a little girl, and had never grown out of the habit. Before the Beckhams left for their hotel, Victoria and Katie decided that they should arrange a girlie shopping trip later in the year.

For years Victoria had chased celebrity, and now she had arrived at its epicentre. In a town where the ruthless pursuit of success, fame, beauty and the elusive 'size zero' was the norm, she had finally found a place where she felt she belonged and truly felt at home luxuriating in the possibility of joining Hollywood's elite. Indeed the ultimate A-lister Tom Cruise later gave them – and her – his personal seal of approval: 'The Beckhams are great friends of mine. I dig Victoria, she's smart and funny. They are a great couple. A go-forward couple.'

The following evening, as she rubbed shoulders with sports stars and showbiz personalities such as Robbie Williams and Diana Ross at the glamorous launch party for David's soccer academy, it may have begun to feel that life in Madrid, and even the comforts of Beckingham Palace, were slowly becoming a distant memory. While she insisted in an interview that week that she loved her life in Spain, Victoria could still feel the seductive siren song of Hollywood. It was a call that one day she was determined to answer.

A few days later, if she needed reminding about the appeal of making a fresh start in Hollywood, then candid photographs published in a British tabloid showing David kissing a girl in a parking bay near the Bernabéu stadium drove the point home. Apparently he had met the statuesque brunette twice in the same street, flashing his headlights at her before she joined him at his car. While both the girl in question and Beckham explained that it was nothing more than a kiss on the cheek from an adoring fan, Victoria was again unsettled, despite telling friends that the incident was a 'pathetic joke'. Once again she had been made to look like a fool – the tabloid sniggers further fuelling her desire for a new beginning.

While she continued to dream, at an isolated Denver ranch a powerful group of millionaires were hatching a plan to turn that fantasy into reality. The ranch owner was reclusive entertainment mogul and Major League Soccer (MLS) patriarch, Philip Anschutz. Alongside other executives from his company, Anschutz Entertainment Group, he listened as the president of LA Galaxy Tim Leiweke waxed lyrical about the 'Beckham Effect'. If any one was going to woo Beckham stateside it would be Anschutz, the soccer-mad billionaire who was pumping millions of dollars into the sport to help it gain a toehold in a country where the holy trinity of basketball, American football and baseball reigned supreme. Known affectionately as 'Uncle Phil', Anschutz first fell in love with soccer when he was given a pair of tickets to the 1994 World Cup Final. He was so inspired by the silky skills of the Brazilian winners that he became the ambassador and moneyman behind America's MLS. For the 2002 World Cup in Japan/South Korea, it was Anschutz who brokered the major TV network deals to arrange coverage in the US.

So while Leiweke outlined a twelve-point strategy that would one day place soccer on a par with the country's three most popular sports, Anschutz listened eagerly to the man who shared his vision and passion for the sport. Everyone in the room realized that soccer in America needed a public face, a poster boy to attract the crowds and enthuse the fans. So why not think big? Why not try for the biggest name in global soccer, David Beckham? Not surprisingly it was music to Anschutz's ears when the English player looked favourably on a move to the MLS league. 'Yeah, I would definitely consider it,' David said in one interview. 'I wouldn't say no to the opportunity.' The question was, when was he likely to make such a life-changing decision, especially as the couple had only just moved into their new home, a £5 million Tuscan-style villa, complete with two acres of manicured gardens, tennis courts, a swimming pool and a practice soccer pitch on the outskirts of Madrid.

There was little doubt that Anschutz and his colleagues knew they had a fight on if they wanted to land their prize. It was not just the fact that Beckham seemed to be putting down family roots in Spain; his paymasters at Real Madrid were also constructing a juicy four-year deal that would make him the highest paid footballer in the world with an annual salary of £36 million. While his feats on the pitch had failed to earn silverware for the club, the cash registers were ringing with shirt sales and other merchandise bearing the Beckham name. In fact his number 23 shirt had outsold those of all the other *galácticos* combined by a factor of four to one. In David's first season at the club, profits had soared from £127 million to £156 million.

Aside from soccer shirts, the Beckham magnet also increased sales of a myriad other products. His face alone sold millions of extra Gillette razors, and to show their appreciation the company presented him with a £20,000 solid gold, diamond-encrusted razor, specially created by American jewellery designer Jacob Arobo, as a Father's Day present.

Brand Beckham was a genuine double act though, with Victoria's burgeoning status as a fashion icon adding to its appeal. Italian designer Roberto Cavalli was quick to spot the advertising potential of the most photographed couple in the world, and signed up Victoria in a lucrative deal to wear his clothes. Gone were the days when the Beckhams had to strike under-the-table deals with paparazzi photographers to ensure their pictures ended up in the papers. Now they were the darlings of the mass media, every detail of their enviable lifestyle became front-page news. In spite of consistent reports of marital infidelity, the couple had robustly maintained the illusion of glamour and success within a wholesome family setting. The Beckhams seemed to have it all. They had become the couple everyone envied, yet aspired to emulate.

With the couple's every move being watched and photographed, their summer holiday to St Tropez attracted more media attention than Princess Diana in her heyday. They made headlines when they kissed and cuddled on a crowded public beach, while David set pulses racing when he posed in a pair of skimpy, white, Speedo swimming shorts. Even though Victoria said she 'looked awful naked', millions of women disagreed, and her beachside look of straw Stetson hat, pendant necklace and cheesecloth kaftan was instantly copied on the High Street.

The Beckhams were top of the guest list for every celebrity bash, joining models, entertainers and royalty at Elton John's White Tie and Tiara summer ball in June. A month later, in London's Hyde Park, they headed the galaxy of stars taking part in Live 8, the charity pop concert organized by Bob Geldof under the slogan: 'Make Poverty History.' Egged on by his wife, David agreed to join actor Brad Pitt and comedian Ricky Gervais as one of the guest presenters at the prestigious event. As comfortable as he was with his celebrity, he was still nervous behind the microphone, and spent a sleepless night worrying that he would fluff his lines when he came to introduce Robbie Williams before an estimated 3 billion worldwide TV audience. Backstage, Victoria was quick to assert her status as showbiz royalty, holding court with a host of celebrities. She smartly intervened when rapper Snoop Dogg invited her husband out for a night on the town. 'Look Mr Snoopy, you're not taking my husband out. I know all about your reputation!' she was heard to say.

A further sign of David's global appeal became apparent when the British Government harnessed his celebrity to back London's 2012 Olympic bid. In early July 2005, the Beckhams flew to Singapore where the successful host nation was to be announced, to join Prime Minister Tony Blair and celebrities such as supermodel Kate Moss in frantic last-minute lobbying to boost the capital city's bid. In a passionate speech Beckham, who grew up in London's East End where it was proposed that the Games should be held, talked about his humble roots. 'I have got friends who have children growing up in the East End of London,' he said, 'and they have said to me that to have the Olympics in our manor would be a special thing for kids to have inspiration from different athletes from all around the world.'

The lobbying seemed to work. In a surprise victory, London was chosen to host the 2012 Olympic Games, beating off strong challenges from Paris, New York and Barcelona.

David's evident love of his country led to renewed speculation that he was thinking of returning to a London soccer club, while conversely the US media pondered a possible move to the States and a place as the star attraction in the MLS. There simply wasn't enough Beckham to go around. The man himself insisted he was staying in Spain. 'At the moment, all I'm thinking about is playing and ending my career at Madrid and winning titles,' he explained. 'We've not won anything this season, so next season we have to win the league and the Champions' League. I want to win all the titles there are.'

Much as Victoria was seduced by Hollywood, her husband was adamant that he had to focus on his football career. Not only did he genuinely want to win trophies with Real Madrid, but there was also the 2006 World Cup to think about. At the age of thirty, it would probably be his last chance to aim for a coveted winner's medal. Furthermore, his family was happy and settled. The boys were learning Spanish, they had made friends at their new schools, and they loved playing outside in the garden during the long, warm Mediterranean evenings. As much as Victoria was keen to move on, she had to admit that sunshine and Spanish life suited her young family.

Despite their jet-set lifestyle, family would always come first for the Beckhams. Away from the cameras and the glamour, they have always insisted that they lead a very normal life. Having both come from strong families, Victoria and David have always tried to create security and stability for their own children. They even took legal action against a British Sunday tabloid for suggesting that their 'happy family' image was merely a front to protect their lucrative brand. In a statement, they said, 'We do not deny that we promote ourselves as a happily married couple. We say that because it is true.' However, the fact that they would have to prove this in court against a background of tabloid allegations pertaining to David's infidelity caused the couple to drop the case.

They had paid a high price for Brand Beckham. The couple had become increasingly guarded about whom they let into their world. From their beautician to their nanny, everyone who worked for them had a story to tell – and to sell. When the couple discovered that David's father was planning to release a book about his famous son, it seemed the last straw. A 'glowing tribute' it may have been – complete with snaps from the family album – but David is believed to have been surprised that his father had not consulted with him first.

Wary about whom to trust, Victoria relied heavily on the help and support of her own parents. Even though three boisterous boys is a handful for any young mother, Victoria refused to entrust her sons' safety to anyone outside her family – especially after Abbie Gibson's actions. While Victoria could always depend upon her parents or sister Louise for extra childcare, she also genuinely enjoyed being a hands-on parent. It was she who got the kids up and ready each morning before David took Brooklyn and Romeo to school. As parents, they insisted on old-fashioned good manners. Routine and order was the rule in the Beckham household, while any bad behaviour was punished by a spell on the 'naughty step'.

Behind closed doors, the Beckhams lived out scenes of comfortable normality, with David enjoying a kickabout with his boys in the back garden just as he did when he was a youngster. 'Brooklyn is the most amazing footballer,' said his doting dad. 'I'd love it if he did play for England one day. That would make me so proud.'

For the Beckham family, a night in front of the television rather than a celebrity party was the norm. Scoffing at reports that her husband enjoyed watching pornography, Victoria explained to readers of *Marie Claire* magazine that David was much more likely to be found watching TV gardening shows. As for Victoria, even though her father was building an extra wing on Beckingham Palace to make one of the world's biggest walk-in wardrobes, when she slipped out of her Roberto Cavalli gown or Dolce & Gabbana outfit she was perfectly happy romping about with her boys in jeans, T-shirt and flip-flops.

The importance of family was brought sharply into focus when, in November 2005, their middle son Romeo developed a fever. With his temperature soaring to 104°F, his anxious parents rushed the three-year-old to a private clinic in Madrid. His illness was all the more worrying because it was the fourth time in three months that he had been taken to hospital, on all occasions suffering a dangerously high temperature and frightening convulsions. His parents insisted on extensive tests to find out what was wrong with their son, but this time it seemed to be nothing more than a case of bronchitis. Even so, David and Victoria were understandably jittery and insisted on more tests. Eventually, the youngster was diagnosed with epilepsy, a condition that can be brought on by exposure to flashing lights.

It was the cruellest of ironies. While the diagnosis was worrying for any parent, for the Beckhams, who lived their lives under the constant glare of paparazzi flashbulbs, the implications were dramatic. Before the devastating news, they had been more concerned about the emotional impact the constant tabloid intrusion would have on their boys. Now Romeo's health would be placed in jeopardy by the very lifestyle they embraced.

On one occasion, Victoria and her son were ambushed by photographers when they arrived at London's Heathrow airport. As a terrified Romeo tried to shield his eyes from the flashes, his mother screamed at the photographers to stop. Once she had bundled him into the safety of a waiting blacked-out car, she held her son tight, consumed by guilt, anger and fear. In fairness to the responsible photographic agencies, once they were informed of Romeo's condition, they promised not to use flashbulbs. But that did not stop maverick photographers or curious members of the public taking snapshots of the youngster.

Romeo's condition went to the heart of the dilemma facing the couple. On the one hand they objected to their children being photographed, but on the other they did everything they could to ensure maximum exposure. It was particularly difficult for Victoria, her attentions torn between a glamorous career and caring for her children. 'All I want to do now is stay in the shadows and look after my children,' she told a Spanish writer, confiding that she was desperate for a baby girl to complete her family. For the woman who once said she wanted to be more famous than 'Persil Automatic', her modest familial ambition did not really suit. Life in the shadows was clearly not for her.

Like a moth to a flame, she was drawn to the spotlight. At the star-studded Fashion Rocks event in Monaco in October 2005, for example, she guaranteed herself maximum attention by wearing a Cavalli dress slashed to her navel. The outfit raised eyebrows not least because it was known that David had wanted her to stay in Spain to care for Romeo who had been unwell again. Victoria's judgement was that their son was in safe hands and she had to fulfil her obligations to her fashion sponsor – and her own career. A few weeks later the woman who 'wanted to live in the shadows' was happily posing on the slopes of the exclusive Spanish ski resort, Baqueira, clad head to toe in £8,000 worth of designer skiwear – with her three boys in tow, all dressed in matching designer outfits.

The international fashion plate, who had loved dressing up when she was little, now had a worldwide following – and she was determined to exploit it. With the help of a British fashion journalist, Victoria put her name to a 'how to' fashion stylebook called *That Extra Half an Inch*, which was to be published in autumn 2006. As a taste of what was to come, she also divulged her 'fashion commandments' in an American fashion magazine. Even though she wore size zero dresses and confessed to buying children's clothes to fit her slim frame, Victoria still admitted to 'fat days', and recommended a slouchy Stella McCartney sweater dress for 'days when you don't feel that great about yourself'. For a star who had become famous for flashing her flesh, she then went on to warn, 'Don't let it all hang out. It's much sexier to leave a little to the imagination.' It was very much a case of 'wear as I say, not as I wear.' As well as the fashion manual there was even talk of writing a children's book. The audacious Mrs Beckham, who once boasted that she had never read a whole book, was now seemingly eager to follow in Madonna's footsteps and pen a story for children.

Like Madonna and model Kate Moss, who had both put their names to fashion labels, Victoria was no longer prepared simply to be a spectator or a fashion plate. When she joined the fashion editors on the front row at Paris Fashion Week in January 2006, she revealed that she planned to further her fledgling career as a designer by starting up her own fashion range under the logo dVb – David and Victoria Beckham. As well as men and women's clothing, she aimed to launch a range of sunglasses, bags and other accessories. She was confident that her label would be successful because in her view 'people love dressing like me.' It was a move inspired as much by her fallout with Michael Ball, the US owner of Rock & Republic who sold her jeans label, as her own growing fashion confidence. Relations between the two had been strained since having a 'blazing row' at a fashion show in October 2005 because Ball had decided not to show her limited edition jeans collection on the catwalk.

A year later it was announced that the partnership was over, but there were still some unresolved matters, notably concerning the thorny issue of money. Although Victoria had been paid £490,000 since signing the deal in September 2004, she believed that the success of her designs had warranted a much larger payout. Thus she found herself in dispute with Ball, and reportedly threatened legal action to claim a share of the profits.

While she looked forward to her new career,

David had his eyes on the ultimate football prize – the 2006 World Cup. Even Victoria was caught up in the excitement and anticipation surrounding the June tournament. While the World Cup could prove to be the crowning moment in David's soccer career, she was determined to lift the social trophy by hosting a ball at Beckingham Palace that would seal their position at the apex of celebrity society and send off the England team in style. So while David was spending sleepless nights worrying about the forthcoming sporting event, Victoria was fretting about making a success of her 'Full Length and Fabulous' party.

She planned the occasion to the last detail, ensuring a glittering array of stars, an after party with rapper P Diddy as the DJ, and a banquet organized by celebrity chef Gordon Ramsay. There was even a proposed fly-past by Battle of Britain fighter planes. Unfortunately, the £2,000-a-head event, which eventually raised £1 million for children's charities, did not get off to a flying start: the Battle of Britain plane spectacle was cancelled after angry protests from war veterans, Gordon Ramsay had injured his knee in a charity football match and spent the evening directing other chefs while balancing on a pair of crutches, and the local council threatened to ban the party outright because of a 'ring of steel' security fence that had been erected without official permission.

These were the least of Victoria's worries, though, as she faced every hostess's nightmare when a number of high-profile guests failed to appear. They included Prince Charles and his new wife, the Duchess of Cornwall, his sons Princes William and Harry, as well as the King of Spain. Even the ever reliable Sir Elton John was double booked, while

Tom Cruise and Katie Holmes were too preoccupied with baby Suri. If that wasn't enough, newspaper reports revealed that the Beckhams and Adams families were once again at loggerheads because David's parents had not been invited to join Tony and Jackie Adams at the top table. To add to Victoria's troubles, a torrential downpour put the damper on a spectacular firework display and even threatened to flood the splendidly decorated marquee.

Ironically, the Beckhams' World Cup party turned out to be the perfect metaphor for England's World Cup tournament – an all too familiar tale of high expectation that ended in crushing disappointment. For once this was a competition that the youthful and talented England team stood a real chance of winning, but in the opening matches the team stuttered and spluttered, as brilliant club players collectively failed to replicate their domestic form on the world stage. The team scored a shaky 1–0 win against the unfancied Paraguay and then left it late to take the spoils against tournament minnows, Trinidad and Tobago. A 2–2 draw against Sweden ensured that England went through to the knockout stages, but it was an unconvincing, laboured performance. And no one looked more ordinary than the team's one-time talisman and playmaker, David Beckham.

While he was making headlines on the newspaper back pages, his glamorous wife was making a splash on her own as she joined the partners of the other players at the exclusive Brenner's Park Hotel in Baden-Baden. The antics of the players' other halves – quickly dubbed the 'WAGs' to signify 'wives and girlfriends' – generated more attention than their partners' lacklustre performance on the pitch. Young, pretty and fashionable, the WAGs lapped up the attention of the paparazzi, posing in skimpy bikinis, enjoying extravagant shopping trips and creating havoc in the sleepy town's bars and nightclubs where they danced on tables and drank until dawn. Their riotous lifestyle mirrored the outlandish antics made famous in a barely fictional British TV drama, *Footballers' Wives*.

By contrast, Victoria Beckham ensured that she kept her distance from their headline-grabbing behavior, the mother of three deliberately remaining above the boozy affray. She arrived with her sons by private jet, dined with her family and went to bed early. On the night the WAGs drank the hotel bar dry, she took her sons to see the stage musical *Mamma Mia!* in Stuttgart. During the tournament she portrayed herself as the elder stateswoman, grabbing the front pages for what she wore rather than what she did. After all she had a brand to promote. Every time she was photographed in a new designer outfit, she ensured that it was always accessorized with a pair of her own dVb designer sunglasses. Yet the presence of the WAGs ensured that the focus was fixed not so much on her clothes as her skeletal physique. While they looked healthy as well as glamorous, by contrast Victoria seemed skinnier than ever. Fellow WAG Carly Zucker, a fitness instructor who was dating England's Joe Cole, allegedly described Victoria as 'emaciated'.

Not only did Victoria arrive with three different-sized pairs of jeans in case she lost even more weight, but a picture of her looking painfully thin, dressed in a tiny tank top and hot pants, featured heavily in websites highlighting anorexia and other eating disorders. She was the uncrowned queen of lean, the patron saint of skinny. Along with US actress Nicole Richie, she found herself at the centre of a debate about how celebrities help to perpetuate eating disorders in impressionable youngsters. Several months later, she admitted that she had suffered from eating disorders in the past, but that these days she simply controlled what she ate.

Back on the pitch, after beating Ecuador in the second round, the England campaign stepped up a gear as the team prepared to take on Portugal in the quarterfinals. A frustrating game, it saw David limping off with a knee injury at half-time, while Wayne Rooney was sent off in the second half. The match ultimately went to penalties and predictably England failed from the spot.

As David watched helplessly from the touchline, tears of frustration and bitter disappointment streamed down his cheeks as he realized his childhood dream of lifting the World Cup was just that – a dream. With a heavy heart and a trembling voice, he faced the press the next day to announce his resignation as England captain. 'It has been an honour and a privilege to captain our country,' said the man who had led the national side for 58 of his 94 caps, 'and I want to stress that I want to continue to play for England and look forward to helping both the new captain and Steve McClaren [the new coach] in any way that I can. I have lived the dream.'

After he left the pressroom he was physically sick, deeply depressed by his – and the team's – failure. It was the manner of the defeat that was so galling. England, like Beckham, had promised much, but delivered little. It was a highly unsatisfactory end to his captaincy. His only consolation was that he was still in the England squad and would, injuries and selection permitting, join the elite band of players who had won 100 caps for their country. A few days later, though, even that ambition appeared to have been thwarted when he received a phone call from Steve McClaren. At first David thought he was calling to ask about his injured knee, but he was badly misguided. 'David, I want to move forward, but there will be casualties along the way,' explained McClaren. 'And you're one of them.'

For a few minutes, David was too stunned even to comprehend what the England manager had told him. Then, as McClaren's words began to sink in, a wave of anger and disappointment swept over him. As he later admitted, 'It surprised me. I was gutted. Playing for England meant everything to me. But I did not plead with him, as he has made his decision.'

A true professional with an inner core of toughness that few recognize, David resolved to prove McClaren wrong and redeem himself through his efforts for his club side. He returned to Spain eager to prove his point on the pitch, but his plans seemed destined to founder. New Real Madrid team coach Fabio Capello made it clear that he no longer considered Beckham an automatic first-team choice. Instead the Englishman was now part of the thirty-four-man squad and had to fight every week for a place in the starting line-up. As the new season got underway, Beckham often found himself relegated to the bench.

It seemed that his career was in freefall, the glittering prizes no longer in his grasp. In quick and cruel succession he had lost the England captaincy, his England shirt and a place in the line-up of *galácticos* for Real Madrid; the one-time star attraction now reduced to a series of walk-on parts. However, the ultimate soccer showman was not finished yet. It was time to take centre stage at another theatre of dreams.

Sixteen

Hooray for Hollywood

It was a sophisticated new look that marked a coming of age of sorts, a significant change in the glamorous life of Victoria Beckham. When she unveiled what quickly became known as the POB, a shorter, sophisticated bobbed haircut, Victoria was signalling much more than a simple switch of look. The new style, first revealed in August 2006, marked a genuine new-found confidence in who she was and where she was headed, both as a woman and a fashion icon.

Ostensibly, the fresh look was inspired by a man, top fashion photographer Thiemo Sander, who suggested a radical rethink when he was snapping her for an Australian glossy magazine. Victoria, who admitted that she was 'sick' of her much-imitated hair extensions, responded positively to the suggestion, as did her long-time hairdresser, Ben Cooke, who designed the iconic POB. While her new approach inevitably drew praise and criticism from the media, it was generally much admired – and copied. There was no escaping the fact that the look was much more grown up, framing her razor-like cheekbones and jaw in a way that was chic, yet uncomplicated. It also uncovered the Hebrew tattoo that ran down the nape of her neck, which again gave her an edgier, street persona. It was a look that wasn't trying too hard and yet worked.

Just as the late Diana, Princess of Wales changed her hairstyle to mark a change in her life, be it separation or divorce, so it seemed that Victoria too was making a statement about who she was, consciously indicating a fresh start.

For years she had lived with the knowledge that her fame was as fake and transitory as her hair extensions. As she was the first to admit, she was an 'ordinary girl who got lucky'. During her days with the Spice Girls she knew that she was the weakest singer. 'I never used to be able to wake up in the morning knowing "I'm brilliant at what I do,"' she explained, a state of mind underscored by her failed career as a solo artiste. Even her marriage was a mixed blessing, with David adored for his soccer brilliance, his effortless style and his sex appeal. 'I always used to say to David, you've got much more going for you. You're so naturally talented and good-looking, so much more than me.'

As far as Victoria was concerned, throughout her adult life she was valued not for who she was, but for who she was with, be it the Spice Girls, her husband or her three boys. It gnawed away at her very being, eating at her self-confidence and sense of who she was. In public she was never really relaxed, and in the moment her poses always studied and highly self-aware, as though she was always outside herself looking nervously on. Yet this conflicted creature, vexed by self-doubt, loved to be looked at and admired, always thrilled to be the centre of attention. Fashion designer Roberto Cavalli, who styles some of the world's most beautiful women, was also aware of the tensions within her, and observed that her lack of self-confidence was no act. 'She asks me, "What do I look like? Am I OK?" Her uncertainty is so different from other stars.'

During the summer and autumn of 2006, Victoria truly began to grow into herself and discover who she was. Her new career as a full-time stylist and trend-maker defined her as a woman with a real flair for fashion. She began to feel truly valued for herself, not for her image. It was as much a revelation to her as it was the watching world. 'Now it's amazing. I'm doing something I'm actually very good at,' she remarked to writer Caroline Hedley. 'I can confidently sit in a room with Donatella Versace or anyone in the fashion business, and be respected as I know what I am talking about. It's the first time I've ever felt like that and I can't explain how good that feels.'

Indeed it was Donatella who first 'lit the fuse' years earlier, encouraging the young Spice Girl to choose whatever she wanted from her store before she went to her first fashion show in Italy. It was the beginning of a journey that propelled her to the front rank in the fashion world. While she has made many fashion mistakes on the way – most embarrassing, she says, was the night she and David appeared at a party in matching black leather Gucci outfits – she now felt that her look was more laid-back and less contrived. 'I've made fewer mistakes as I've grown older,' she says.

As she has become increasingly more relaxed with who she is, that inner certainty has started to be reflected in her clothes. Throughout the autumn of 2006, she unveiled a series of fashion-forward outfits as she went from the front row of various top designers' shows in Paris and New York. In just five days she had paraded in no fewer than ten different looks in Manhattan, from a Sixties inspired 'Twiggy' outfit to a white shirt, tartan pencil skirt teamed with black leather gloves. However, in Paris her most important accessory was her friend, actor Katie Holmes. The pair appeared in complimenting outfits, at one show arriving in tightly belted, grey trenchcoats and over-sized Jackie O style sunglasses.

The Victoria roadshow was not simply about capturing the limelight. It was a subtle – and at times not so subtle – way of selling Brand Beckham, specifically dVb, the eponymous label the couple had recently launched. They initially marketed his-and-hers sunglasses and perfume, while jeans designed by Victoria went into stores in spring 2007. She also expanded her existing collaboration with Japanese designer Samantha Thavasa from just handbags to designer jewellery. Her commercial efforts were reinforced by a website dedicated to all things Victoria, including a jaunty video diary where she confided that she once dreamed of being a ballerina and appearing in *Swan Lake,* and that she never wore a seatbelt on planes as death did not scare her. She also performed a karaoke version of the Spice Girls' hit 'Wannabe'. The presenting image was a woman who was chic, coiffed and confident, yet utterly down to earth with a sharp sense of humour. The site had more hits than the Spice Girls ever had, and proved so popular that it crashed in the early days because of the sheer volume of traffic.

However, in the backstabbing world of the fashionista, her self-deprecating personality was regarded as uncool. Worse still, her style was deemed altogether too considered and overdone. She was dubbed a fashion liability with the capacity to kill a style stone dead if she was pictured wearing it. During New York Fashion Week, a PR for a cool label was seen looking through newspapers 'checking that the dreaded VB hasn't managed to get hold of any of our clothes'. Fashion writer Liz Jones sneered that Victoria was trying too hard – a failing that the former Spice Girl herself admitted during her early struggles to find her groove. It was not an isolated view: TV presenter and stylist Hannah Sandling also argued that Victoria was a fashion follower rather than a leader. 'I think she puts too much effort into thinking about what she's going to wear,' she said.

Despite such disparaging remarks, it was not a view shared by the 3,000 or so fans who, in October 2006, queued for hours at a central London store to meet their icon when she signed her fashion book *That Extra Half an Inch*, her own style bible on what, how and when to wear clothes. Her signing session was vindication of her instincts – that ordinary women genuinely admired and emulated her taste. It was a look shaped by her own love of the fashions of the 50s and 60s, particularly the clothes of actress Audrey Hepburn. The self-styled girl-next-door had found an avid and eager following, several fans even flying from Spain to meet their heroine, others bursting into tears in her presence.

Her ghost writer, *Guardian* fashion journalist Hadley Freeman, nicely captured the chatty, self-deprecating manner of the former Spice Girl, a style that was parodied by Freeman's own newspaper: 'The idea that once you have a bit of money you . . . live on caviar and champagne is just nonsense. They've both got far too many calories.' Victoria, though, was able to dine out on the fact that her book was an instant bestseller, reinforcing her status as one the High Street now watched.

While the world kept a weather eye on Victoria's rising fashion barometer, David was in the doldrums, spending much of the new season with Real Madrid on the bench. By early November he had only started in four games, the former England captain clearly no longer figuring in the long-term plans of Real coach, Fabio Capello. Though David insisted that he had plenty of football left in him, his situation was a recipe for uncertainty and speculation. 'Every day I feel sad and very frustrated as a footballer because I am not playing for my country or my club,' he complained. 'Two more years on the bench would be very difficult.' While he was he linked with a move to Celtic in Glasgow or London clubs Arsenal and Tottenham Hotspur, he was also being courted openly by the Major League Soccer in America, whose deputy commissioner Ivan Gazidis said that if Beckham's name could help activate the potential in the States, US soccer and Beckham would be a 'marriage made in heaven'.

Certainly all the signs were that David and his Spanish football partner were heading for the divorce court – especially after it emerged that Capello would not allow him to attend the wedding of his friends Tom Cruise and Katie Holmes in November 2006. Even though he had been sidelined with a knee injury, his coach insisted that David was present in Spain to undergo medical treatment and to watch his team play their weekend match. The Spanish side did give him permission to attend the pre-wedding party with Victoria, however, which was held on the outskirts of Rome, but he had to return to Madrid the following day. 'That's not my problem,' retorted Capello, when informed that David would miss the ceremony.

Instead Victoria, dressed in a striking satellite-dish hat and black cocktail dress, arrived alone at Orsini Odescalchi, the medieval castle north-west of Rome, where she joined fellow celebrities Jennifer Lopez, Will Smith, Jim Carrey and Brooke Shields to watch Tom and Katie plight their troth in a ceremony based on the tenets of Scientology, a controversial cult founded by science fiction writer L. Ron Hubbard over fifty years ago. Victoria and the rest of the congregation looked on as Tom was told: 'Girls need clothes and food and tender happiness and frills, a pan, a comb, perhaps a cat.'

Perhaps the most moving moment of the occasion was when the blind Italian opera singer Andrea Bocelli serenaded the assembled throng. Certainly Victoria was singing for her supper, making useful Hollywood contacts to add to her bulging address book. She hit it off well with Hollywood entertainer and fashionista Jennifer Lopez, as the two women decided to start a 'seriously sexy fashion range' after realizing they shared similar tastes. JLo also agreed to act as a 'guinea pig' to try out the first samples of Victoria's dVb denim jeans range. She was keen to hear feedback from the Golden Globe nominated actress and singer, to make sure that the shape and fit of her range was right for a woman of her shapely proportions.

A few days later, Victoria flew to Los Angeles for a first-person assessment from her new best friend. Her clothing range was not the only thing on her mind. During her flying visit to the States in December 2006, she took time out to look at several mansions in Beverly Hills, a provocative move that caused a flurry of speculation that the Beckhams were about to decamp to the USA. For once the gossips were spot on.

In early January 2007, the biggest open secret in football was finally confirmed: David Beckham was moving to planet Hollywood, swapping the *galácticos* for the Galaxy, the Los Angeles Galaxy. The deal was out of this world: at £125 million it made him the highest paid soccer star in history, earning £500,000 a week during the five-year contract. Marketing analysts reckoned that in a few years' time, Brand Beckham would be worth a staggering £500 million once his wages, endorsements, ticket sales and Victoria's fashion line were added in. The much-anticipated marriage between the biggest name in soccer and the largest untapped market in the world was finally consummated. As his agent Simon Fuller, the entertainment mastermind behind the Spice Girls and *American Idol*, said, 'I always wanted to create history with the biggest sports deal ever and David Beckham is the only athlete in the world who could have made this happen. His decision to move to Galaxy and play in Major League Soccer is the beginning of probably the greatest and most important adventure of all.'

He had, though, exchanged glory for gravy, passing up the opportunity to finish his playing career at Real Madrid or a top British side for the chance to spearhead a change in the way that Americans viewed soccer. It was an enticing prospect, an opportunity to make an indelible mark on the future of the sport in the United States. Even so, for David, still only thirty-one, it was the hardest decision of his career, as it dawned on him that he was turning his back on top-flight football and possibly saying goodbye to any realistic hope he may have harboured of playing for his country again. In the past he had joined clubs that were bigger than the player. Now he was poised to sign on for a new team where not only was he bigger than the club, his name was bigger than the entire league. David had now become a sporting Goliath, his face on every Galaxy match ticket.

In spite of the sums on offer, it had been a tough choice for a young man whose boyhood dream had been to wear the England number-seven shirt. He was reported to have wept tears of despair as he weighed up the pros and cons of the deal, at one point making two hour-long phone calls to his 'wise' friend Tom Cruise for advice. The Hollywood actor walked him through the possibilities of life in California as well as the pitfalls, notably the ever-present paparazzi. 'Living in LA is going to be a great experience for my whole family,' David said, after he had inked the deal. 'It was a big decision, but it is going to be great. I've played in top-class football now for fifteen years for two of the biggest clubs in the world . . . so stepping away from that was always going to be difficult.'

In a televised press conference he was keen to emphasize that it was more than the mountain of money that had lured this sporting Mohammed to the States. He was keen to spread the word about 'the beautiful game'. 'The main thing for me is to improve the soccer and to improve the standard and be part of history,' said David.

Typically, his decision excited controversy in all corners, with some of the biggest names in sport – and fashion – going head-to-head. Surprisingly, his former manager Sir Alex Ferguson, who had a difficult relationship with Beckham in the latter stages of his career at Manchester United, wished him well, believing that the young man would never have returned to England because deep down he was always a Manchester United fan. 'Everyone at our club hopes he does well,' said Ferguson. 'It's a big career change, from playing for Real Madrid to go and play in America.' Even Giorgio Armani, not known for his soccer wisdom, got in on the drama, indicating that the move was part of David's ambition to become a Hollywood actor. However, it was a notion that the soccer star quickly quashed. 'I'm a terrible actor,' he said.

In contrast, the move from the European soccer elite to the premier league of celebrity drew a scornful response from the Real Madrid president Ramón Calderón, who believed that Beckham would 'end up as a B-list actor living in Hollywood'. (He later apologized for his remarks.) While the Real Madrid executive reacted like jilted lovers – his coach Fabio

Capello indicated that Beckham would never play for the Spanish side again, even though his contract did not end until June 2007 – other soccer figures such as former England manager Sir Bobby Robson and Arsenal manager Arsène Wenger were more temperate, suggesting that the decision to axe Beckham from the England squad had finally made up his mind. 'American soccer has nothing to do with top-level football in Europe,' noted Wenger drily, while a 'surprised and disappointed' Robson commented, 'David no longer has the appetite to challenge at the very highest level. Some have the fire burning in their late thirties; Beckham's seems to have gone out at thirty-one.' According to Bayern Munich manager Uli Hoeness, it was all the fault of Posh Spice, whom he described as 'the death of football'. 'It's terrible that Beckham's going to Hollywood,' complained Hoeness. 'He's a gifted footballer.'

It was the fact that David had seemingly shirked the manly challenge of fighting for silverware at the top table of European soccer that irked many in the world of football, particularly at a time when his former Manchester United teammates Paul Scholes, Ryan Giggs and Gary Neville were part of a resurgent squad challenging for European and national honours. 'Beckham has decided to unroll the beach towel and reach for the sun-tan lotion,' noted sports writer Des Kelly scornfully, comparing Beckham unfavourably with his former teammate Ryan Giggs who was honoured 'as one of the greats' at a Football Writers' tribute dinner, in the week at Beckham announced his departure. It was a theme developed by England World Cup medal-winner

Jimmy Greaves, who declared, 'Beckham will not be remembered as an England great. More someone who epitomized a time of bling and pampering which turned our "stars" into lightweights on the biggest of stages.'

Ironically, with England stuttering in the European qualifying games in 2007, there were calls to bring David back into the squad, and he received a standing ovation when he was given an Outstanding Contribution to British Sport trophy at the Sports Industry Awards in March 2007.

In many respects, David's decision had gone way beyond the soccer pitch, becoming part of a long-running morality play of how the behaviour of the Beckhams defined the ethical temperature of the nation. The couple certainly got commentator Leo McKinstry hot under the collar. 'It seems to me that he and his wife embody the worst of modern British culture,' he fumed, 'in its celebration of excess, its enthusiasm for a quick buck, its lack of dignity, its preference for show over substance, its obsession with fame.'

The starchy, censorious reaction of the Brits con-trasted with the cool, laid-back Californian take on the couple's decision to move to the land of oppor-tunity. Joel Stein of the *Los Angeles Times* wondered wryly, 'Do we need another breast-enhanced wife who is famous for nothing but shopping and party-ing, as evidenced by the fact that she lists her occupation as "fashion designing"? Hell, yes we do! These are exactly the kind of people who keep LA the most culturally important city in the world.'

No sooner had the Beckhams told the world that they were heading for Hollywood than they became the hottest ticket in Tinsel Town. As LA mayor Antonio Villaraigosa proclaimed, 'We've got the beaches, the glitz and the glamour, and now we even have David Beckham.' He was not the only one caught up in the excitement, as stars such as director Steven Spielberg, Jennifer Lopez, and singers Robbie Williams and Rod Stewart all bought season tickets to watch David play, while Hollywood legend Clint Eastwood announced that he was looking forward to making the soccer star's day. 'I love soccer, I used to play it when I was younger. It's a great game,' said the veteran actor. Perhaps the ultimate seal of respectability was when Hugh Hefner invited the couple to a party at the Playboy Mansion.

Even Victoria Beckham was taken aback by the genuine interest, when her arrival at LAX to view possible properties was greeted by a jostling throng of film crews, reporters and photographers. She was further amazed at a party in Beverly Hills when Oscar-winning actor Tom Hanks not only recognized her, but pronounced himself 'thrilled' that she and her husband were coming to Hollywood. He promised to join the crowds at the Home Depot Center, while *Rocky* actor Sylvester Stallone reckoned that Beckham would punch well above his celebrity weight: 'David will be received as a superstar. He has the looks, the whole thing. He will bring tremendous interest and support to the sport. Twenty per cent of America is Latino, and they just live for soccer. With Beckham there it'll really take off.'

Certainly ticket and shirt sales rocketed to new heights, not just at LA Galaxy but at other MLS teams in places such as Toronto, Salt Lake City and Boston, where special 'Build It Like Beckham' ticket packages ensured that fans had to buy extra match tickets to guarantee the chance of seeing Beckham play. His scheduled appearance against Boston in August 2007, for example, was already shaping up to have the biggest crowd for a MLS-only regular season match in New England history. Television networks also got on board, planning to show sixteen of the seventeen Galaxy games, while for the first time network stations such as ESPN, the Fox soccer channel and Univision were paying rights fees to carry MLS games. Advertising during the games on ESPN was already sold out for the entire 2007 season, the station's play-by-play announcer Dave O'Brien identifying Beckham's sex appeal as a major factor in bringing teenage girls and soccer moms to watch him play: 'He is a worldwide star. David Beckham transcends sports and goes right to rock-star status.'

On the pitch, the Beckham Effect helped to draw top-class foreign players to the league. When the Mexican striker Cuauhtémoc Blanco – who is as famous as Beckham among the Hispanic community – signed with Chicago Fire, his arrival at the Toyota Park stadium was greeted by 6,000 fans. There was heated talk that Aston Villa's Juan Pablo Angel, Liverpool's Robbie Fowler and others had been offered MLS contracts, though French soccer legend Zinedine Zidane decided against coming out of retirement to play in the States. LA Galaxy coach Frank Yallop revealed that he had received enquiries from several top players in the English league. 'Players who would make you go "wow" if I named them,' said the former Ipswich Town player.

For once the billboards and newspaper ads with

lines such as, 'The dawning of a new era', 'He's coming' and 'Words are not enough' were no exaggeration, vindicating the commercial vision of Tim Leiweke, President of the Anschutz Entertainment Group which owns the LA Galaxy, who had spent four years stalking his target. Leiweke had first aired his thoughts about Beckham playing in the US to Simon Fuller when they met in 2003 at an adidas sports convention at the Galaxy's ground. Both agreed it would be 'fantastic' to have someone like David with his standing and stature in the States. 'We wondered how he would adapt to football in America, how different it was to England, how big a success he could be and those types of things,' recalled Leiweke. 'That's really when my thoughts about him playing in the United States started.'

It was perhaps no coincidence that AEG funded David's first soccer academy, which opened in 2005 at the Home Depot stadium. The gentle wooing continued when the Beckhams invited Fuller, Leiweke and another AEG executive Shawn Hunter for dinner at their Hertfordshire mansion, shortly after David had joined Real Madrid. During their late-night conversation, Leiweke realized that there was a chemistry between his company and Beckham and his family. 'I was confident – but not over-confident – that he would come to play his football in America in the future,' revealed the astute businessman.

There were further dinners, including one in Madrid in August 2005, after an all-star MLS side had lost 5–0 to Real Madrid. Once the player's talks with Real had stalled in autumn 2006, AEG were ready with a coherent business plan, ready to sign their man.

Beckham and Fuller fully appreciated the 'vision thing' of Leiweke and Phil Anschutz, the billionaire owner of AEG. Everyone concerned was keen to avoid a remake of the Pele disaster movie of the 1970s, which was the lavishly-funded epic known as the North American Soccer League, when a group of US businessmen dug deep into their pockets to hire the Brazilian icon as well as ageing European soccer legends such Johan Cruyff, George Best and Franz Beckenbauer to promote the game to a disinterested public. After a few heady seasons of financial excess and big crowds, the soccer greats hung up their boots, leaving the public watching second-raters and also-rans. The NASL ended in 1984 and it was another decade before America flirted with soccer again, when they played host to the 1994 World Cup, which led to NASL's successor, Major League Soccer.

This time around the team owners were building from the bottom, using Beckham's name to add the buzz, but most importantly they were thinking like entrepreneurs and managing the venture like a global business. The idea was that with Beckham's arrival, the game had reached a 'tipping point', tapping into a much wider audience than the 15,000 average MLS crowd.

While the talk was positive and upbeat – certainly sponsors and TV companies were buying into the idea – it was clear that life in sunny California was not going to be an unopposed coronation for the blond superstar and his wife. Away from the publicity and hype, the cold reality was that LA Galaxy was a poor team, missing the play-offs the previous season after coming fourth in the Western Conference. Moreover, as David was not joining until July – his first game was to be an exhibition match against Chelsea – he would be hard pressed to rescue them if they made a poor start to the 2007 season. In any event, he would have little chance to enjoy the California climate, for as soon as he arrived in the States, the player was due to travel one and a half times round the world on a rolling roadshow, as he and his team played every other MLS opponent in the country.

The gruelling 38,000 mile schedule raised other issues: could he avoid injury, would referees favour the greatest asset in the league and how would Beckham, who had struggled to learn Spanish during his time in Madrid, relate to the under-appreciated Hispanic soccer community? In fairness, this was not just Beckham's problem – the MLS ownership, coaching and administration was mainly white European, while the potential soccer fan base was Hispanic. However, it was a problem that the league was addressing, as it directed 40 per cent of its marketing towards the 42 million strong American Hispanic community. As Jonathan Weinbach, LA correspondent for the *Wall Street Journal*, noted, 'There will undoubtedly be a short-term bump when he first arrives and all the Hollywood folk turn out to watch him play. But what remains to be seen is whether the city's huge Hispanic community come out in their droves to watch after that.'

While the commercial and professional pitfalls had to be faced by Beckham and MLS management together, only he could overcome the day-to-day reality of his life at LA Galaxy. The plain fact was that his lifestyle was light years apart from that of his teammates, which was something he had never experienced before. For example, at Manchester and Madrid, when he bought himself a flash new car, he had been able to talk about it at training with his teammates, secure in the knowledge that they were also in a position to pay out a small fortune for a Bentley or a Porsche. But this would not be the case at his new club, where the entire salary budget for the twenty-five-strong squad was £1.05 million – the equivalent to two weeks' money for Beckham. Thus, while David arrived at the training ground in a customized super car, other squad players, some earning only £15,000 a year, made the trip to Carson, 30 miles south of Los Angeles, in beaten up second-hand autos.

As the Beckhams searched for a £5 million plus house in Beverly Hills with a swimming pool and tennis courts, several Galaxy players shared apartments to make ends meet. Barbecue cookouts with a couple of beers or chips 'n' dips in front of the TV was the social norm for Galaxy players; not for them the high life in Hollywood, going to the fashionable Ivy restaurant with TomKat (the media nickname for Tom Cruise and Katie Holmes). Galaxy midfield player Peter Vagenas, who played for the US Olympic team, let the cat out of the bag when he told BBC radio that there was a degree of hostility to Beckham's huge salary – roughly 500 times what Vagenas earned. 'Of course there is resentment. I'd be lying if I said there wasn't,' he admitted. 'On the one hand, more power to him, and on the other you say, "Why can't I be getting some of that."' Interestingly, most of the Internet responses to his comments were hostile, as fans pointed out that the reason why Vagenas was relatively poorly paid was because he was *not* David Beckham.

This was the new reality that David had to accept. At LA Galaxy he was no longer a star in a firmament of talent as he had been at Manchester United and Real Madrid. In Hollywood he was unique. More than a soccer player, he and his wife were a brand, a formidable marketing combo that was going to be exploited to the hilt by their billionaire backers, Phil Anschutz and Simon Fuller. As MLS commissioner Don Garber noted, 'They are one of the world's power couples. David is not just about the sport; he and Victoria are about fashion and trendsetting.'

As Fuller had recognized from the get go, the Beckham brand was about much more than soccer. The days when the Beckhams did deals with paparazzi photographers to garner headlines were long gone. Fuller had already negotiated a reported £5 million deal for a six-part reality TV show on the fabulous life of David and Victoria, due for broadcast in summer 2007. Each episode, shown on TV network NBC, would slavishly chart the couple's move to California, focusing on Victoria's house-hunting and shopping. There was also heated speculation in the US media that Fuller had suggested to fellow Brit Simon Cowell that he let Victoria join the panel of judges on *American Idol*, replacing singer Paula Abdul. In the end, though, it was decided that the panel should remain the same for fear that ratings could be damaged if too many Brits were judging American acts.

Fuller also rolled out the annual media chestnut that the Spice Girls would tour again, even though Mel C quickly dismissed the notion.

Perhaps a surer sign of genuine brand recognition was that not only did David appear in an advertisement during the 2007 NFL Superbowl, watched by much of male America, he was also chosen to feature in an advertising campaign to promote Disney. Together with singer Beyoncé and actress Scarlett Johansson, the glamorous trio were captured by celebrity photographer Annie Leibovitz in different Disney scenes. David was photographed on a white charger playing Prince Charming about to rescue Sleeping Beauty. The sword-wielding knight later confessed, 'I'm the prince, and I'm sort of slaying the dragon, which is something I've never done before, obviously.' While he enjoyed the experience, he dismissed the notion of a film career once his playing days are over. 'I am not an actor and I never will be,' he said.

While Fuller orchestrated the marketing plan, Victoria made sure that she was never far from the headlines. She changed her hairstyle again, opting for a boyish blonde look modelled on another style icon, Edie Sedgwick, while her eye-catching outfits seemed to be busting out all over the place. One American magazine was prompted to pen her an open letter urging her to buy a bra. 'There is nothing Posh about forgetting to wear a bra when gallivanting about in thin T-shirts as you've unfortunately been known to do,' sniffed the editors of *US Weekly* magazine. Of course the letter was entirely self-serving, as the magazine simply gained worldwide publicity on the back of the former Spice Girl.

They quickly learned what their British counterparts had understood for years: the Beckhams moved product. In March 2007, for example, Victoria was on the cover of no fewer than five weekly women's magazines. Katie Grand, the editor of underground fashion magazine *Pop*, described her as 'the most important woman in Britain'.

Victoria was rapidly making her mark in Hollywood as well, as both a fashion label and a stylist to the stars. For the Golden Globe Awards she helped Jennifer Lopez choose her stunning black Marchesa dress, while her friend Katie Holmes asked her to style her when she appeared on the cover of American *Harper's Bazaar*. Under Victoria's tutelage, Katie dressed in a manner reminiscent of the golden age of Hollywood. Certainly the PR machine was working overtime. There was heated talk that Katie and Victoria were going to start their own children's clothing line and even, more improbably, that Victoria, who has admitted to never finishing a book, was going to start a girls-only book club for her A-list friends, where they would discuss English classics by such authors as Charles Dickens, the Bronte sisters and Jane Austen.

While the story was the kind of classic celebrity froth they had long become used to, in Hollywood they soon discovered that there were traps for the unwary, however seasoned and sophisticated. From the outside Hollywood is a mass-market fantasy factory, a place that draws thousands of young hopefuls dreaming of becoming the next big thing. From the inside, the town is a shark tank, a place of desperate ambition and greed where, as writer Charles Fleming reports, you can hear a late-night conversation in the plush Four Seasons hotel that goes something like this:

> FIRST MAN: 'You're lying! You're lying to me!'
> SECOND MAN: 'Yes, I know . . . but hear me out.'

It is a land of smoke and mirrors, hype and hope, rumour and gossip, where nothing is really as it seems. Hollywood is as beguiling as it is deceptive, a social code that is tough to crack. As Victoria discovered when she was house-hunting in Bel Air and Beverly Hills, she felt instinctively that the prices were unrealistically high as news of David's multi-million-dollar deal percolated through Hollywood. As a result, the Beckhams decided to wait until the price was right.

There were also other predators lurking in the Hollywood undergrowth. Novelist Jackie Collins warned Victoria of the beautiful man-hunters who would smile at her, and then make a play for David. 'There are so many girls in LA that are more beautiful than any you see on the screen and they are predators,' she advised. 'They go after men with a vengeance.'

Other pitfalls were more subtle and sophisticated. Any celebrity who has been in Hollywood for any length of time will have been approached by the controversial Church of Scientology, an organization that *Time* magazine famously described as a 'thriving cult of greed and power'. Its founder L. Ron Hubbard believed that celebrities were the key to the organization's success, their high profile giving it a patina of respectability. Over the years they have successfully recruited numerous Hollywood stars, notably John Travolta, Isaac Hayes, Jenna Elfman and Tom Cruise. They are used as missionaries to recruit other celebrities, targeting those who have high standing in their particular communities. They have focused on Michael Jackson, Will Smith and Oprah Winfrey to bring in the black community and are currently putting pressure on Jennifer Lopez because of her standing within the Latino population. Hollywood veterans know how to avoid the social tentacles of Scientology, but for the newly arrived Beckhams – revered in Europe and the Far East – they provide a juicy target for the cult. Tom Cruise has made a point of befriending the couple, and, on the way, gently introducing them to the basic tenets of his faith. He has given Victoria booklets on its teachings, who in turn has described their work as 'cool'.

Even if they were attracted, the Beckhams would have trouble following Cruise's creed. Their middle son Romeo suffers from epilepsy, a condition that needs medication, but Scientology teaches that its members should avoid the use of prescription drugs. So if they decided to join, Romeo Beckham would not be allowed to take any medicines for his illness, and instead he would be offered vitamins and counselling.

With a wily agent, big money backers and a network of celebrity friends, the Beckhams are unlikely to be seduced by the excesses of Hollywood. In many ways it has been their spiritual home, as they have enjoyed a long-distance love affair with Californian culture for years. David was into LA rapper Tupac Shakur long before he was famous, loves the hip car renovation show *Pimp My Ride* because of his own fascination with fashionable automobiles, and lately has had a Michael Scofield-style sleeve tattoo based on the hit US drama show, *Prison Break*. He even has a gold card for his weekly hit of McDonalds. With his relaxed sense of fashion and laid-back style he has long been an honorary Californian, a young man who has gone into this new stage of his career with a master plan – to enjoy promoting soccer on the pitch as a player and then, when his legs give out, become an ambassador for the game, focusing on giving youngsters every opportunity to play the sport he adores.

While David 'loves' the US cosmetic surgery show *Extreme Makeover*, Victoria has long modelled herself on the Beverly Hills ideal of beauty, a place where botox, breast implants and beach bodies are de rigueur. For a woman who admits to having spent much of her life dressing up and preening in front of the mirror, Hollywood is a reflection of who and why she wants to be. It is a place where size zero women like Victoria reign supreme. Indeed her diet has already been parodied by Drew Barrymore on the TV sketch show *Saturday Night Live*, when the blonde actress, who impersonated the former Spice Girl, told the amused audience that she wouldn't eat 'meat, vegetables, grains, liquids or dairy products'.

For years Victoria has worried that she has lived her life as a fake, a fraud waiting to be found out. A woman who intrigues not because she is obviously talented, but because she seems troubled. A woman famous for being famous. So it is a supreme irony that she has truly found what she really, really wants in a place where the false is real and where the look is the life. As a style icon and a fashionista she is thriving, and, with her edgier European sensibility, she will shine in Hollywood which, for all its glamour, has rarely set the fashion pace. She has found her true métier as a fashion plate where the fake, the fabulous, and the freaky hang out. Already her arrival in America has fascinated those fashion gurus who truly shape the direction of the style seasons. At a recent charity party in Paris where Raquel Welch was guest of honour, designer Rolf Snoeren (of cutting-edge designers Viktor & Rolf) was intrigued by the slim blonde waif whose face was on virtually every magazine. 'What do you think of Victoria Beckham?' he asked the assembled throng rhetorically. 'She's SO everywhere and now she's planning to take over America. There is just no stopping that girl.'

For all the criticism and mockery, millions admire and ape the Beckham lifestyle, their continuing success based on the simple equation that these days celebrity sells. They are more than just a name, they are a brand, an advertiser's dream. In a world saturated with celebrity, no one sells it like David and Victoria Beckham. As commentator Jason Cowley points out, 'Global capitalism has, at present, no greater ambassador than David Beckham. His life is dedicated to conspicuous consumption and ostentatious display. In this he represents all that is worst and most excessive about our winner-takes-all society.'

They have endeavoured to present an image, now somewhat tarnished, of wholesome family life, just ordinary folks living an extraordinary life. People like you and I – but much richer. Certainly their lives have struck a chord in the international psyche, so that, in an uncertain and dangerous age, they represent the comfortable predictability of a favourite soap opera, there to amuse, entertain and occasionally inspire. Their move to Hollywood seems somehow destined, a natural part of the script of their lives.

And just when England's fans had thought they had seen the last of David in an England strip, in May 2007 he received an unexpected recall to the England squad for a friendly against Brazil and a crucial European Championship qualifying game against Estonia. Once again, David's self-belief had proved the doubters wrong – his form for Real Madrid helping the Spanish side to mount a positive challenge for the La Liga title, which proved himself worthy of a place in the England side. And with Prime Minister Tony Blair considering a knighthood for the football star in his resignation honours list, it was yet another incredible twist in the story of David and Victoria Beckham as they embraced their greatest – and perhaps happiest – adventure yet. Truly a real-life Hollywood ending.

Select Bibliography

David Beckham: My Son, Ted Beckham (Boxtree, 2005)

Just for the Record, Geri Halliwell (Ebury Press, 2003)

Learning to Fly, Victoria Beckham (Michael Joseph, 2001)

Managing My Life, Alex Ferguson (Hodder & Stoughton, 2000)

My Side, David Beckham with Tom Watt (Collins Willow, 2003)

That Extra Half an Inch, Victoria Beckham, (Michael Joseph, 2006)

The Comings and Goings of David Beckham, Anon (David and Charles, 2005)

VII: David Beckham, Amy Lawrence (Weidenfeld & Nicolson, 2006)

Wannabe: How the Spice Girls Reinvented Pop Fame, David Sinclair (Omnibus Press, 2004)

Index

319